Grassland Ecology

To I. S.

Grassland Ecology

C. R. W. SPEDDING

ASSISTANT DIRECTOR AND
HEAD OF THE ECOLOGY DIVISION
THE GRASSLAND RESEARCH INSTITUTE
HURLEY, BERKSHIRE

VISITING PROFESSOR OF AGRICULTURAL SYSTEMS
THE UNIVERSITY OF READING

OXFORD · AT THE CLARENDON PRESS
1971

Oxford University Press, Ely House, London W. 1

GLASGOW NEW YORK TORONTO MELBOURNE WELLINGTON
CAPE TOWN SALISBURY IBADAN NAIROBI DAR ES SALAAM LUSAKA ADDIS ABABA
BOMBAY CALCUTTA MADRAS KARACHI LAHORE DACCA
KUALA LUMPUR SINGAPORE HONG KONG TOKYO

PRINTED IN GREAT BRITAIN

Preface

THERE is an increasing need to achieve a synthesis of ecology and agriculture. The latter is sometimes described as applied ecology but this is true only in a very limited sense. Where agriculture is concerned only with short-term profit, ecological principles—even where they are known—may be ignored. But agriculture represents a great deal more than the business of farming, and has considerable influence on people in general and the kind of world in which they live.

Ecologists, however, have often preferred to study those environments that are least affected by man's activities and have thus made less impact on, or contribution to, the relatively artificial ecosystems represented by agriculture.

Yet each activity has much to contribute to the other. The approach and outlook characteristic of ecology is greatly needed in agriculture, but it is not always clear to what extent and in what way ecological principles are applicable. On the other hand, ecologists often struggle to understand complex situations from which relatively little information can be extracted, and ignore the slightly simpler agricultural systems about which accumulates a vast amount of carefully recorded information, derived from both research and practice.

Nowhere do these arguments apply with greater force than in the field of grassland ecology.

Clearly, the understanding of ecological principles must not be inhibited by agricultural necessities, and agricultural application must not be inhibited by ecological theory. But neither should deprive itself of the considerable benefits of the other.

In this context ecology must include both animals and plants, another synthesis fraught with difficulty but indispensable to an understanding of grassland.

The difficulties are of two kinds, one much more serious than the other. The less serious is the idea that plants and animals and ecology and agriculture are separate subjects and that any combination must therefore be a mightier proposition, even to contemplate, as if the result aimed at was the sum of the components. This need not be so, as a moment's thought about the components of any well-recognized subject will show. Each subject must recognize units and levels appropriate to it, whether they be molecules, cells, individuals, populations, or planets, rendering the whole content understandable by one person. Nor is lack of information a good reason for failing to recognize and describe a subject.

The second and more serious difficulty is exemplified by the differences between animals and plants. There is clearly a sense in which it is more difficult to comprehend systems involving both, simply because the background knowledge of the underlying biological processes has to be greater.

The greatest difficulty, however, is the attitude of mind which really believes that the definition of subjects is in some way decided once and for all, and fails to see that a subject can be created around any focal point and must include whatever part of any other subject impinges at that point.

This book is written in the belief that grassland ecology is a subject, of great importance biologically, agriculturally, and socially. This preface may be said to be *about* grassland ecology, but the book is primarily an attempt to describe what grassland ecology is about. There is a great temptation to expand in all directions with examples to illustrate the wide range of the subject, but this has been resisted in order to present a concise picture of the complex to be comprehended.

The account is therefore a functional anatomy of the subject rather than a comprehensive description of the completely clothed body of knowledge.

Since it is written for readers who may be specialists in some of the components but relatively new to others, the treatment has been kept simple without being elementary.

For those who dislike mathematics, it is worth pointing out that a quantitative approach is indispensable for a full understanding of the subject, and a degree of abstraction is necessary in order to manipulate even the minimum of factors involved. Figures have been used to help in conveying a picture of the main processes, and an introduction to the use of mathematical models is provided in the Appendix.

C.R.W.S.

Hurley, Berks.
August 1969

Acknowledgements

I WISH to acknowledge my indebtedness to Professor E. K. Woodford, the Director of the Grassland Research Institute, and to the Governing Body, for facilities made available to me in writing this book and for permission to use both published and unpublished data. I am most grateful to the many colleagues who have allowed me to draw freely upon their results and who have helped in the compilation of figures and tables. These contributions are acknowledged in the text but I wish especially to record my thanks to Mr. R. V. Large and Miss J. M. Walsingham, both of whom helped me enormously during the preparation of the book, and, in particular, of the tables and figures. The latter were drawn by Mr. B. D. Hudson. I am greatly indebted to my colleague Mr. N. R. Brockington for his major contribution to the Appendix and to Professor J. L. Harper and Professor E. K. Woodford for helpful comments and criticisms of parts of the text.

Thanks are due to the editors of the following journals for permission to reproduce tables or figures: *Journal of Agricultural Science* (Figs. 3.3, 3.4, and 3.5); *Agricultural Progress* (Table 16.1; Figs. 16.3, 16.4, 16.5, and 16.6); *Australian Journal of Agricultural Research* (Fig. 5.1); *N.A.A.S. Quarterly Review* (Figs. 5.2 and 8.1); *Journal of the British Grassland Society* (Figs. 2.1 and 10.1); *Journal of Applied Ecology* (Figs. 3.6, 5.1, and 5.3); *Proceedings of the Nutrition Society* (Fig. 10.1); *World Review of Animal Production* (Table 15.1). I also wish to make acknowledgement to Methuen and Co., Ltd., for permission to reproduce the equation from Professor T. R. E. Southwood's book, on p. 135.

Finally, I wish to thank Mrs. H. L. B. Stone for her rapid and accurate typing of successive drafts of the manuscript, and Miss A. Hoxey for her helpfulness during the later stages of preparation of the book.

Contents

1
Introduction

'GRASSLAND' and 'Ecology' are both terms that bear many different meanings. It is not so much a rigid definition that is required in each case, however, but a brief description of the ways in which the the terms will be used in the following chapters.

Grassland

Grassland may be of two main kinds, natural or artificial. Many other terms are used to describe these two categories and a brief examination of any of them illustrates the problem and casts doubt on the validity of even this first distinction.

Natural grassland has been defined as 'a plant community in which the dominant species are perennial grasses, there are few or no shrubs, and trees are absent' (Moore 1964), although the provision of shelter belts is often part of grassland improvement (Shamsontdinov 1966). It is often called 'permanent' grassland, but this is clearly a relative term and simply implies a relatively stable community. Since this stability often depends upon the direct or indirect influence of man (see Davies 1960), it is doubtful whether 'natural' is a particularly accurate description. Whether trees are included or not really depends upon the areas involved and in some cases the presence of trees cannot be regarded as merely incidental, since their products may contribute essential components to the diet of grazing animals. Tansley (1939) pointed out that in Britain the vast majority of the grasslands were best regarded as 'biotic plagioclimax vegetation, i.e. vegetation stabilized by pasturing'.

Within agricultural use there are certainly examples of artificial grassland that are clearly distinguishable. They have been created from quite different kinds of vegetation by considerable intervention including deliberate sowing. Thus an agricultural distinction may be made between 'natural' and 'sown' grassland (Woodford 1965).

After a sufficiently long interval, of course, the botanical composition of the sward reflects its management rather than its seed mixture and it ceases to matter precisely how and by whom the seed was sown. If origin is ignored, grassland can be divided into cultivated and uncultivated (Davies 1960).

The world's grasslands have been classified in many different ways, related chiefly to climate (see Moore 1964) because this is often considered to be the major factor in determining the distribution of grasslands. Other factors are also important, however, notably soil, topography, and the biotic factors, including fire (Thomas 1960).

Any reasonable definition of grassland must include dominance by grasses, but this does not usually mean that the number of grass species is greater than the number of other plant species. On the contrary, natural grassland is characterized by its large number of species, and grasses may represent only 10–20 per cent of that number; in sown grassland the number of grass species is usually low and generally outnumbered by the non-grass weed species. Indeed, as Hartley (1964) has pointed out, grass species are very widely distributed and are present in almost all types of vegetation, being represented by a similar percentage of the total number of species (15–23 per cent) over a range of vegetation types. The grasses as a family (Gramineae) are outstanding in their ability to adapt themselves to diverse ecological conditions and it is surprising that so few (about forty) of the 10 000 or so known grass species are used on any important scale as cultivated pasture plants (Hartley 1964).

Grassland, then, is considered here as a plant community in which the bulk of the herbage consists of grasses but which can occur in a wide range of types, varying from the floristically rich vegetation of the natural pasture to the single species sward characteristic of some extreme agricultural situations. One important qualification is necessary in relation to legumes. Grasslands are extremely important as pastures for grazing livestock and it is of increasing importance to adopt an ecosystem approach (Moule 1964, Puri 1966, Naveh and Ron 1966): a great many of the world's grasslands are used agriculturally and much valuable information relevant to grassland ecology derives from this. In many of these situations legumes play a vital part as contributors of nitrates and without them agricultural productivity would be very much lower.

The legume has therefore been considered here as a major constituent of grassland, even to the extent of sometimes being the species of primary importance and sown alone for agricultural purposes. It is also true that a great many natural pastures contain several legume species which contribute a substantial proportion of the ground cover and of the primary production.

Ecology

Ecology is often concerned with a particular organism in relation to its environment: some ecological studies may even be confined to the relationship between one organism in one physiological state and one aspect of its environment.

Such studies fall into categories, like 'plant' or 'animal' ecology, according to the kind of organism selected.

Generally speaking, such relationships are not one-sided and the organism has important effects on the environment, just as the environment influences the organism. It is characteristic of an ecological approach, therefore, to consider whole ecosystems, the components of which include climate, physiography, soil, animals, and plants. A particular organism may still remain the focal point, or, as in the present instance, an ecosystem (grassland) is chosen that does not necessarily even contain one dominant species. Furthermore, the ecosystem cannot very sensibly be regarded as predominantly botanical.

As Tansley (1946) has pointed out, 'anything like a *complete* study of the ecology of a plant community necessarily includes a study of the animals living in or feeding upon it'. This is, of course, a vast undertaking and involves a synthesis of data from many disciplines. It is probably still true that 'there is as yet no single complex ecosystem of which we have anything approaching a satisfactory knowledge' (Tansley 1939). It may be doubted whether we will ever have enough information to construct complete and detailed descriptions of the range of ecosystems that constitute grassland. There should, however, be a basic model that can be distinguished as common to all such systems. If there is not, it is doubtful if they can be validly grouped together for ecological purposes.

It may still be argued that there is insufficient information for the construction of the basic model and, again, perhaps there never will be, depending on the nature of the model envisaged.

Three points should be noted.

First, the only way to be sure whether the information is adequate or not is to collate and organize it as would be required in building a model; in other words, to attempt the construction.

Secondly, only by such attempts can the gaps and deficiencies in our knowledge be convincingly demonstrated and their importance assessed; this is the first step in correcting them.

Thirdly, it should not be expected that a synthesis of these dimensions should deal in the same kind of detail as is customary in smaller-scale studies. Astronomy would be impossible if the units of microscopy were insisted upon. It is essential to use the units that are appropriate to the kind of study envisaged. Just as a study of each individual cell separately would produce a very poor concept of a whole animal body, so a study of the components of ecosystems does not necessarily lead to a picture of the whole. Furthermore, it is not necessary to know all about each component before it becomes legitimate to study the whole.

There is one other aspect of ecology that must be mentioned. The environment selected is commonly referred to as the 'natural' environment of the organism. In terms of a complete synthesis of results from the contributory disciplines, 'involving a really scientific description of the ecosystems of the world', this is a 'work of the future, scarcely likely to be completed before most of the "natural" ecosystems have been destroyed, broken up, or at least profoundly modified by human activity' (Tansley 1939).

In any event, 'natural' habitats are rarely as free from human influence as they appear and many of the man-dominated habitats *are* the natural ones to their inhabitants. Parasites of man would find it difficult to accept as 'natural', environments that excluded their host.

The desire to study organisms uninfluenced by man is both understandable and necessary for a great many purposes but it does not characterize any particular branch of study, and ecology ought to have room for the human situation also.

Certainly no comprehensive study of grassland ecology can exclude the vast areas influenced by man to a greater or lesser degree and, in any case, the study of controlled situations is one of the roads to understanding the less controlled ones.

The study of ecosystems

Miller (1966) has defined an ecosystem as 'an open system comprising plants, animals, organic residues, atmospheric gases, water, and minerals which are involved together in the flow of energy and the circulation of matter'.

Several processes of great importance are involved, and one useful way of studying ecosystems is to consider them in terms of these main processes. Ovington (1962), for example, selected four:

production of matter;

flow of energy;

flow of water;

cycle of nutrients.

Others have focused more on population dynamics, especially in 'natural' situations, while workers in agriculture have naturally tended to emphasize the output of some product. Agricultural scientists have had increasingly to include in their purview economic considerations, and the planning of farming operations in relation to the use of all resources (Barlow 1966), including climatic resources (Curry 1963), even to the point of considering alternative crops for the efficient use of land (Mitchell 1966).

There are thus several quite different ways of approaching the subject of grassland ecology and the one selected in this book is chosen because it ought to be useful to *all* concerned. The intention is a unifying one but it is not yet possible to achieve either a complete description or a coherent synthesis of the whole subject. As mentioned earlier, this does not invalidate the attempt but it does condition the method.

The first part of the book (Chapters 2–8) deals with the plant, both as an individual and as part of grassland populations, and with the efficiency of primary production.

Chapters 9–16 are concerned with the fauna of grassland, their interactions with the plant population, and the efficiency of secondary production.

The final chapters (17–20) are devoted to agricultural output of the main products derived from grassland that are of benefit to man.

In some chapters the issues have been greatly simplified in order to describe the major processes with greater clarity. In others, some of the detail and complexity are indicated to illustrate the range of additional material with which these simple outlines have to be clothed.

Essentially, we are engaged in the building of models, of one sort or another, of the biological processes we describe. They may be represented by ideas in the mind of how it all works and fits together, by qualitative accounts, or by quantified descriptions involving formulae to describe precise relationships. If complex ecosystems are to be fully comprehended, the assistance of mathematical models must be sought. Mathematical expression has all the advantages of precision, clarity, and brevity that are needed in handling complexity without over-simplification. The fact that it also opens the door to the use of computers makes calculations possible that would not have been physically possible otherwise.

It seems clear that one major ecological activity will involve the construction of such mathematical models, and it is essential that the biologist, whatever his own competence in mathematics, should not be afraid of this development. It would be a great pity if the mathematical and non-mathematical approaches separated: it is of the essence of ecology that the biologist and biometrician should co-operate and combine, rather than allow development to proceed in distinct compartments.

Because ignorance makes model-making seem much more difficult and abstruse than it really is, a simple account of the way in which it is undertaken is given in the Appendix.

The rest of the book attempts to describe the grassland ecosystem in more familiar terms; but, eventually, a more precise and comprehensive picture will have to be formulated by the greater use of mathematical models.

The present account is concerned more with the anatomy of the subject, but from a functional point of view.

References

BARLOW, C. (1966) *Expl. Agric.* **2**, 317–29.
CURRY, L. (1963) *Econ. Geogr.* **39**, 95–118.
DAVIES, W. (1960) *The grass crop*, 2nd edn. Spon, London.
HARTLEY, W. (1964) *Grasses and grasslands* (editor C. Barnard), chapter 3. MacMillan, London.
MILLER, R. B. (1966) *Proc. N.Z. ecol. Soc.* **13**, 49–52.
MITCHELL, K. J. (1966) *N.Z. agric. Sci.* **2**, 23–9.
MOORE, C. W. E. (1964) *Grasses and grasslands* (editor C. Barnard), chapter 11. MacMillan, London.
MOULE, G. R. (1964) *Proc. N.Z. Soc. Anim. Prod.* **24**, 90–110.
NAVEH, Z. and RON, B. (1966) *Proc. Xth int. Grassld Congr.*, Helsinki, pp. 871–4.
OVINGTON, J. D. (1962) *Adv. Ecol. Res.* **1**, 103–203.
PURI, G. S. (1966) *Proc. Xth int. Grassld Congr.*, Helsinki, pp. 818–23.

SHAMSONTDINOV, I. S. (1966) *Proc. Xth int. Grassld Congr.*, Helsinki, pp. 960–2.
TANSLEY, A. G. (1939) *The British islands and their vegetation.* Cambridge University Press.
—— (1946) *Introduction to plant ecology.* Allen & Unwin, London.
THOMAS, A. S. (1960) *Proc. IXth int. Grassld Congr.*, Reading, pp. 405–7.
WOODFORD, E. K. (1965) *Grass tomorrow.* Lecture at Seale–Hayne Agricultural College, Devon.

2

The Individual Plant

GRASSLAND ecology is not greatly concerned with the individual plant but it is a useful starting-point from which to explore the whole soil–plant–animal complex. In this chapter the individual plant will be considered briefly and from this point of view.

Since grassland may contain many different plant species it is necessary to be extremely selective. It was argued in the previous chapter that a major characteristic of grassland is the formation of a more-or-less continuous canopy consisting of plant species that may be described as sward-forming, especially under the influence of grazing. The most typical of these species are grasses and legumes and this chapter will confine itself to these as examples.

The features of greatest ecological significance are:

structure—morphology and growth habit;
nutrition—the needs of the plant;
photosynthesis—the provision of energy;
growth—rate and pattern;
reproduction—methods and seasonality;
senescence and decay—of leaves and roots;
longevity and perenniality—of all plant parts.

These will be discussed briefly for both pasture grasses and legumes.

Structure

Grasses

The majority of grasses possess the following features, embodied in growth forms varying from tufted tussocks to prostrate, creeping, or straggling types (Barnard 1964):

(1) The stems are cylindrical and jointed with short basal internodes;

(2) branches of successive orders are arranged in alternating planes at right angles;

(3) the leaves are long and narrow with parallel veins and sheathing bases;

(4) the leaf arrangement is in two opposite rows;

(5) the root system is fibrous and consists mainly of adventitious roots arising from nodes of the stem;

(6) the flowers and embryos have characteristic structures, the seeds are albuminous, and the fruits of caryopsis type. (For detailed descriptions see Armstrong 1948, Hubbard 1954).

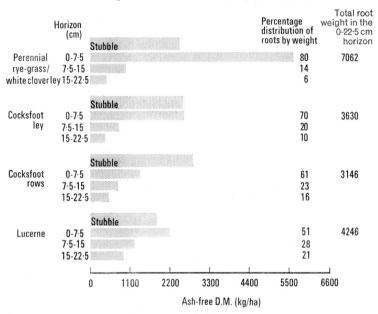

FIG. 2.1. The average weight of stubble and the quantity and percentage distribution of roots under different types of sward. (From Baker and Garwood 1959.)

The fact that the majority of the roots are to be found in the top layer of the soil has considerable significance (see Fig. 2.1) but should not obscure the fact that penetration down to depths of several metres is quite common; this greatly influences the reaction of the plant to drought.

The roots of grasses such as *Spartinia michauxiana* have been recorded down to depths of 2·4–3·3 m (Troughton 1957) and of

Phalaris tuberosa down to 2·1 m (McWilliam and Kramer 1968). The distribution of root dry matter with depth is shown for a grass and a legume in Table 2.1.

TABLE 2.1

Percentage of root dry matter (From Troughton 1957)

Species	Depth (cm)				
	0–10	10–20	20–30	30–40	40–50
Lolium perenne	80.3	9.3	4.6	3.5	2.3
Trifolium repens	82.4	5.9	8.1	2.6	1.0

Probably the most important feature in relation to sward formation is the tendency to branch or tiller (see Langer 1963), although in some species the development of rhizomes or stolons may have the same effect.

Legumes

The structure of legumes also varies between erect and creeping. In the latter forms all the meristematic activity occurs near to ground level, with implications to possible damage by grazing, except in those legumes that climb up other plants. Erect forms possess a well-marked crown, so that if the plant dies a space is left in the sward.

The leaves are arranged alternately on the stem and, apart from the first produced, are compound, usually forming three leaflets, the shape of which varies greatly between genera. The terminal leaflet is often modified to form a tendril in climbing plants. The flower is characteristic, brightly coloured, and adapted to insect pollination; the fruit is a pod, often of considerable food value to animals. The root system usually involves a well-developed tap-root as well as profusely branched secondary roots and the depth of soil penetration in some species is considerable (up to 2 m in *Medicago sativa*, for example).

Many creeping legumes have stolons that remain close to the soil surface and root at the distal nodes. These roots develop in a similar manner to the main root system.

A most important feature of the roots is the development of nodules in which nitrogen-fixing bacteria form a symbiotic relationship with the legume. These bacteria, of the genus *Rhizobium*, are host specific and the correct strain must be present. They occur as free-living soil organisms but may not be present where required; plants may then be inoculated. When nodules are ineffective, they are small, numerous, and whitish; when they are effective, they are usually few, large, and reddish in colour (Davies 1969).

Growth and nutrition

The growth of grasses and legumes is influenced by the same factors that affect all plant growth, primarily the supply of light, nutrients, and an adequate temperature.

The main differences between the two are that legumes are independent of soil nitrogen, in the sense that if they are effectively nodulated they can make use of nitrogen from the air. Legumes tend to prefer less-acid soils than do grasses.

Van Burg (1966) has found that the maximum growth-rate from grass cannot be obtained if the internal nitrate concentration in the herbage is less than about 100 mmol/kg dry matter. This figure can be used as a criterion for the application of fertilizer as ammonium nitrate, limestone, and calcium nitrate, but not for ammonium sulphate.

Water-supply is always important for growth but the availability of soil water depends greatly on the root system. Here there is often an important difference between grasses and legumes. If the water table is low it may still be available to both grasses and legumes, if their roots penetrate deeply enough. Frequently, however, the water available at depth is deficient in plant nutrients, especially nitrates. In this situation grasses may fail to grow but continue to transpire at a high rate, whereas the legume may grow simply because it is independent of the supply of soil nitrogen.

The optimum temperature for growth has been found to vary with the species. For legumes, for example, *Trifolium repens* grew at a maximum rate at 23·9 °C and subterranean clover at 18·9 °C (Mitchell 1956). Nitrogen fixation in subterranean clover was optimal between 22 and 26 °C, and at 5 °C was only 10–17 per cent of that at 18 °C (Gibson 1963).

In grasses, the optimum temperature for growth also varies with species. For *Lolium perenne* and *Dactylis glomerata*, growth is most rapid at a temperature between 13 and 18 °C. *Paspalum* spp., on the other hand, grow most rapidly at much higher temperatures, in the region of 30 °C. In general, temperate species have optima at about

20 °C, will grow at temperatures down to 5–10 °C, and exhibit light saturation between 20 000 and 30 000 lx (Cooper and Tainton 1968). Tropical grasses, on the other hand, have optima between 30 and 35 °C, often fail to grow below 15 °C, and continue assimilation and growth up to 60 000 lx or even higher.

Growth can occur at a range of light intensities: Blackman and Black (1959) recorded maximum relative growth-rates (g/g/day) of lucerne at $2\cdot51 \times$ daylight, of red clover at $1\cdot00 \times$ daylight, and of Italian rye-grass at $0\cdot71$.

In addition to oxygen and carbon dioxide, derived mainly from the atmosphere (6 per cent of carbon dioxide needs may come from biological processes in the soil (Monteith, Szeicz, and Yabuki 1964)), the following major nutrients are regarded as essential and they have to be taken up in aqueous solution by the root system: N, Ca, P, K, S, and Mg. In addition, the following minor or trace elements are required: Fe, Mn, Cu, B, Mo, and Zn. Other minor elements often occur in plants but may not be essential; they include: Na, Cl, Al, Si, Se, and Co.

Legumes not only derive their own needs of nitrogen from the atmosphere but contribute substantial quantities to the soil (see Chapter 12).

The energy for growth, as for all other processes in green plants, is provided by photosynthesis.

Photosynthesis

Sunlight is absorbed by the green system of the plastids, mainly chlorophyll, and the energy liberated is used to produce chiefly sugars and carbohydrates but also proteins, fatty acids, fats, and a variety of other compounds required for the regeneration of chloroplasts (Bassham and Jensen 1967). The supply of light to an isolated individual plant is determined by the daylength, season, cloud cover, and other factors related to the general environment. Much more important in most circumstances is the supply of light energy to a crop or plant population, or to the individual plant growing in a community (see Chapter 3).

At low light intensities the photosynthetic function may be described as about $3\cdot6$ kg carbohydrate/ha/hour for each $0\cdot01$ cal/cm^2/min absorbed by the leaves, with a maximum for individual leaves of agriculturally important species of about 20 kg carbohydrate/ha/hour (de Wit 1967). De Wit points out that leaves that absorb a light intensity of 0·2 cal/cm²/min already operate close to this maximum. Since this light intensity can occur on an overcast day, the light intensity on a clear day (up to 0·8 cal/cm²/min) may be largely wasted on plants with large, horizontally displayed leaves.

Light also has considerable influence on reproduction in both grasses and clovers, especially in terms of daylength.

Senescence and decay

The longevity of plants and of the individual parts of plants is of great importance ecologically. In general, grasses and legumes are characterized by the short time for which a high proportion of the plant lives. Grass plants are difficult to define and it is often difficult to say when an individual is still present or has ceased to exist, because of the tillering habit of growth, or the development of rhizomes or stolons. Grass plant units and certainly grass swards may live for very long periods (decades at least), but individual leaves and roots are relatively short-lived.

Grass tillers may live for a few weeks or for more than a year, producing some thirty leaves in that time, at the rate of, perhaps, one a week during the summer. Relatively few leaves of agricultural grasses live longer than about 8 weeks. The rate of leaf appearance is affected by many factors (Anslow 1966), as is the rate at which they senesce. Amongst the more important are light, temperature, and soil moisture deficiency.

Individual grass roots also vary greatly in longevity and it is not always easy to determine when a root has died. Garwood (1967) estimated that the mean length of life of *Lolium perenne* roots varied from month to month, from 61 to 188 days. Roots produced in the autumn lived longer than roots produced at other times of the year.

Young grass roots are reported to decay fairly rapidly, usually disappearing within 2 years (Troughton 1957).

Comparable information is not available for legumes, in spite of the importance of root death and decay as a means of liberating nitrogen fixed from the atmosphere.

The function of plants

Plants are often referred to as though their main function was the trapping of light energy, and many calculations have been made as to the efficiency with which they do this. No one would suggest that photosynthesis is not of very great importance but attention must not be concentrated on it to such an extent that other processes are ignored.

In a sense, all the plant nutrients are of equal importance also, for without them the sun's energy could not be used productively. Similarly, the gases, oxygen, carbon dioxide, and nitrogen are vital. It may be argued that the sun's energy is the only component that has to come from outside the earth, though it is not easy to see the precise significance of this; nor are the gaseous boundaries absolutely clear. Indeed, in most circumstances, light may be regarded as the least limiting factor, even though light energy once used never re-appears as usable light.

Nor is there necessarily any good reason why the sun's rays should be used with maximum efficiency. Present usage is very inefficient; Army and Greer (1967) quote photosynthetic efficiencies of 2–2·5 per cent for agriculturally advanced areas. Net efficiency, corrected to absorbed visible radiation, was 7·3 per cent for the most active part of the growing period for a corn crop at Ithaca, New York (Lemon 1966). It follows that the current problems of food production could be solved without approaching maximum photosynthetic efficiency over a wide area, and there is, in any case, no reason why the world should support the maximum possible human population.

However, whatever efficiency grassland plants operate at, it is generally not as individual plants but in very closely knit communities.

References

ANSLOW, R. C. (1966) *Herb. Abstr.* **36**, 149–55.

ARMSTRONG, S. F. (1948) *British Grasses*. Cambridge University Press.

ARMY, T. J. and GREER, F. A. (1967) *Harvesting the sun* (editors A. S. Pietro, F. A. Greer, and T. J. Army), pp. 321–32. Academic Press, New York.

BAKER, H. K. and GARWOOD, E. A. (1959) *J. Br. Grassld Soc.* **14**, 94–104.

BARNARD, C. (editor) (1964) *Grasses and grasslands*, chapter 4. Macmillan, London.

BASSHAM, J. A. and JENSEN, R. G. (1967) *Harvesting the sun* (editors A. S. Pietro, F. A. Greer, and T. J. Army), pp. 79–110. Academic Press, New York.

BLACKMAN, G. E. and BLACK, J. N. (1959) *Ann. Bot.* **23**, 51–63.

COOPER, J. P. and TAINTON, N. M. (1968) *Herb. Abstr.* **38**, 167–76.

DAVIS, W. ELLIS (1969) *Crop grasses and legumes in British agriculture* (editor C. R. W. Spedding), chapter 24. Commonwealth Agricultural Bureau.

GARWOOD, E. A. (1967) *J. Br. Grassld Soc.* **22**, 121–30.

GIBSON, A. H. (1963) *Aust. J. biol. Sci.* **16**, 28–42.

HUBBARD, C. E. (1954) *Grasses: a guide to their structure, identification, uses, and distribution in the British Isles.* Penguin, Harmondsworth, England.

LANGER, R. H. M. (1963) *Herb. Abstr.* **33**, 141–8.

LEMON, E. R. (1966) *Plant environment and efficient water use* (editors W. H. Pierre, D. Kirkham, J. Pesek, and R. Shaw), pp. 24–48. Am. Soc. Agron., Wisconsin.

MCWILLIAM, J. R. and KRAMER, P. J. (1968) *Aust. J. agric. Res.* **19**, 381–95.

MITCHELL, K. J. (1956) *N.Z. Jl Sci. Technol.* **38A**, 203–16.

MONTEITH, J. L., SZEICZ, G. and YABUKI, K. (1964) *J. appl. Ecol.* **1**, 321–37.

TROUGHTON, A. (1957) *The underground organs of herbage grasses. C.A.B. Bull.* No. 44.

VAN BURG, P. F. J. (1966) *Proc. Xth int. Grassld Congr.*, Helsinki, pp. 267–72.

DE WIT, C. T. (1967) *Harvesting the sun* (editors A. S. Pietro, F. A. Greer, and T. J. Army), pp. 315–20. Academic Press, New York.

3

The Plant Population

THE main difference between isolated plants and those growing in populations, as in a grass sward, is that the environment of the latter includes the presence of the surrounding plants. These may be of the same or different species and they may interfere or compete with each other to a greater or lesser extent. The question of competition is further discussed in Chapter 7 and will not therefore be dealt with specifically here.

What must be considered is the manner in which plants interact with each other when they grow in populations, especially in relation to energy and nutrient supplies.

The effect on the individual plant

Light

Plants growing in a stand have two sources of light, direct sunlight and diffuse skylight. The foliage area that actually receives direct sunlight can be calculated for any particular foliage-area index, given the inclination of the foliage (α) and of the sunlight (β), provided certain assumptions are made (Warren Wilson 1967). The area of sunlit foliage (in the case of *Medicago sativa*) increased with β when α was greater than β but was independent of β when α was less than β.

The flow of light through the foliage is clearly influenced by sward structure (Anderson 1966, Cowan 1968) and this is affected by many factors, including the pattern of defoliation (Hunt and Brougham 1967). A major aspect of the attenuation of light is the amount of leaf displayed. Watson (1947) introduced the concept of leaf-area index (L) to denote the leaf area per unit of land area. This indicates the relative area available for photosynthesis, although stems, petioles, leaf sheaths, and inflorescences also intercept light and contribute to varying degrees in photosynthesis (Brown and Blaser 1968).

The vertical distribution of L and the associated illumination profiles of many plant communities have been studied by Monsi and Saeki (1953), who found that their observations fitted the Bouguer–Lambert law: $I = I_o e^{-KL}$, where I and I_o refer to the illumination of a horizontal surface within and above the canopy, respectively, and K is the extinction coefficient. For grass-type canopies, K generally fell between 0·3 and 0·5. Differences have been demonstrated between grassy and clovery swards, however (Stern and Donald 1962).

Although only the 0·4 to 0·7 μm wave region of sunlight is important for photosynthesis, the spectral modifications that occur within plant communities are relatively small (Loomis, Williams, and Duncan 1967).

The main effect on the individual plant of growing within a dense population is thus on the light intensity received by its photosynthetic regions. The area of leaf is thus important, as is leaf duration, and it is an important attribute of some plant populations that water loss is not increased by increasing the amount of leaf (Bunting 1958). This argument will not apply, however, to crops with less than full ground cover.

Water

The effect on water-supply may be rather different since the roots of one plant do not reduce the water available to another plant, except in conditions of drought, although early-growing components of a mixture may reduce the water available for a later-growing component (but see Milthorpe (1961) for a discussion on the interactions involved in competition between plants with different root distributions). When a grass crop has extracted water from a soil at field capacity†, resulting in a soil moisture deficit of 7 cm, transpiration is likely to be reduced (Penman 1958) and growth may cease. As the water deficit approaches this level, however, herbage growth may progressively decrease and may be measurably depressed by a deficit of 2·5 cm (Stiles and Garwood 1963). Since a deficit of this magnitude can be reached in one week in fine summer weather in England, for example, water shortage may affect large areas for short periods. Where water-supply is not limiting, transpiration of a crop is dominated by meteorological conditions, especially incident

† Field capacity is represented by a saturated soil in which the maximum amount of water is held against gravity. The soil moisture deficit is the amount of rain or irrigation water required to restore field capacity.

radiation. The water consumption of a complete, relatively uniform cover of short green plants, as in a grass sward, is then related to the evaporation from a free surface during daylight (Penman 1948). Water consumption under these conditions is known as the 'potential transpiration'.

Maximum plant growth occurs when the actual transpiration equals the potential transpiration.

Rather more energy is available for transpiration than for photosynthesis, from solar radiation alone but also from thermal or re-radiation and convected sensible heat in the air (Lemon 1966).

In practice, irrigation can greatly increase pasture production (Smith 1960, Campbell 1967).

Minerals

As with water, in which the minerals are dissolved, the effect on an individual plant of growing in a pasture is only significant at times of shortage. In both cases the volume of soil that can be explored by one plant alone is much less in a sward, but this is unlikely to prove disadvantageous when nutrient supplies are plentiful.

Carbon dioxide

The requirements of grassland plants for carbon dioxide have to be met by passage of the gas from the air through the stomata to the chloroplasts. The process is therefore influenced by the size of the stomatal opening and by the rate of transpiration (Zelitch 1967). Since pasture may form a dense canopy with a distinct microclimate within it, the supply of carbon dioxide to the individual plant may be greatly affected by the structure of the sward.

The difference between the carbon dioxide concentration in the atmosphere and within the sward must depend on such factors as wind speed (Lemon 1967), but atmospheric mixing is usually vigorous enough to maintain CO_2 concentration close to 300 ppm at the assimilating leaves of a field crop (Monteith, Szeicz, and Yabuki 1964). Also, in a grass crop growing rapidly in early spring, the soil supplies about 6 per cent of the total carbon assimilated. The possibility of such carbon dioxide remaining within the canopy depends on the structure of the sward and is less relevant for an isolated individual plant. The carbon dioxide produced by a plant during respiration, however, is generally used by the individual plant during photosynthesis.

Oxygen

Oxygen is also affected by sward structure, but there is no evidence that individual plants or the sward as a whole are ever deficient in it. The oxygen produced during photosynthesis probably supplies the current needs for respiration, but production is greatly in excess of these needs.

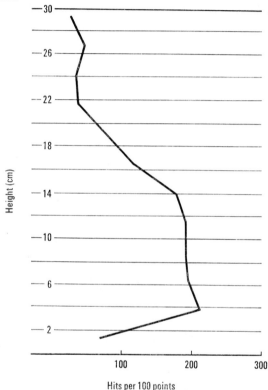

Fig. 3.1. Profile of height and density (as estimated by point quadrat) of a perennial rye-grass sward. (After Spedding and Large 1957.)

Sward structure

This is important for many reasons, some of which have been mentioned already. The structure of individual plants influences whether they shade or are shaded by others, whether they are grazed or damaged by the hooves of grazing animals, and how different their microclimate is from that of the atmosphere. The appropriate description of sward structure varies with the aspect being considered.

Height and density are obvious features but turn out to be extremely difficult to describe for a sward. The fact is that there are serious deficiencies in the criteria of 'average' height (the mean height of all the component plants or the mean height of all the leaves and stems) and in the maximum height of the community (that of its tallest plant). Similarly, density is difficult to describe usefully unless a particular height stratum is specified. The difficulties are obvious from an examination of Fig. 3.1.

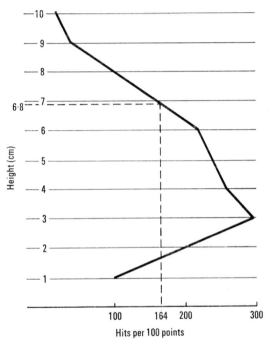

FIG. 3.2. The derivation of a 'height index' from a sward with a maximum height of 10 cm (R), with a total number of hits (T) at all heights of 1540, and with a maximum density at 3 cm. (After Spedding and Large 1957.)

Height index = the height at which the mean number of hits (T/R = 164) occurs = 6·8 cm.

(Since the mean number of hits can occur at more than one height, the strict definition is 'the height above which density is always less than the mean'.)

One of the ways in which height and density can be expressed is therefore to combine them in an index that expresses the height below which some large proportion of the crop lies (see Fig. 3.2). This could be based on weights of herbage (fresh or as D.M.) or on volume (as indicated by point–quadrat estimations). Such descriptions of the disposition of plant material per unit area of soil and per unit of height may be relevant in studying the grazing animal but they are unlikely to be very useful in considering the growth of the plant. Crop structure in relation to growth, and especially in relation to photosynthesis, has also been expressed quantitatively, as in the leaf-area index already referred to, and in terms of the amount of chlorophyll in a sward. The optimum value of chlorophyll for Ladino clover regrowth, for example, has been found to be 1·2–2·5 g/m² (Nishimura, Okubo, and Hoshino 1966).

For some purposes, however, such as an understanding of crop physiology, a more detailed description is required. The importance of leaf arrangement (see Jewiss 1967) varies with the leaf-area index. In general, a horizontal arrangement is advantageous at low values of leaf-area index and a more erect habit at higher values; leaf arrangement appears to matter less at high leaf-area index values, however.

The structure of grassland vegetation has a considerable bearing on productivity (Mitchell 1966) and will therefore be considered again in Chapters 4 and 5. The same is true of plant growth-rate but there are characteristic patterns of growth that are relevant to a description of the grassland plant population.

Pattern of growth

In most temperate grasslands the pattern of growth is largely determined by temperature, usually by the periods of low temperature. Shelter can therefore influence the productivity of grassland by modifying the local climate (Marshall 1967). Extremes of high temperature can have the same effect but drought is the most common major determinant of growth pattern apart from low temperature. (For a discussion on the effect of climate on forage grasses, see Cooper 1965.)

It might be expected that, within a tolerable temperature range, the pattern of growth would be closely related to incident light supply, either in terms of day length or light intensity. This is by no means always the case, however, and such factors as the rhythm of flowering and tiller regeneration may be important determinants of a sward's capacity to sustain herbage growth (Anslow 1965).

The seasonal growth of pasture grasses in Britain has been extensively investigated by Anslow and Green (1967), some of whose

C

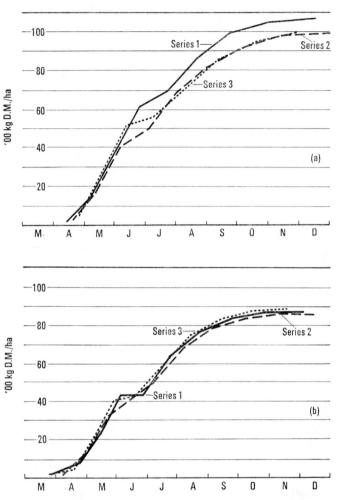

FIG. 3.3. The accumulation of the annual yield of herbage from three series of plots, cut in staggered sequence. The interval between cuts was the same in each series, but the dates of cut varied between series by one-third of the current growth interval. (a) of timothy (var. *S*.48) in 1963; (b) of timothy (var. *S*.51) in 1964. (From Anslow and Green 1967.)

results are illustrated in Fig. 3.3, and by Alberda and Sibma (1968) in Holland. Anslow and Green assessed growth-rate by a series of cuts of monthly regrowth, three pairs of plots being cut in staggered sequence; fertilizer applications and irrigation use were designed to supply an abundance of plant nutrients and adequate soil moisture.

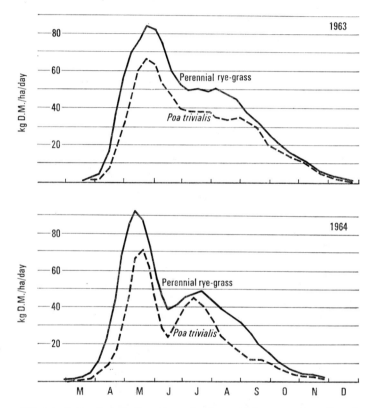

FIG. 3.4. Rates of production of swards of perennial rye-grass (var. *S.* 101) and *Poa trivialis*. (From Anslow and Green 1967.)

The very marked seasonal pattern of growth that they found could not be entirely related to the changes in temperature and radiation. At relatively low temperature in the spring higher rates of production were found than at the same temperature in the autumn. Maximum rates of production occurred at average temperatures of only 10–13 °C and did not coincide with the maximum daily receipt of solar energy (see Fig. 3.4).

Efficiency of conversion of incident solar energy was calculated for perennial rye-grass (variety *S.* 101), assuming (*a*) that 'the illumination active in photosynthesis was 46 per cent of the total radiation recorded', and (*b*) that the calorific value of grass dry matter was 4·25 k cal/g. Efficiency varied up to about 2 per cent (see Fig. 3.5), but, as Anslow and Green point out, this relates only to the energy contained in harvested herbage and not the energy of the whole

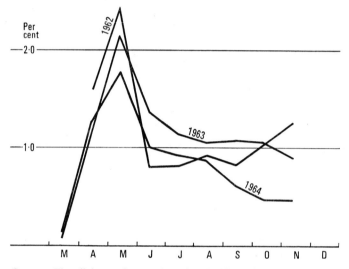

Fig. 3.5. The efficiency of conversion of the incident solar energy, active in photosynthesis, into the energy of grass harvested from swards of perennial rye-grass (var. *S.* 101). (From Anslow and Green 1967.)

plant. Maximum growth-rates, as determined by Anslow and Green (1967), were of the order of 88 kg dry matter/ha/day: rates exceeded this over short periods of the undisturbed growth of a sward, reaching 220–330 kg dry matter/ha/day during April/May (Anslow and Back 1967) in southern England.

The pattern of growth for legumes (Fig. 3.6) usually shows a rather different distribution, although it is primarily influenced by the same environmental factors.

In the longer term, other considerations influence the yield of a pasture, such as the accumulation of pests and diseases, changes in plant nutrient status of the soil, and changes in botanical composition. One of the expressions of such changes is the occurrence of what have been called the 'years of depression', a period of some years of poor production, lower than that of the first year after sowing, from which pastures recover eventually. Hoogerkamp and Minderhoud (1966) have discussed this in relation to grassland in the Netherlands. They concluded that the prime cause in young grassland with a good botanical composition was a decreased nitrate supply (mineralization of organic matter) on soils with a low humus content.

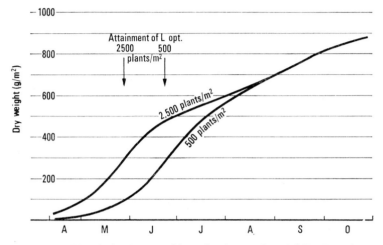

FIG. 3.6. The calculated course of dry-weight increase in undefoliated swards of subterranean clover, 1950 (in Adelaide). (From Black 1964.)

Whatever the annual yield of herbage, however, grass growth is usually characterized by marked seasonality. This can be greatly modified by the patterns of fertilizer application and of defoliation. There are also marked differences between herbage growth-rate in different habitats, that are related to differences in soil temperature (Alcock, Lovett, and Machin 1968).

References

ALBERDA, T. and SIBMA, L. (1968) *J. Br. Grassld Soc.* **23**, 206–15.
ALCOCK, M. B., LOVETT, J. V. and MACHIN, D. (1968) The measurement of environmental factors in terrestrial ecology. *Br. Ecol. Soc. Symp.* No. 8, pp. 191–203.
ANDERSON, M. C. (1966) *J. appl. Ecol.* **3**, 41–54.
ANSLOW, R. C. (1965) *J. Br. Grassld Soc.* **20**, 19–26.
—— and BACK, H. L. (1967) *J. Br. Grassld Soc.* **22**, 108–111.
—— and GREEN, J. O. (1967) *J. agric. Sci., Camb.* **68**, 109–22.

BROUGHAM, R. W. (1962) *J. Ecol.* **50**, 449–60.

BROWN, R. H. and BLASER, R. E. (1968) *Herb. Abstr.* **38**, 1–9.

BUNTING, A. H. (1958) *Agric. Prog.* **33**, 42–50.

CAMPBELL, A. G. (1967) *Proc. N.Z. Soc. Anim. Prod.* **27**, 126–38.

COOPER, J. P. (1965) The biological significance of climatic changes in Britain. *Inst. Biol. Symp.* No. 14, pp. 169–171.

COWAN, I. R. (1965) *J. appl. Ecol.* **2**, 221–39.

—— (1968) *J. appl. Ecol.* **5**, 367–79.

HOOGERKAMP, M. and MINDERHOUD, J. W. (1966) *Proc. Xth int. Grassld Congr.*, Helsinki, pp. 282–7.

HUNT, L. A. and BROUGHAM, R. W. (1966) *J. appl. Ecol.* **3**, 21–8.

JEWISS, O .R. (1967) Fodder conservation. *Occ. Symp. Br. Grassld Soc.* **3**, 53–65.

LEMON, E. R. (1966) *Plant environment and efficient water use* (editors W. H. Pierre, D. Kirkham, J. Pesek, and R. Shaw), chapter 3. *Amer. Soc. Agron. and Soil Sci. Soc. Amer.*

LEMON, E. (1967) *Harvesting the sun* (editors A. S. Pietro, F. A. Greer, and T. J. Army), pp. 263–90. Academic Press, New York.

LOOMIS, R. S., WILLIAMS, W. A. and DUNCAN, W. G. (1967) *Harvesting the sun* (editors A. S. Pietro, F. A. Greer, and T. J. Army), pp. 291–308. Academic Press, New York.

MARSHALL, J. K. (1967) *Fld Crop Abstr.* **20**, 1–16.

MILTHORPE, F. L. (1961) Mechanisms in biological competition. *Symp. Soc. Exp. Biol.* xv, 330–55.

MITCHELL, K. J. (1966) *Proc. N.Z. ecol. Soc.* **13**, 52–8.

MONSI, M. and SAEKI, T. (1953) *Jap. J. Bot.* **14**, 22–52.

MONTEITH, J. L. (1962) *Neth. J. agric. Sci.* **10**, 334–46.

——SZEICZ, G. and YABUKI, K. (1964) *J. appl. Ecol.* **1**, 321–37.

NISHIMURA, S., OKUBO, T. and HOSHINO, M. (1966) *Proc. Xth int. Grassld Congr.*, Helsinki, pp. 117–20.

PENMAN, H. L. (1948) *Proc. R. Soc.* A193, 120–45.

—— (1958) The biological productivity of Britain, pp. 91–9. *Inst. Biol. Symp.* 1957.

SMITH, L. P. (1960) *J. Br. Grassld Soc.* **15**, 203–8.

STERN, W. R. and DONALD, C. M. (1962) *Aust. J. agric. Res.* **13**, 599–614.

STILES, W. and GARWOOD, E. A. (1963) Climatic factors and agricultural productivity. *Memo* No. 6. Geography Dept., University College of Wales, Aberystwyth.

WARREN WILSON, J. (1967) *J. appl. Ecol.* **4**, 159–65.

WATSON, D. J. (1947) *Ann. Bot.* **11**, 41–76.

ZELITCH, I. (1967) *Harvesting the sun* (editors A. S. Pietro, F. A. Greer, and T. J. Army), pp. 231–48. Academic Press, New York.

4

Concepts of Efficiency in Primary Production

EFFICIENCY of production simply means the ratio of output of products to input of resources. It can therefore be calculated for any product, which may relate to one or more constituents of the plant, and for any of the resources employed. There is no reason, for example, why the efficiency of protein production should not be expressed in terms of the water used to produce it; in an arid area this might be extremely important.

There are thus many different calculations all perfectly valid and of interest in certain circumstances. The most important are those concerned with the major resources and the most important products. All resources are important but the major ones may be listed as follows:

land   nitrogen   carbon
light   water   time

The appropriate one to choose depends on whether the intrinsic interest or the practical value of the calculation is uppermost.

Clearly, in many circumstances, land simply summarizes the supply of nitrogen and water, and the opportunity to collect light.

Time is included because where a resource is not limiting, frequently the case with carbon as carbon dioxide, the important calculation is the rate at which it is incorporated into the plant, the soil, or the system as a whole.

The product is superficially easier to define, but in practice production is extremely difficult to measure and these difficulties are often reflected in the definition.

Agriculturally, the problem is simpler since grassland vegetation is grown for some purpose and this helps to specify the product. Furthermore, the product is only that part of the vegetation (often called the yield) that is harvested, by man or by grazing animals. Even this is often very difficult to measure or estimate. In general, harvested herbage for use in agriculture can be described in terms of

(1) fresh weight—of only limited value;
(2) dry weight (dry matter)—of value only if additional data are available on quality;
(3) digestible matter (D.D.M. = digestible dry matter, D.O.M. = digestible organic matter), related to how digestible the herbage is to a particular animal;
(4) weight of protein (generally derived from nitrogen content: crude protein = C.P. = $N \times 6.25$);
(5) energy (the energy content of grass appears to be relatively constant at $4.2–4.5$ kcal/g D.M. (Harris 1969)).

The problem of assessing the food value of herbage will be discussed in later chapters (8 and 10) but it may be helpful to give some indication at this point. Blaxter (1964) has pointed out that the energy that grass supplies to an animal can be conveniently measured as metabolizable energy (M.E. = the heat of combustion of the food less the heat of combustion of the faeces, the urine, and the combustible gas, mostly methane, that is produced from it). Metabolizable energy can be estimated by multiplying the apparently digested energy by 0.82; alternatively, but with slightly greater error, by assuming that each gramme of digested organic matter has a metabolizable energy value of 3.6 kcal.

The choice of expression does not greatly affect the method of calculation or the general concept and tends to be largely determined by the resource being considered.

For non-agricultural purposes there is much less justification for excluding any part of the plant (Troughton 1960, Holliday 1966) or for measuring production at a particular series of harvests; but there are considerable difficulties in measuring all the herbage grown, including that which is lost by senescence and decay in periodic harvesting, and in measuring the production of the whole plant, including the roots (Troughton 1957, Leith 1968, Newbould 1968). For a detailed discussion of the components of plant production, see Warren Wilson (1967).

If production is assessed in terms of foliage, it has to be assumed that this is an approximately constant proportion of the whole plant, or that the foliage is a suitable index of total production, or that foliage production is of direct interest as the basis of secondary production; all these assumptions involve some degree of over-simplification.

At this point it is worth noting that in *Bromus marginatus* some 33–52 per cent of the plant's weight was recorded in the roots (Troughton 1957); the figures for *Agropyron smithii* were 61–4 per cent, and for *Agropyron ciliare* 48–50 per cent. Selected maximum yields are shown in Table 4.1.

TABLE 4.1

Weight of roots (kg dry matter or air-dry weight/ha) produced by swards (From Troughton 1957)

		kg/ha
Europe	*Molinia caerulea*	46 477
	Phalaris arundinacea	35 396
	Lolium perenne	13 310
U.S.A.	*Agropyron smithii*	15 235
	Panicum virgatum	23 342
South America	*Paspalum notatum*	15 270
Africa	*Cynodon dactylon*	11 825
Ceylon	*Tripsacum laxum*	49 280

The calculation of efficiency will now be considered in relation to the resources previously listed.

Land

Production per unit area of land is the commonest expression of agricultural output and is always likely to be important while crops are grown in soil, since the total area available is limited and is also subject to other demands.

It should be borne in mind that even with a given *area* of land, the extent to which the soil is explored for water and nutrients by the plant root system varies with the species (Tadmor, Cohen, Shanan, and Evenari 1966).

Light

Efficiency is commonly expressed in terms of the use of light because of the unique property of plants to engage in photosynthesis. But, in fact, very little of the incident light is ever used by plants. Solar radiation is not entirely useful to vegetation, only about 45 per cent of the energy received is in the photosynthetically useful range of

0·4–0·7 μm. Of the visible light received by leaves, about one-quarter is reflected and the rest absorbed. The latter is largely converted to long-wave radiation and re-emitted or used in the evaporation of water in transpiration. The total quantities of energy received are very large; Mitchell (1966) refers to an average of solar energy equivalent to over 10 000 kW/acre/day (about 22 000 kW/ha). Yet less than 2 per cent of this is generally used for photosynthesis and for heating and cooling the soil. Most leaves become light saturated at 25–30 per cent of full noon daylight in midsummer, and additional light makes no further contribution to photosynthesis (Jewiss 1967). Thus full exploitation of light requires a more complex receiving surface than a single horizontal layer, and maximum production should be obtained when water and nutrients are non-limiting and plant density is optimal. Under these conditions Donald (1951) found that *Trifolium subterraneum* could produce 930 g/m² year. Blackman and Black (1959) confirmed the importance of solar radiation and leaf area under such conditions, and calculated the efficiency of utilization of light energy as 4–10 per cent over short periods, 2–3 per cent for the whole year.

Army and Greer (1967) estimated that it was theoretically possible to produce about 77 g dry matter/m² on a bright sunny day, and de Wit (1967) has also estimated potential output as greatly in excess of current production. The interest in efficiency of light use is not because it is a limiting resource but because there is much scope for increasing production from the light already received. Efficiency is therefore commonly expressed per unit of land or the light that falls on it and is often calculated as the crop growth-rate (defined as rate of dry matter production per unit area of land).

There is not necessarily a relationship between harvested yield and crop growth-rate since the rate of senescence may vary greatly. Morris (1967) found that cocksfoot swards, maintained at different leaf area index values, produced similar amounts of 'gross aerial growth' but that senescence accounted for about one-third of it in each case. Senescence was thus equal to about half of the quantity harvested and, in this experiment, amounted to 3·8 g dry matter/m²/day. Brougham (1962), in quite different circumstances, estimated a daily loss of about 1·2 g/m² from Italian rye-grass.

As mentioned earlier, dry matter is only one of several ways of expressing production. It has the merit of being a relatively easy thing to measure accurately, provided that harvested top growth is all that is required. It is not, however, what plants actually create, nor is it what animals eat. It is impossible to regard dry matter as in any way the real substance of a living plant and it is interesting to note that it is rarely used in relation to the measurement of growth in animals. It is not what herbivores value in a feed, and they only absorb a part of it.

It is important to bear this in mind continually and not to become so accustomed to the convenience of the expression (dry matter) that one ceases to question its relevance.

An index of photosynthetic efficiency in relation to dry-matter yield is the net assimilation rate. This is the mean rate of dry-matter production per unit of leaf area; it thus measures the balance of photosynthetic gain over respiratory loss.

The output side of these calculations may be one component only of the dry matter gained, carbohydrate being a commonly used product. The resource used is a straightforward matter when it is land or time, but if it is light it is usually expressed as the proportion of the solar energy that is used by the vegetation. Generally, as in this chapter, the energy used is expressed as a percentage of that which is available to plants, that is, some 45 per cent of the total incident solar radiation.

Nitrogen

In a world that is short of protein, it is not surprising that nitrogen has been considered as a major product. Since nitrogen is also one of the major plant nutrients and the one most amenable to manipulation for agricultural production from grassland, one of the most important calculations of production efficiency is the output of nitrogen per unit of fertilizer nitrogen applied to the soil.

Output is also commonly expressed as dry matter and many estimates have been made of dry matter (D.M.) production per unit of applied nitrogen (N). Reid (1966) applied thirty-three rates of fertilizer nitrogen, ranging from 0 to 800 lb/acre (i.e. up to 880 kg/ha), to grass swards composed largely of *Lolium perenne* with about 10–15 per cent of *Phleum pratense*. The relationship between dry-matter yield per annum (Y_{dm} in 100 lb/acre) and the nitrogen application ($= X$ in lb/acre) could best be expressed by the following formula (where e = the base of natural logarithms):

$$Y_{dm} = 123 \cdot 18 - 69 \cdot 63 e^{-0 \cdot 00130\, X^{1 \cdot 32}}.$$

Similar calculations for yield of crude protein ($= Y_{cp}$) resulted in the following:

$$Y_{cp} = 28 \cdot 23 - 20 \cdot 35 e^{-0 \cdot 00060\, X^{1 \cdot 32}}.$$

Up to 150 lb/acre of applied nitrogen, the response was over 26 lb dry matter/lb nitrogen applied, but thereafter each additional pound of nitrogen produced less, reaching 13 lb of dry matter between 200 and 250 lb nitrogen/acre and less than 1 lb at rates over 500 lb nitrogen/acre.

The crude protein-yield response remained high up to 300 lb nitrogen/acre (about 330 kg/ha) and only fell below 1 lb when the application rate exceeded about 600 lb nitrogen/acre.

Crude protein is simply calculated from the nitrogen content and Reid (1966) found that there was a rapid increase in the nitrate content of the herbage at the higher rates of application (see Table 4.2).

TABLE 4.2

Mean content of nitrate–nitrogen in herbage (mostly Lolium perenne, *with about* 10–15 *per cent* Phleum pratense) *in relation to fertilizer nitrogen application (as nitro-chalk with* 21 *per cent N). Content expressed as percentage of total dry matter* (After Reid 1966)

Applied nitrogen (kg/ha)	NO_3–N (%)
0	0.011
110	0.019
220	0.035
330	0.084
440	0.254
550	0.313
660	0.408
770	0.492
880	0.531

The yield of nitrogen depends greatly on the presence or absence of a legume. Cowling and Lockyer (1967) studied seven species or varieties of grass, grown both with and without white clover. Yields of nitrogen differed little between the grass/clover mixtures: the nitrogen yields of the grass components were significantly different and tended to be negatively related to the nitrogen yields of clover. Pure grass swards required over 220 kg of fertilizer nitrogen/ha/year in order to yield the same amount of nitrogen as the mixtures. The percentage recovery of applied nitrogen tended to increase with level of nitrogen applied (Table 4.3) but, as Cowling and Lockyer (1967) point out, was generally lower than the 66–75 per cent suggested by Cooke (1964).

TABLE 4.3

Percentage recovery of fertilizer nitrogen (nitrogen yield in excess of control as a percentage of nitrogen applied). 3-year weighted mean (From Cowling and Lockyer 1967)

Grass	Fertilizer nitrogen (kg/ha)		
	90	180	360
S. 24 perennial rye-grass	35	48	61
S. 23 perennial rye-grass	39	48	63
Irish perennial rye-grass	38	46	50
S. 48 timothy	48	58	63
S. 215 meadow fescue	44	54	64
S. 37 cocksfoot	59	63	70
Agrostis tenuis	34	53	63
S. 24, S. 37, S. 48 mixture	48	58	67
Standard error	±3.60	±2.32	±1.20
Mean of all grasses	43	54	62

In all this it should again be remembered that only part of the plant is harvested.

The most relevant measure of efficiency in legumes is the quantity of nitrogen fixed in total per year. Different legume species vary greatly in this, as will emerge in later chapters (7 and 12). For very high-yielding plant populations, the annual yield of crude protein may be very large. Cooper (1967), for example, recorded 3500 lb/acre/year (about 3850 kg/ha) from heavily fertilized and irrigated small plots of S. 23 perennial rye-grass.

Water

Since water is mainly used by the plant in transpiration and only a very small proportion of the water absorbed by the roots is incorporated in plant material, it is in no sense a product of any real significance, although the herbage water content may be the main source of this element for many herbivores. The water content of herbage does vary, especially with the stage of growth, but not very much because of variations in soil moisture content.

The efficiency of water use is therefore generally expressed as the dry-matter yield per unit of additional water applied as irrigation.

It has been pointed out many times (Penman 1962, Stiles and Williams 1965) that, unless rainfall can be accurately predicted, irrigation water may have to be used wastefully. Whatever plan is adopted, when irrigation is applied it can immediately rain and the use of the applied water is rendered inefficient.

Apart from this, the general response to irrigation will be determined by the extent of the soil moisture deficit at the time. It has been suggested that, in Britain, working to a deficit not exceeding 1·5 in (about 3·7 cm) leads to annual yields being about 5 per cent below maximum and that for 2 in (about 5 cm) the reduction is 10 per cent (Tayler 1965).

What has already been said about the effect of nitrogenous fertilizer on the yield of grasses makes its obvious that the influence of irrigation must also be affected by the nitrogen status of the soil. It is also clear that the effect may be different for legumes.

Williams, Stiles, and Turner (1960) have recorded responses of 560 lb dry-matter/inch water/acre (approximately 250 kg/cm/ha) from a rye-grass/white clover pasture receiving about 460 lb nitrogen/acre/year (506 kg nitrogen/ha).

It is as well to remember that in many parts of the world (for example, in three-quarters of Australia (Perry 1967)), water shortage is the major factor limiting production.

Carbon

Photosynthesis involves the use of carbon dioxide and water in the production of oxygen and a great many carbon-containing compounds. Carbon fixation is thus a central activity in primary production and carbon dioxide a major resource.

There are many similarities between carbon and light as resources for plant production. Only a small proportion of the total resource is ever used by plants but local shortage can occur. When it does so plant growth-rate may be reduced and an increase in the supply will cause a response in growth-rate. At saturating light intensities and in normal air, photosynthesis is strongly affected by variations in carbon dioxide concentration (Gaastra 1962). If a shortage of carbon dioxide occurred more frequently and it was practicable to increase the supply, efficiency would probably be computed as in irrigation, that is, the quantity of dry matter produced per unit of resource added.

In general, the efficiency of carbon dioxide use is not separately calculated except to the extent that dry-matter production per unit area of land or per unit of light energy are both expressions of carbon fixation. The carbon dioxide produced by respiration is used within the plant whilst photosynthesis is taking place.

Efficiency of primary ecosystems

It will be obvious from what has been said that any discussion of efficiency in primary production suffers at the present time from two main disadvantages. First, it is rarely that whole plants have been measured in such a way that a complete balance can be calculated for any element within the whole plant ecosystem. Secondly, the purpose of such calculations must be defined. This is not difficult within agricultural contexts, since products and resources can be pinpointed with some precision. It is a very different matter where we are simply concerned with understanding the biological processes involved.

The use of light, for example, seems so obviously important that some effort is required to pose questions like 'Is a plant community necessarily more efficient if it fixes more carbon per unit of incident light energy?' Clearly it does not necessarily mean that the plant community will survive longer, or reproduce to a greater extent. It may be argued that 'purpose' should not be attributed to the plant community, but it certainly should be to the calculation. In short, it is essential to be clear as to what the calculated efficiency means. In general, it means only what was stated at the beginning of this chapter: the ratio of product output to resource input within a context defined for the status of the other resources.

References

ARMY, T. J. and GREER, F. A. (1967) *Harvesting the sun* (editors A. S. Pietro, F. A. Greer, and T. J. Army), pp. 321–32. Academic Press, New York.

BLACKMAN, G. E. and BLACK, J. N. (1959) *Ann. Bot.* **23**, 131.

BLAXTER, K. L. (1964) *J. Br. Grassld Soc.* **19**, 90–9.

BROUGHAM, R. W. (1962) *J. Ecol.* **50**, 449–60.

COOKE, G. W. (1964) Nitrogen fertilizers. *Proc. Fertil. Soc.*, No. 80.

COOPER, J. P. (1967) *W.P.B.S. Rep. for 1966*, p. 14.

COWLING, D. W. and LOCKYER, D. R. (1967) *J. Br. Grassld Soc.* **22**, 53–61.

36   *Concepts of Efficiency in Primary Production*

DONALD, C. M. (1951) *Aust. J. agric. Res.* **2**, 355.
GAASTRA, P. (1962) *Neth. J. agric. Sci.* **10**, 311–24.
HARRIS, C. E. (1969) Crop grasses and legumes in British agriculture (editor C. R. W. Spedding) Commonwealth Agricultural Bureau. (In Press.)
HOLLIDAY, R. (1966) *Agric. Prog.* **41**, 24–34.
JEWISS, O. R. (1967) Fodder conservation. *Occ. Symp. Br. Grassld Soc.* **3**, 53–65.
LEITH, H. (1968) Functioning of terrestrial ecosystems at the primary production level. *UNESCO Symp.*, Copenhagen, pp. 179–84.
MITCHELL, K. J. (1966) *Proc. N.Z. ecol. Soc.* **13**, 52–8.
MORRIS, R. M. (1967) Pasture growth in relation to pattern of defoliation by sheep. Ph.D. thesis, Reading University.
NEWBOULD, P. J. (1968) Functioning of terrestrial ecosystems at the primary production level. *UNESCO Symp.*, Copenhagen, pp. 187–90.
PENMAN, H. L. (1962) *J. agric. Sci.* **58**, 349–64.
PERRY, R. A. (1967) *Proc. Ecol. Soc. Aust.* **2**, 1–14.
REID, D. (1966) *Proc. Xth int. Grassld Congr.*, Helsinki, pp. 209–13.
STILES, W. and WILLIAMS, T. E. (1965) *J. agric. Sci.* **65**, 351–64.
TADMOR, N. H., COHEN, O. P., SHANAN, L. and EVENARI, M. (1966). *Proc. Xth int. Grassld Congr.*, Helsinki, pp. 897–906.
TAYLER, R. S. (1965) *Outl. Agric.* **4**, 234–42.
TROUGHTON, A. (1957) The underground organs of herbage grasses. *C.A.B. Bull.* No. 44.
—— (1960) *Proc. IXth int. Grassld Congr.*, Reading, pp. 280–3.
WARREN WILSON, J. (1967) *The collection and processing of field data* (editors E. F. Bradley and O. T. Denmead), pp. 77–123. Interscience, New York.
WILLIAMS, T. E., STILES, W. and TURNER, P. J. (1960) *Exps. Grassld Res. Inst.* **12**, 55.
DE WIT, C. T. (1967) *Harvesting the sun* (editors A. S. Pietro, F. A. Greer, and T. J. Army), pp. 315–20. Academic Press, New York.

5

Factors Affecting Efficiency in Plant Production

THE most important factors influencing efficiency in plant production depend somewhat, of course, on the method of expressing efficiency. They are most likely to be concerned with the rate of sward growth in one way or another.

Mitchell (1966b) has pointed out some of the deficiencies of a typical pasture in terms of photosynthetic efficiency. He has argued that efficient production requires the establishment of a large weight of photosynthetic tissue and its maintenance for an extended period in a condition where photosynthesis continues; he has pointed out that pasture typically requires defoliation after a relatively short period, or it becomes 'self-choking', with old leaves dying off as fast as new ones are formed. Two further principles are involved. First, the dependence of photosynthetic rate on the existence of a high-capacity 'sink' to draw off rapidly the products of carbon dioxide fixation. This occurs to a greater extent in plants with grains or tubers. Secondly, plant species differ in their maximum rate of carbon dioxide fixation at medium to high light intensities and in warm temperatures; pasture grasses are intermediate in this.

Not all pasture plants are grasses, however, and the efficiency of production of a plant community will depend upon its botanical composition. For any given grassland community, efficiency will be chiefly determined by: (1) sward structure and the use of light; (2) other factors affecting growth-rate; and (3) the extent of losses due to disease, decay, and pests, before the herbage has contributed to the 'output'.

Sward structure and light use

Sward structure has already been referred to (Chapter 3), chiefly in

terms of problems in describing it, and its importance in the use of
light. In this chapter it is necessary to consider the significance of
sward structure in the widest sense, including the importance of leaf
area (Jewiss 1967). Since pasture continues to grow, the quantity
of leaf and the structure of the sward continually change. No
optimum state can be maintained, therefore, but it is possible to
try and manage pastures so that they fluctuate as little as possible
about some optimum state.

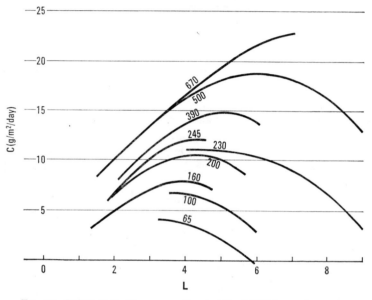

FIG. 5.1. Relationship of crop growth-rate (*C*) of *Trifolium subterraneum*
and leaf-area index (*L*) at nine levels of illumination (in cal/cm²/day).
(From Black 1963.)

The usefulness of the leaf area concept in pasture management
has recently been reviewed by Brown and Blaser (1968). Clearly, the
crux of this matter lies in the relationship between crop growth and
leaf-area index. An optimum leaf-area index value at which growth-
rate was maximal has been reported by many workers (Davidson
and Donald (1958); Black (1963) for *Trifolium subterraneum*) but
others (Brougham 1956) have found that swards reached an almost
constant maximum growth-rate, with no indication of an optimum
value for leaf-area index. Stern and Donald (1962*b*) pointed out
that the optimum varied with the level of radiation. This was

confirmed by Black (1963, 1965) and expressed in a diagram relating crop growth-rate of *Trifolium subterraneum* and leaf-area index (see Fig. 5.1) at a range of values of solar radiation. Wilfong, Brown, and Blaser (1967) found that the optimum leaf-area index for *Medicago sativa* and Ladino clover (*Trifolium repens*) occurred over a broad range, there being a decreased respiration rate per unit of leaf area at high values of leaf-area index.

This emphasizes the fact that any term representing the total leaf area present tends to ignore differences between different leaves in, for example, photosynthetic efficiency (Milthorpe 1963, Jewiss and Woledge 1967); the whole concept tends, of course, to ignore the photosynthetic activity of other tissues (for example, flowering stems).

Any system that uses light as an energy source must involve some relationship between rate of production and photosynthetic area. This will be most marked where no other factor limits growth and least marked where another factor is limiting. Thus, in extreme drought, one would hardly expect crop growth-rate to reflect either the quantity of incident light or the quantity of leaf intercepting it.

If we consider practically bare ground as a starting-point, plant density† is the first important factor in determining whether sufficient leaf area is present. Very rapidly, however, increasing plant density leads to competition for light (see Donald 1961, Stern 1965) and results in a rise in leaf-area/leaf-weight ratio, a decline in root/shoot ratio, and a reduction in the rate of leaf unfolding in individual plants affected by shading.

Careful distinctions must be made between final plant density, and variations in seed-rate which may be used agriculturally to influence density. The effect of seed-rate (what weight of seed or how many seeds sown per unit area of land) will vary with time and whether species are sown alone (Lazenby and Rogers, 1965*a, b*) or in mixtures, especially of grasses and clovers (Green and Corrall 1965). In both cases there may be extensive interactions with the level of nitrogen available in the soil (Stern and Donald 1962*a*).

Since herbage used agriculturally has to be defoliated frequently, with consequent large effects on leaf-area index, the application of concepts relating crop growth and leaf-area index is nowhere more important than during the period of regrowth after defoliation. Brown and Blaser (1968) found that many authors attributed the rate

† For a discussion of plant growth and density, see Harper 1964.

of regrowth to residual leaf area (Brougham 1956, Davidson and Donald 1958, Langer 1959), while others had emphasized the importance of the concentration of carbohydrate in storage organs, such as stem bases and roots (Smith 1962, Dobrenz and Massengale 1966). In a study of regrowth in *Lolium perenne*, Anslow (1966) found that there was no apparent relationship between growth-rate and light interception and drew attention to the possible influence of other factors. Carbohydrate levels have been found to influence regrowth in rye-grass (Davies 1965), although May (1960) could find little evidence at that time of a correlation between initial carbohydrate level and rate of subsequent regrowth. May (1960) pointed out that 'reserves' might be a misleading term for the carbohydrates involved.

In Australia, Humphreys and Robinson (1966) found that growth of sub-tropical grasses was more positively dependent on leaf-area index than on carbohydrate status, when moisture and nutrients were in adequate supply. As Davidson and Milthorpe (1965) have shown for *Dactylis glomerata*, however, the reserve carbohydrates form only part of a labile pool used for synthesis of new compounds and for respiration when photosynthesis is restricted.

Anslow (1965) reported that the growth of perennial grass swards, cut at a suitable stage for grazing, was lower in (British) midsummer than in late spring, even with abundant supplies of water and fertilizer. Yields tended to be correlated with average tiller size, rather than with solar radiation, and it was suggested that the rhythm of flowering and tiller regeneration seemed to be a major determinant of the sward's capacity to sustain herbage growth. Subsequent discussion (Brougham and Glenday 1967, Anslow and Back 1967) clearly illustrated the difficulties that may attend the measurement and interpretation of grass growth. One of these difficulties is associated with the fact that leaf is the dominant contributor to both leaf area and production, as the latter is usually measured.

The problems of mathematical expression involved in growth analysis have been recently discussed by Radford (1967). In so far as tiller populations and flowering rhythms are important, it is as well to note that light has a notable effect on these (Bean 1964, Ryle 1966*a*, *b*) and the influence of temperature should not be ignored (Baker 1956, Ryle 1964, Robson 1967, Tow 1967).

In concluding this section, it is salutary to refer back to a paper by Blackman in 1905 on optima and limiting factors in plant growth.

He concluded 'that the way of those who set out to evaluate exactly the effects of changes in a single factor upon a multi-conditioned metabolic process is hard, and especially so when the process is being pushed towards the upper limits of its capacity'.

The factors affecting growth-rate

The effect of light and other related factors has already been dealt with. It will be obvious that frequency and severity of defoliation may influence crop growth-rate by decreasing the sward's capacity for intercepting light or by exhausting carbohydrate 'reserves' (Alberda 1966).

It is well established that cutting management will influence yield of harvested material. For example, Reid (1967) found that the yield from a rye-grass/white clover sward was greater when five successive cuts were taken at a height of 1 in (2·5 cm) above soil surface than at 2·5 in (6·3 cm); the average yield difference was about 13 per cent.

Frequency of cutting often influences yield, depending somewhat on how this is measured (for example, dry matter or digestible organic matter), how it is harvested, and what fertilizers are applied. Lambert (1962) found that cutting every 4 weeks resulted in similar yields from timothy (*Phleum pratense*) and meadow fescue (*Festuca pratensis*) whereas with a hay cut and two subsequent cuts, the yield of timothy was greater.

Frequent defoliation usually induces a more prostrate habit of growth (Struik 1967) and may greatly change sward structure and botanical composition. It may also retard growth in length of roots and thus the weight of roots in the lower layers of the soil. This may be of some consequence in drought (Troughton 1957). In lucerne (Mitchell and Denne 1967), after defoliation, two things are chiefly important in relation to roots. The first is immediate availability of reserves (only sufficient in lucerne for 2–3 days) to allow growth of buds to the point of photosynthesis. Secondly, the ability of the root system to absorb enough minerals and maintain nitrogen fixation.

The physiological significance of defoliation has been discussed by Alcock (1964), who drew attention to the rapidity with which existing roots may decompose after grazing: roots of orchard grass and of brome-grass, for example, decomposed within 36 to 48 hours after defoliation of top growth (Oswalt *et al.* 1959). The effect of defoliation varies with the species. Struik (1967) found that daisy (*Bellis perennis*) biomass was little affected by management (perhaps because few managements actually result in defoliation of the daisy), whereas increasing degree of defoliation greatly influenced plant radius, root length, and plant form in *Taraxacum officinale, Hypochaeris radicata,* and *Leontodon taraxacoides.* Relative root dry weight varied from 17 to 57 per cent.

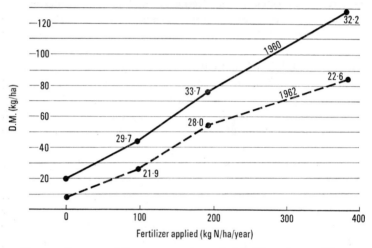

Fig. 5.2. Response of *S.* 24 rye-grass to applied fertilizer nitrogen. (From Whitehead and Cowling 1967.)

Within quite a wide range of harvesting procedures yields may not be greatly changed. This can also be true for the use of fertilizer, where little shortage exists, and even for nitrogen in the case of pastures with a large legume component.

In general, increasing the level of applied nitrogen increases the yield of pure grass swards in a linear manner up to about 330 kg nitrogen/ha (see Fig. 5.2). No other factor has such a large and widespread effect on agricultural grassland ('t Hart and van der Molen 1966), including natural grassland that is poor in clovers (Regal 1966). Nitrogen, however, is taken up by the plant at a greater rate than that required for maximizing the growth response. Immediately after nitrogen is applied a great deal of it may be taken up by the crop. If the latter is cut soon afterwards there will have been too little time for a large crop growth response and nitrogen will have been used inefficiently (Holliday and Wilman 1965).

Efficiency in the use and recovery of nitrogen thus depends upon the pattern of fertilizer application and of defoliation (Brockman 1966), and on the herbage species and time of harvesting in spring (Cowling 1966, Bland 1967). Less frequent harvesting generally improves the efficiency of nitrogen use for dry-matter production but may have little effect on yield of nitrogen (Mortensen, Baker, and Dermanis 1964). Lazenby and Rogers (1965a, b) studied the effect of nitrogen and spacing on yield of *Lolium perenne*. The nitrogen harvested per unit area in sward herbage increased in a linear manner up to an application of 880 kg nitrogen/ha/year.

There are, of course, many other factors that influence the growth-rate of herbage. Little mention has been made of the microclimate within the sward and the influence of sward structure on such facets as plant temperature (see Mitchell 1966a, Priestley 1967).

The importance of growth-rate is well illustrated by the work of Cooper (1967). In small, simulated swards of rye-grass with high nitrogen and ample water, the maximum crop growth-rate varied from 7 to 26 g/m²/day, with light-energy inputs from 21 to 79 cal/cm²/day and optimum leaf-area index values varying from 7 to 12.

The percentage energy conversion ranged from 8·6 up to 19·2 at these maximum crop growth-rates. Total annual production of *S*. 23 was between 19 800 and 20 900 kg dry matter/ha and the percentage conversion over this total was 2·6 per cent; total production of crude protein was 3850 kg/ha/year.

Finally, it is worth noting again how often this kind of discussion tends to leave out of account the importance of root growth and its effects on the gaseous composition of the soil environment (Currie 1962) and the distribution of roots seasonally and within the soil (Baker and Garwood 1959). Effects of the grazing animal on soil compaction and herbage production (Brougham 1966) are discussed in Chapter 13.

Losses due to disease, decay, and pests

There are two senses in which such losses contribute to inefficiency. First, where production is measured as a harvested part of the crop, plant tissue that is grown but not harvested represents a reduction in output of any product at some cost in resources used to produce it. The loss may not be complete and some elements may be re-used (this aspect is further considered in Chapter 12) but this does not apply to energy and may only be true to a limited extent for water and nitrogen.

The initial cause of such loss may be disease or pests, but it may also be trampling by grazing animals or anything else that causes plant material to die or fall below some harvesting level (as in cutting) or render it unpalatable (as in grazing). Normal senescence of plant material that is not harvested may account for much of this kind of loss.

Secondly, losses may be incurred as a result of pest or disease attack that actually reduces the amount grown. In this category the most serious damage is that which affects critical points of the plant or its growth cycle. Slug damage to seedlings, for example, can cause direct loss of a small amount of herbage, that is, small as far as a grazing cow is concerned, but an immensely greater loss in terms of a reduced potential production.

Agriculturally, fauna other than domesticated herbivores cause loss and inefficiency in production (see Chapter 9) simply by consuming herbage before it can be harvested by the farm stock. This is hardly an inefficiency in primary production but it is so assessed where the same processes prevent the herbage from contributing to the measured harvests.

There is here a major difficulty in assessing such losses, precisely because they frequently occur in such a way that harvesting methods may not record them. This is the primary difficulty in assessing losses due to senescence.

Frequent but lax defoliation systems have been found to involve a build-up of dead matter (Hunt and Brougham 1967) and senescence and decay at the base of the grass canopy may have several deleterious effects (Hunt 1965, Thomas 1966).

In general, diseases and pests affect primary productivity by reducing plant growth-rate, mainly by damaging growing points or by dislocating metabolic processes within the plant. Damage may occur below ground as well as above it and many common pests are root feeders.

The importance of growth-rate

The major determinant of efficiency in primary production is thus plant growth-rate. As with the growth-rate of animals, there are two main effects on the efficiency of production. The first is the direct loss of production per plant or per unit area, due to a reduced growth-rate (see, for example, Fig. 5.3). The second is the reduced efficiency directly associated with slower growth. The distinction is less clear with plants than it is in animal production and probably less important, but it is worth making in principle.

Any reduction in output reduces efficiency unless it is matched by a reduction in input. If an animal grows more slowly, it matters less if it also eats less. As will be seen from Chapters 15 and 16, the

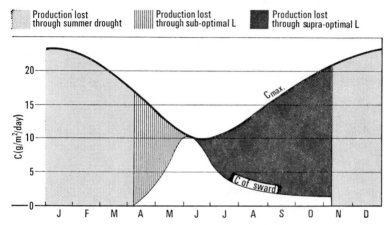

FIG. 5.3. A diagrammatic summary of the sources of losses of potential production of subterranean clover in Adelaide. Area enclosed by curve $C_{max.}$ = potential annual production; area enclosed by curve of C of sward = actual production. (From Black 1964.)

reduction in input never matches the reduction in output, except at zero values, when the animal dies. There is a maintenance cost of keeping it alive and this has to be met however low the rate of production.

With plants there are some similarities but many differences also.

The area of land and the quantity of incident light remain the same when plants grow slowly, so they are less efficient in the use of these resources because there is no alternative use for them. In the case of water, plants in a drought may continue to transpire large quantities of water without growing very much, if the water available at depth lacks nitrogen (Garwood and Williams 1967). The water used to keep the plants alive is thus used inefficiently because there is little production. By contrast, many plants can survive severe water shortage (Gates 1964) but efficiency of carbon or light use is limited by the reduction in growth induced by water stress.

If plants continue to respire during conditions in which they cannot grow (for example, in the dark or at the base of a tall sward) then a similar situation exists to that of the animal at maintenance. The difference lies in the relationship between maintenance requirement and growth-rate. The greater the amount of plant material, the greater will be both 'maintenance' needs and potential growth-rate. In the animal, however, bigger animals have bigger maintenance requirements but do not necessarily have a greater growth potential (especially within a species), and the ratio of resources used for maintenance to those used in production is generally much higher.

In the plant, it has been estimated that respiration accounts for approximately 25 per cent of the products of photosynthesis during a 24-hour cycle (Jewiss 1967). If the same factors control both processes, this will remain roughly constant.

In the animal, however, the entire energy intake can be absorbed simply in maintaining bodily functions and essential processes, including respiration and the maintenance of body temperature. This last point is, of course, a characteristic of warm-blooded animals and the differences between plants and cold-blooded animals is less in this respect.

References

ALBERDA, T. (1966) *Proc. Xth int. Grassld Congr.*, Helsinki, pp. 140–7.
ALCOCK, M. B. (1964) *Grazing in terrestrial and marine environments* (editor D. J. Crisp), pp. 25–41. Blackwell, Oxford.
ANSLOW, R. C. (1965) *J. Br. Grassld Soc.* **20**, 19–26.
—— (1966) *Proc. IXth int. Grassld Congr.*, Sao Paulo, pp. 403–5.
—— and BACK, H. L. (1967) *J. Br. Grassld Soc.* **22**, 108–11.
BAKER, H. K. (1956) *J. Br. Grassld Soc.* **11**, 235–7.
—— and GARWOOD, E. A. (1959) *J. Br. Grassld Soc.* **14**, 94–104.
BEAN, E. W. (1964) *Ann. Bot.* **28**, 427–43.
BLACK, J. N. (1963) *Aust. J. agric. Res.* **14**, 20–38.
—— (1964) *J. appl. Ecol.* **1**, 3–18.
—— (1965) *Proc. Nutr. Soc.* **24**, 2–8.
BLACKMAN, F. F. (1905) *Ann. Bot.* **19**, 281–95.
BLAND, B. F. (1967) *J. agric. Sci., Camb.* **69**, 391–7.
BROCKMAN, J. S. (1966) *Proc. Xth int. Grassld Congr.*, Helsinki, pp. 234–40.
BROUGHAM, R. W. (1956) *Aust. J. agric. Res.* **7**, 377–87.
—— (1966) *J. N.Z. Inst. agric. Sci.* **2**, 19–22.
—— and GLENDAY, A. C. (1967) *J. Br. Grassld Soc.* **22**, 100–7.
BROWN, R. H. and BLASER, R. E. (1968) *Herb. Abstr.* **38**, 1–9.
COOPER, J. P. (1967) *W.P.B.S. Rep. for 1966*, p. 14.
COWLING, D. W. (1966) *Proc. Xth int. Grassld Congr.*, Helsinki, pp. 204–9.
CURRIE, J. A. (1962) *J. Sci. Fd Agric.* **7**, 380–5.

DAVIDSON, J. L. and DONALD, C. M. (1958) *Aust. J. agric. Res.* **9**, 53–72.
—— and MILTHORPE, F. L. (1965) *J. Br. Grassld Soc.* **20**, 15–18.
DAVIES, ALISON (1965) *J. agric. Sci.* **65**, 213–21.
DOBRENZ, A. K. and MASSENGALE, M. A. (1966) *Crop Sci.* **6**, 604–7.
DONALD, C. M. (1961) *Soc. Expl Biol. Symp.* No. xv, pp. 282–313.
GARWOOD, E. A. and WILLIAMS, T. E. (1967) *J. agric. Sci., Camb.* **69**, 125–30.
GATES, C. T. (1964) *J. Aust. Inst. agric. Sci.* **30**, 3–22.
GREEN, J. O. and CORRALL, A. J. (1965) *J. Br. Grassld Soc.* **20**, 207–11.
HARPER, J. L. (1964) Genetics today. *Proc. XIth int. Congr. Genet.*, The Hague. Pergamon Press, Oxford.
'T HART, M. L. and VAN DER MOLEN, H. (1966) *Proc. Xth int. Grassld Congr.*, Helsinki, pp. 36–44.
HOLLIDAY, R. and WILMAN, D. (1965) *J. Br. Grassld Soc.* **20**, 32–40.
HUMPHREYS, L. R. and ROBINSON, A. R. (1966) *Proc. Xth int. Grassld Congr.*, Helsinki, pp. 113–16.
HUNT, L. A. (1965) *J. Br. Grassld Soc.* **20**, 27–31.
—— and BROUGHAM, R. W. (1967) *N.Z. Jl agric. Res.* **10**, 397–404.
JEWISS, O. R. (1967) Fodder conservation. *Occ. Symp. Br. Grassld Soc.*, No. 3.
—— and WOLEDGE, JANE (1967) *Ann. Bot.* **31**, 661–71.
LAMBERT, D. A. (1962) *J. agric. Sci.* **59**, 25–32.
LANGER, R. H. M. (1959) *J. agric. Sci., Camb.* **52**, 273–81.
LAZENBY, A. and ROGERS, H. H. (1965a) *J. agric. Sci.* **65**, 65–78.
—— —— (1965b) *J. agric. Sci.* **65**, 79–89.
MAY, L. H. (1960) *Herb. Abstr.* **30**, 239–45.
MILTHORPE, F. L. (1963) *The growth of the potato* (editors J. D. Ivins and F. L. Milthorpe), pp. 3–16. Butterworths, London.
MITCHELL, K. J. (1966a) *Proc. N.Z. ecol. Soc.* **13**, 52–8.
—— (1966b) *J. N.Z. agric. Sci.* **1**, 23–9.
—— and DENNE, M. P. (1967) *The lucerne crop* (editors R. H. M. Langer and A. W. Reed), pp. 22–7. New Zealand and Australia.
MORTENSEN, W. P., BAKER, A. S. and DERMANIS, P. (1964) *Agron. J.* **56**, 316–20.
OSWALT, D. L., BERTRAND, A. R. and TEAL, M. R. (1959) *Proc. Soil Sci.* **23**, 228–30.
PRIESTLEY, C. H. B. (1967) *Sci. J.* **3**, 67–73.
RADFORD, P. J. (1967) *Crop Sci.* **7**, 171–5.
REGAL, V. (1966) *Proc. Xth int. Grassld Congr.*, Helsinki, pp. 245–9.
REID, D. (1967) *J. agric. Sci., Camb.* **68**, 249–54.
ROBSON, M. J. (1967) *J. appl. Ecol.* **4**, 475–84.
RYLE, G. J. A. (1964) *J. Br. Grassld Soc.* **19**, 281–90.
—— (1966a) *Ann. appl. Biol.* **57**, 257–68.
—— (1966b) *Proc. Xth int. Grassld Congr.*, Helsinki, pp. 94–9.
SMITH, D. (1962) *Crop Sci.* **2**, 75–8.
STERN, W. R. (1965) *Aust. J. agric. Res.* **16**, 541–55.
—— and DONALD, C. M. (1962a) *Aust. J. agric. Res.* **13**, 599–614.
—— —— (1962b) *Aust. J. agric. Res.* **13**, 615–23.
STRUIK, G. J. (1967) *N.Z. Jl agric. Res.* **10**, 331–44.
THOMAS, P. T. (1966) *J. Br. Grassld Soc.* **21**, 1–6.
TOW, P. G. (1966) *Neth. J. agric. Sci.* **15**, 141–54.
TROUGHTON, A. (1957) The underground organs of herbage grasses. *C.A.B. Bull.* No. 44.
WHITEHEAD, D. C. and COWLING, D. W. (1967) *N.A.A.S. q. Rev.* **78**, 56–67.
WILFONG, R. T., BROWN, R. H. and BLASER, R. E. (1967) *Crop Sci.* **7**, 27–30.

6

Natural Grassland

MOST of the world's grasslands are natural plant communities, in the sense that they have not been sown by man. The latter, often called 'leys', are generally less complex botanically and the species sown are chosen for their productivity and nutritional value as well as for their suitability for the local environment. Indeed, the cost of sowing may not be justified unless the environment can be substantially improved by fertilizers, fencing, and management.

The distinction between 'natural' and 'sown' grassland is misleadingly obvious and should not be pursued rigidly. Many natural grasslands, like the permanent pastures of England, do not represent climax vegetation (Davies 1960) but depend upon grazing, by wild or agricultural animals, to prevent them proceeding to woodland or forest; Tansley (1939) classified them as 'subclimax or (better) biotic plagioclimax vegetation'. Even where the grazing animal may not be essential to maintain grassland, its exclusion results in great changes in botanical composition. Exclusion of sheep from Pennine grasslands, for example, resulted in a decrease in bryophytes, lichens, and flowering plants other than grasses (Welch and Rawes 1964), and within the latter, non-palatable species such as *Nardus stricta* and *Juncus squarrosus* also declined; the number of species fell from ninety-three to sixty-seven. In North America, Merton Love (1961) concluded that 'the domestic animal has as great or greater an impact on the "natural vegetation" as the plough'. The range, therefore, is no longer a climax but a modified ecosystem.

Many of the grasslands of America and Africa are considered by Thomas (1960) to owe their existence to fire, which stimulates some grasses, reduces competition from woody species, and does not deplete the organic matter of the soil.

Natural grasslands are extremely variable and may be subdivided into many different categories. Consider the U.S.S.R., in which natural pastures are estimated to occupy 318 million hectares, or 14·4 per cent of the whole territory. If the tundra, forest-tundra, and northern part of the forest zone, which are utilized as pastures for reindeer, are included, the total becomes 30 per cent of the whole of the U.S.S.R. (Larin 1960). These areas are estimated to contain between 10 000 and 11 000 plant species but only in the steppe zones do grasses contribute as much as 55 per cent to the plant cover.

There are thus differences within natural grassland that are quite as great as between this category and sown grassland. In some regions this variety is essential to the grazing animal. In north Scandinavia, for example, reindeer range consists of different types of vegetation (Steen 1960): in summer the grass/herb communities are used and the higher the proportion of grass the better; during winter-grazing the lichen/dwarf-shrub communities are grazed and the higher the lichen percentage the better.

Even the distinction between sown and unsown grassland is somewhat artificial. When a particular pasture is considered, it obviously matters very little who sowed it, or even whether it was sown or propagated vegetatively. What matters is the composition and structure of the plant community, the purpose for which it is being managed, or some other aspect of its biological or social importance.

It is nevertheless convenient to discuss separately the sown pasture and the extent to which it can be treated as a crop (see Chapter 8), and natural pastures and the extent to which they can be exploited for various purposes. The latter is the subject of the present chapter and thus far it may be said that the characteristics of natural grassland are variety of types, number and variety of species, variety of purpose, and method of utilization.

It is quite possible that there are great advantages associated with this variety. A large number of varied species may confer stability on the populations that live on or visit the pasture. The implications of mixed plant populations will be considered in the next chapter.

Changes in botanical composition with time depend upon factors influencing the spread of one species in competition with others. The method of spread varies from increases in the size of the individual plant, vegetative reproduction and growth by stolons, runners, and tillers, or by seeding. Quite apart from botanical change, since individual plants do not live for ever the same mechanisms must also operate to perpetuate the pasture. A natural pasture must be continually renewing itself, and is characterized only by the gradualness of the process.

Agriculturally, natural grassland sustains a very large proportion of the domesticated grass-eating animals; its exploitation is thus of some consequence to man's food supplies.

Agricultural exploitation of natural grassland

The use of natural grasslands is often referred to as 'exploitation' because it is largely based on deriving production from land with the minimum input of resources. It is perfectly possible to raise the output of permanent grassland, by the use of fertilizers and by improved methods of utilization, to the level of output associated with well-managed leys. Wherever a particular element is limiting, quite spectacular improvements can be made over large areas by supplying it.

Changes in soil pH by liming, and changes in soil moisture content by irrigation or drainage, may make it possible for more-productive plant communities to thrive. Alterations in grazing management and fertilizer use also result in changes in botanical composition, often in the same direction as that achieved more quickly by sowing. Seed can, of course, be added to an existing pasture without ploughing, with or without herbicide treatment.

Very often the limiting factors are of the kinds referred to, but even where no specific deficiency of an element exists, productivity may be low because of a shortage of available nitrogen. This is a complex matter (see Chapter 12) but, as with sown grass swards, an additional supply of nitrogen greatly increases herbage production. At the same time nitrogen accumulates in the soil under leys (Williams and Clement 1966) and under permanent pasture (Woldendorp, Dilz, and Kolenbrander 1966).

The main reasons why more resources are not used to raise productivity of natural pastures are as follows:

1. The owner or farmer has no need to increase output because his income is derived from a great many hectares.
2. The resources required are virtually unobtainable, as with fertilizer in some parts of the world.
3. The capital is not available for the initial resources or for the stock and machinery required to utilize the increased output (see McMeekan 1960).

4. Even where (1), (2), and (3) do not apply, the farmer may be convinced, rightly or wrongly, that higher profit would not result.

There are other reasons, of ignorance, fear, and lack of skill, but the most potent are basically economic. For example, even where fertilizer is available to the farmer, the terrain may prevent transportation to his land. This has been tackled by using aircraft, notably in New Zealand, but is still basically an economic question.

There are therefore several good reasons at present, and some which may remain for a long time, why some natural grassland will continue to be exploited without major inputs of additional resources. The main reasons for continuation of such natural grassland will probably be in circumstances where

it is economically unavoidable,
it is desirable as an amenity,
it is actually more profitable.

Where inputs are limited or the environment imposes severe restrictions, the herbage species adapted for survival may well be those considered less valuable from other points of view. Some climatic restrictions, like the long winter in north Scandinavia, lead to a decrease in permanent pasture; intensive production has to be practised in order to grow enough in the short growing season available.

A part of successful exploitation depends also on using the most appropriate animal species or, in some circumstances, animals in the most appropriate physiological state. Very often the same climatic factors that limit the productivity of natural grassland also place some limits on the kind of animals that can be kept and on the level of performance that they can achieve. In these circumstances integrated use of natural and sown grassland, or of improved and unimproved areas, may have advantages. It has also been argued that natural grasslands, on the British uplands for example, should be utilized by several different kinds of animal (Cragg 1958) and, clearly, the greater the variety of plant material, the greater the variety of animals that can be, and perhaps should be, supported.

There are other natural grasslands that will remain in the 'permanent' category because they cannot be ploughed: for example, the flood meadows of Western Germany (Voigtlander 1966) and of the U.S.S.R. (Rabotnov 1966). These areas can be fertilized, however, and improved in many other ways. Since these improvements could include the addition of seed, it is clear that if taken far enough the process of improvement could result in exactly the same pasture as might have been sown.

There is thus no fundamental difference between natural and sown grassland, and no sharp line can be drawn between the two. Arguments as to which is more productive have little meaning unless the pastures are much more rigorously defined.

In most circumstances natural grassland will tend to consist of more plant species under much less controlled conditions of growth, and its major advantage will lie in its cheapness. In many parts of the world it will have special advantages, one of the most important being the prevention of soil erosion, as in India (Whyte 1964) and Australia (Costin 1964).

References

Costin, A. B. (1964) *Grasses and grasslands* (editor C. Barnard), Chapter 14. MacMillan, London.

Cragg, J. B. (1958) The future of the British uplands. *The biological productivity of Britain.* Institute of Biology, London.

Davies, W. (1960) *The grass crop*, 2nd edn. Spon, London.

Larin, I. V. (1960) *Proc. VIIIth int. Grassld Congr.*, Reading, pp. 823–8.

Love, R. Merton (1961) *J. Br. Grassld Soc.* **16**, 89–99.

McMeekan, C. P. (1960) *Proc. VIIIth int. Grassld Congr.*, Reading, pp. 45–9.

Rabotnov, T. A. (1966) *Proc. 1st Meet. Eur. Grassld Fed.*, Wageningen, pp. 109–19.

Steen, E. (1960) *Proc. VIIIth int. Grassld Congr.*, Reading, pp. 998–1003.

Tansley, A. G. (1939) *The British islands and their vegetation.* Cambridge University Press.

Thomas, A. S. (1960) *Proc. IXth int. Grassld Congr.*, Reading, pp. 405–7.

Voigtlander, G. (1966) *Proc. 1st Meet. Eur. Grassld Fed.*, Wageningen, pp. 93–104.

Welch, D. and Rawes, M. (1964) *J. appl. Ecol.* **1**, 281–300.

Whyte, R. O. (1964) The grassland and fodder resources of India, *Sci. Mon.* No. 22. I.C.A.R., New Delhi.

Williams, T. E. and Clement, C. R. (1966) *Proc. 1st Meet. Eur. Grassld Fed.*, Wageningen, pp. 39–45.

Woldendorp, J. W., Dilz, K. and Kolenbrander, G. J. (1966) *Proc. 1st Meet. Eur. Grassld Fed.*, Wageningen, pp. 53–68.

7

Mixed Populations of Plant Species

As was pointed out in Chapter 6, natural grassland is characterized by its varied botanical composition, and it is important to know whether a large number of plant species growing together possesses advantages over the simpler mixtures and single species of sown pastures (see Chapter 8).

It has been pointed out that one logical extension of the idea of 'niche specialization' is that 'complex ecosystems are more efficient than simple ones in using environment resources' (Harper 1967, MacArthur and Connell 1966) and that Darwin (1859) considered that several genera of grasses would yield more than one species. For agricultural purposes the yield has to be in a particular form and there appears to be no conclusive evidence on this point (Woodford 1966).

Nor is yield over a short period the only useful criterion. Stability is often important and may influence average yield over a longer period. A complex mixture may be a more stable producer than a monospecific pasture (Morley 1966) but this is not necessarily so.

If there are insufficient resources available for the whole plant population, then they tend to be shared unequally and the yield per unit area approximates to that of the higher yielding species in the mixture (Harper 1964). The results of competition between plants (see de Wit 1960, 1961) are rarely straightforward, however, partly because competitive ability has to be related to environmental and other factors that are by no means static. Even when only two plant species are involved, the advantages may not be consistently with one or the other. Thus the more controlled the environment, the more likely it is that one species will thrive at the expense of another; and competition must involve both advantage and disadvantage.

Competition

The nature, and indeed the definition, of plant competition has received much attention (de Wit, Ennik, Bergh, and Sonneweld 1960). Some authors have preferred to consider the 'interference' that results from two plants growing in such proximity that they modify each other's growth (Harper 1964). Clearly, 'interference' includes both beneficial and damaging influences, and competition is only one aspect of it. 'Competition' often conjures up certain anthropomorphic ideas involving purposeful activity, but it does vividly describe one category of situations. For example, grasses may be said to compete with clovers in Britain, mainly by growing earlier in the spring (Cowling 1962). This results in the clover being shaded during its early growth, unless grazing is sufficiently intensive to remove the grass as it grows. This situation fits quite well the general use of the term 'competition', since it involves a common need for a limiting resource. In this example it is light (see also Brougham 1958), and the grass absorbs nearly all the light that falls on the pasture, thus preventing the clover plant from receiving sufficient. The ability of grasses to make so much early growth that clovers are shaded depends also on other requirements being met, including adequate soil nitrogen.

In a situation of very low soil nitrogen, grass growth would be poor but clover growth unaffected, provided that the necessary rhyzobial bacteria were present. Since clover is not only independent of soil nitrogen but also contributes to it, vigorous legume growth will create the conditions required by the grass. Thus grass competes successfully for light in one environment and clover in another. Where the nitrogen supply is moderate, a balance of grass and clover results which is generally more productive than either species alone.

Agriculturally, this is the most important mixed plant population of grassland, because of the very large effect of nitrogen supply on herbage production. It would be quite illogical to suppose that it is the only mixture that is more productive than either species grown separately. It can certainly be argued that nitrogenous fertilizers can be applied in most circumstances, though not necessarily economically, at levels that render the legume unnecessary, and that grass alone is then more productive. The presence of clover is not then a disadvantage but simply no longer needed, and usually its presence is difficult to ensure. But it hardly follows that similar situations will not occur with other mixtures in relation to other aspects of the environment (see England 1968).

It is not difficult to imagine situations with periodic drought in which a mixture of more and less drought-resistant plant species with appropriate seasonal growth patterns might be more productive than either or any of the species grown alone.

In relation to natural grassland, the discussion has to be greatly widened to include differential reactions to grazing animals, pests and diseases, variations in temperature, and a host of other variables.

The more variable the environment, the more likely it is that mixtures may have advantages; the more intensive the agricultural use of grassland, the less variable will be the environment and the greater the advantages of single-species swards (Cowling and Lockyer 1968). There are, of course, economic limits to the extent to which such environmental factors as temperature are ever likely to be controlled, but it would be rash to make too many assumptions even about this.

Competition is not eliminated in a single-species crop, it is merely limited to individual plants or plant units. Obviously, it is possible to have too many individual plants per unit area and there is likely to be an optimum density. Again, since the environment is not constant, the optimum density may not be either. Nor should competition be thought of as only concerning the aerial parts of the plant; it may be just as important below ground. Studies by Donald (1958), Stern and Donald (1962), and more recently by Rhodes (1968) have demonstrated the relative importance of above- and below-ground competition.

Whenever competition is considered it is most important to define the criteria by which success is being judged. It is quite possible that the optimum plant density for dry-matter production is different from that for the production of seed (see Kelly and Boyd 1966, for the effect of environment on seed production in grasses and legumes).

It is as well to bear in mind that, whatever the product, there will be competition *within* the species producing it. If no other species can produce the product (such as the seed of the particular species) then the presence of other species can only hinder the process and its efficiency. In much grazed pasture, however, this is not the case and a number of species may produce herbage on which animals can feed. The concept of weeds even in sown grassland is therefore somewhat different from that appropriate to highly specific crops.

Weeds of grassland

This is a large subject and can only be referred to briefly here. Especially since the advent of efficient herbicides, some of the most important weeds of grassland are themselves grasses. In Britain, one of the most widespread is *Poa trivialis*. Experiments in New Zealand, where this grass is also a common unsown component of perennial rye-grass pastures, showed that, in general, the inclusion of *Poa trivialis* 'resulted in marked changes in the botanical composition of mixed swards, without any apparent marked effect on the annual total herbage production' (Vartha 1965). It did, however, modify the pattern of herbage growth and there would also be some effects on the nutritive value of the herbage produced.

The difficulty of assessing the effect of such weeds on animal production has often been discussed. It has been suggested (Spedding 1966) that the effect of a given proportion of weeds on digestible organic matter production can be expressed as follows.

Percentage reduction in production of digestible organic matter due to presence of weeds =

$$\frac{100 \; (1 - C_w D_c + W D_w)}{CD_c},$$

where C = dry-matter production of weed-free crop grass,

C_w = dry-matter production of crop grass grown with weeds present,

W = dry-matter production of weed,

D_c = digestibility of crop,

D_w = digestibility of weed.

To translate any effect on herbage yield into an effect on animal production would then require the following further information:

the extent to which the weed was eaten by stock;

the extent to which animal performance was dependent on the higher digestibility of the crop grass;

the degree to which the herbage was being utilized or would be utilized if weeds were removed.

Even when weed species are not of equal nutritional value to the sown species, it may be advantageous to achieve a greater total production only part of which is in the form of sown species. This may be relevant where environmental conditions vary sharply and unpredictably to the disadvantage of the sown species. There is thus an element of insurance in mixed populations, which is another way of describing stability.

Biological implications

All the implications of mixed plant populations cannot be pursued here, but it must be pointed out that variety of plant material must influence the populations of animals that live in, on, and under the pasture. These populations may involve large numbers of individuals and a large number of species. The latter is likely to be greater in natural grassland with a variety of plant species; where 'grassland' embraces shrubs and even trees, the variety of small fauna may be very great indeed. In North America, for example, between 1000 and 1200 species of insects have been recorded as resident in a 12-acre area of grassland. If visiting insects were included, the total rose to over 3000. It may be argued that such variety in both plant and animal populations must represent stability (McNaughton 1967, 1968). McNaughton (1967) concluded that (1) diversity is principally a mechanism which generates community stability; (2) dominance is principally a mechanism which generates community productivity; and (3) increasing the number of species in a stand, rather than enhancing efficiency through more efficient exploitation of site resources, decreases efficiency, perhaps through competition. Austin (1968), on the other hand, argued that terms such as 'diversity' and 'dominance' would need to be better defined before a precise meaning could be attached to such statements. There is thus no general agreement as to whether a variety of species results in greater productivity. This must depend greatly on the criteria adopted in measuring productivity and, as was pointed out in Chapter 4, it should not be assumed too readily that there is only one right or best criterion. In some circumstances there is no doubt that a mixture of two plants will be more productive than either alone, almost whatever the criteria adopted. Again, a grass/clover mixture is probably the best example of this. Equally, there is no difficulty in finding examples of pastures that consist of one species being more productive than pastures consisting of several grown together. Perennial rye-grass alone, when heavily fertilized, would be more productive than when mixed with buttercups or plantains or, indeed, many other grasses.

These examples are a little unfair, however, because in most cases it could be argued that in time the most productive mixture for the prevailing environment would be found. If the environment is changed markedly and suddenly, as is often the case in agriculture, the existing plant mixture may be inappropriate; it is in these circumstances and where control of pasture quality is an urgent matter that abrupt changes may be justifiably sought in the botanical composition.

This argument implies an extreme where the environment is so controlled or so constant that one species is more productive than any mixture. This may occur naturally but is more likely in agriculture.

Agricultural implications

There is one further characteristic in the agricultural use of grassland: the product is more rigidly defined, either as a particular plant or plant constituent, or as an animal or animal constituent derived from it.

The foregoing arguments are even more likely to apply within agriculture; where the environment is closely controlled high productivity is likely to be associated with relatively simple populations containing very few species, provided that the product can be produced by them. It is, of course, possible that plant breeders might deliberately select species that would grow together more productively and still represent a satisfactory agricultural product (Harper 1964).

The best example of this so far is undoubtedly the grass/legume association. In Britain the contribution of white clover (*Trifolium repens*) to a rye-grass (*Lolium perenne*) sward without additional nitrogen is of major importance. In Australia subterranean clover (*Trifolium subterraneum*) has made farming possible in extensive areas; it is often grown with Wimmera rye-grass (*Lolium rigidum*) in irrigated pastures (see Davies 1960, Myers 1962, Barnard 1964).

These swards are highly productive in particular environments but might not be more economic. The clear implication is that more efficient use may be made of the environment by mixed plant populations where economic restrictions prevent further modification of the environment. In these examples, the restriction concerns the use of nitrogenous fertilizer to overcome a shortage of one nutrient; the same argument can be applied to a shortage of water and, perhaps, to shortcomings in the temperature and light status of the environment.

There are also much wider implications for the deliberate cultivation of several crops together, where grass is only one component.
Douglas (1967), for example, has suggested a system of land use
based on a concept called '3-D forestry', with alternate strips of
pod- or nut-bearing trees and grass strip-grazed by ruminants,
poultry all over the area, and timber and a substitute for concentrate
feeding being derived from the trees.

References

AUSTIN, M. P. (1968) *Nature, Lond.* **217**, 1163.
BARNARD, C. (editor) (1964) *Grasses and grasslands*. Macmillan, London.
BROUGHAM, R. W. (1958) *Aust. J. agric. Res.* **9**, 39–52.
COWLING, D. W. (1962) *J. Br. Grassld Soc.* **17**, 282–6.
—— and LOCKYER, D. R. (1968) *J. agric. Sci., Camb.* **71**, 127–36.
DARWIN, C. (1859) *Origin of species*. Murray, London.
DAVIES, W. (1960) *The grass crop*. Spon, London.
DONALD, C. M. (1958) *Aust. J. agric. Res.* **9**, 421–35.
DOUGLAS, J. SHOLTO (1967) *New Scient.* **35**, 382–4.
ENGLAND, F. (1968) *J. appl. Ecol.* **5**, 227–42.
HARPER, J. L. (1964) Genetics today. *Proc. XI int. Congr. Genet.*, The Hague.
    Pergamon Press, Oxford.
—— (1967) *J. appl. Ecol.* **4**, 267–90.
KELLY, A. F. and BOYD, M. M. (1966) *Proc. Xth int. Grassld Congr.*, Helsinki,
    pp. 777–82.
MACARTHUR, R. H. and CONNELL, J. H. (1966) *The biology of populations*.
    Wiley, New York.
MCNAUGHTON, S. J. (1967) *Nature, Lond.* **216**, 168–9.
—— (1968) *Nature, Lond.* **219**, 180–1.
MORLEY, F. H. W. (1966) *Proc. N.Z. Soc. Anim. Prod.* **26**, 8–21.
MYERS, L. F. (1962) in *The simple fleece* (editor A. Barnard), Chapter 16. Mel-
    bourne University Press.
RHODES, I. (1968) *J. Br. Grassld Soc.* **23**, 330–5.
SPEDDING, C. R. W. (1966) *Proc. Weed Control Conf.* **3**, 854–60.
STERN, W. R. and DONALD, C. M. (1962) *Aust. J. agric. Res.* **13**, 599–623.
VARTHA, E. W. (1965) *Proc. N.Z. Grassld Ass.* 102–11.
DE WIT, C. T. (1960) *Versl. landbouwk. Onderz.* **66**, 1–82.
—— (1961) Mechanisims in biological competition (editor F. L. Milthorpe).
    Symp. Soc. Exp. Biol. **15**, 315–29.
—— ENNIK, G. C., BERGH, J. P. v. d. and SONNEWELD, A. (1960). *Proc. VIIIth
    int. Grassld Congr.*, pp. 736–41.
WOODFORD, E. K. (1966) *J. Br. Grassld Soc.* **21**, 109–15.

8

Grass as a Cultivated Crop

NATURAL grassland, as described in Chapter 6, may often be regarded as a natural crop and does not differ from sown pastures in any fundamental fashion.

It is true that when grass is grown as an agricultural crop, there must be a clear purpose in mind and this purpose will not be equally served by a host of different plant species. It is probable, therefore, that the aim will be to establish a plant population of particular species; an important way of achieving this is by sowing them. Sowing does not, of itself, guarantee the desired population, and the control of weeds in grassland is now a subject of considerable importance (Fryer and Evans 1968). The whole concept of weeds implies that some species are desired and others not and the idea has increasing validity as grassland is viewed like other crops.

The chief difference here is in the attitude of the user. Natural grassland is improvable from an agricultural point of view and more useful species can be encouraged. In general, the botanical composition has to some extent to be accepted, and the problem is the best way to use the vegetation produced. At the other extreme, the grass crop may have only one species, sown and cultivated for a purpose defined before sowing.

It is not practicable to eliminate every weed, of course, so it is largely a matter of the proportion of the vegetation that is in the desired form. In most cases this will be a very limited number of species, for two main reasons.

1. It is unlikely that many different species are of equal value for the purpose in mind, and clearly there is no point in sowing one that is of inferior quality.
2. Of the short list of those of suitable quality, it is sensible to choose the one that produces the largest quantity.

The purposes of sown grassland

In most cases the purpose will be that of providing food for useful animals. Such a purpose may be more closely defined; for milk production from 3-year-old Friesian cows or for the production of high-quality Merino wool, for example.

Whatever the purpose it cannot automatically be assumed (see Chapter 6) that the optimal diet can be provided by any one species of plant. It may also be argued that the optimal diet is not always accurately known and that there are advantages in allowing the animal to select its own diet from a crop with some variety in it. There are also circumstances in which the needs of the animal population are varied, as in the case of mammals still suckling their offspring. The nutritional needs of the progeny are then different from those of the dam because they are younger, growing, and receiving milk, whilst the dam is lactating. To meet all these nutritional needs from one plant species may be difficult.

Grass as a food for animals will be discussed in greater detail in Chapters 10 and 11, but it is perhaps worth bearing in mind the possibility that grassland herbage might one day be produced for consumption, no doubt after processing, by human beings.

It is also worth considering to what extent the present agricultural purposes can be allowed to determine what crops are grown. There may, in fact, be no conflict, but as the need for human food increases, it becomes more logical to choose the plant population that produces the most energy or protein per unit of land and then to consider how best to process it. If the processing continues to be carried out by animals, it may still be necessary to consider carefully which animals should be used. There is thus a sense in which grass as a crop has a less assured future than natural grassland.

Included amongst the definitions of purpose for which the grass crop is grown must also be a description of the cultural context in which it is to be grown. That is to say that the choice of species must be for quality and quantity of production on certain soils, with given quantities of fertilizer, managed in definite ways, and in certain climates. These ways include the method of harvesting, which may make a great deal of difference to the choice of species. Harvesting by grazing (see Chapter 13), as compared with cutting, may greatly influence the longevity of the plant species. Thus the relationship between grazing and cutting for conservation, and whether grazing is by large or small animals, or whether harvesting is by cutting only (as in zero-grazing), will affect plant survival as well as productivity.

It is obviously unlikely that many different plant species will be equally suitable for particular purposes or production in a particular context and it is clear that suitability must be determined over a period long enough to allow effects on longevity to be expressed.

If the choice of plant species is made in any such fashion, then it follows that the practices of cultivation and management must be carefully planned and consistently applied. It also suggests that the nutritional needs of the animal population should be rigidly defined, if necessary by simplifying the kinds of animal on any one pasture. It is obviously easier to choose an appropriate plant if the animal used can be stated very precisely: it may then be undesirable to graze together cows at different levels of milk yield or ewes with different numbers of lambs.

The characteristics of the grass crop are therefore those of any other crop—defined and controlled crop growth and pattern of cultivation—but it differs from most arable crops in that it can be harvested frequently. Indeed, it must be harvested several times a year, for most species, and each harvest may influence subsequent growth. Since this situation differs in many ways from that of natural grassland, it is worth considering to what extent ecological principles that are appropriate to the latter are also relevant to the former.

Before doing so it is sensible to look more closely at the characteristic pattern of growth in the grass crop.

The pattern of crop growth

The pattern of growth characteristic of grass and grass/clover mixtures has already been referred to in Chapter 3. In most countries seasonality of production is a characteristic, although the precise pattern may be quite different. In New Zealand the output of digestible dry matter varies from 5·5 to nearly 66 kg/ha/day (Joblin 1966). Only 11 per cent of the annual production of digestible material is produced in the four winter months, and 64 per cent in the four spring and early summer months (September to December). The seasonal nature of the growth curve may be modified by harvesting procedures, by fertilizer practices, and by irrigation, but only rarely can it be eliminated. Climate imposes important restrictions, chiefly of temperature and moisture, which generally result in both major and minor irregularities of growth-rate; these irregularities are no more and no less predictable than is the climate.

This combination of variation in growth-rate with a major problem in prediction makes the grass crop a difficult one to harvest efficiently. One advantage of cutting, as opposed to grazing, is the greater extent to which it can be controlled. Thus cutting machinery can be used as required whereas agricultural animals have to be fed each day, whether this is in the best interests of crop growth or not. The differences are not always so clear cut. If cutting is part of a zero-grazing system, fresh grass cut and carted to the animal, then the same need exists for daily harvesting. Even with cutting for conservation, it is rarely possible to have sufficient machinery to cut and process herbage from the whole farm on one day, and for economic reasons it is better to spread the harvesting need over a period. This is particularly so for grass-drying, the most efficient method of preservation, because of the relatively high cost of the drying equipment. The most critical time in this respect is the early spring, or whenever the maximum growth-rate occurs, because the demand for harvesting is then greatest and the consequences of harvesting earlier or later than the optimum time are also greatest.

At this time, when the rate of dry-matter accumulation is most rapid in grasses, the quality of the herbage is declining. The simplest single measure of herbage quality is its digestibility (see Chapter 10); this is at its highest in young spring herbage and declines with in-creasing age of the plant material. The production of animal food, expressed as digestible organic matter, is the resultant of dry-matter increase and digestibility decline (see Fig. 8.1). To a rather less dramatic extent the same is true of the rest of the growing season. There is thus an optimum stage at which to harvest the crop and this depends also on the quality of herbage required by the animals to be fed.

One way of avoiding the situation in which the entire grassland area reaches the optimum harvesting stage at one time, is to sow species or varieties selected for their differing growth patterns. It is then an interesting, and still largely unanswered, question as to whether such an arrangement necessarily involves accepting a lower total yield of herbage.

It appears to be generally the case that maximizing crop yield in grasses tends to widen the disparity between the peak and trough in production. Heavy fertilizer application, with nitrogenous fertilizer especially, increases plant growth at the peak times more than it does at other times; in Britain, for example, nitrogen has its maximum

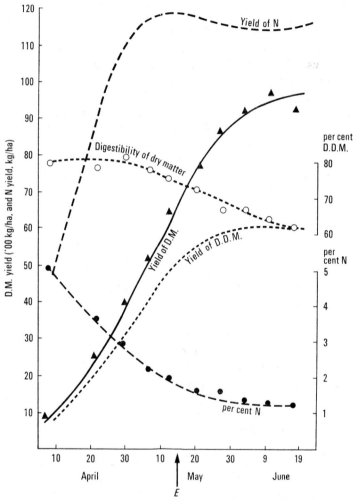

FIG. 8.1. Changes in yield and composition of *S*. 24 rye-grass with increasing maturity following the application of 59·4 kg nitrogen/ha on 25 February 1965, and 77 kg nitrogen/ha on 24 March 1965. *E* indicates date of 50 per cent ear emergence. (From Whitehead and Cowling 1967, after Green and Corrall 1967, unpublished.)

effect in the spring and virtually no effect in midwinter (as can be seen by comparing Figs. 8.2(*a*) and (*b*)). Patterns of defoliation generally increase uniformity of growth only by reducing it at peak times. It is different for irrigation, which is therefore a potent tool in some circumstances for increasing both yield and uniformity.

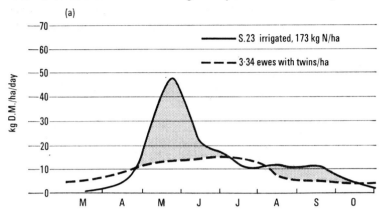

FIG. 8.2 (*a*). Herbage yield with low nitrogen and balanced sheep requirement.

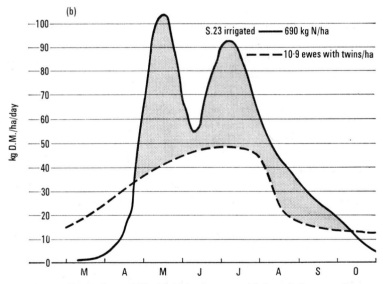

FIG. 8.2 (*b*). Herbage yield with high nitrogen and balanced sheep requirement (i.e. annual requirement = annual yield).

Grass as a crop for grazing possesses one major advantage, that it provides successive harvests within one season; and one major disadvantage, that the pattern of growth is markedly seasonal. It is true that the requirements of an animal population are not constant, but they do not in the agriculturally useful herbivores vary down to nothing. This subject is further considered in Chapter 16, in which the curves of herbage supply and ruminant requirements are illustrated.

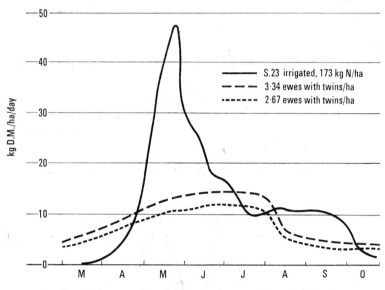

FIG. 8.3. Herbage supply and sheep requirement at two stocking rates.

A simple example is given in Fig. 8.3 in order to show the magnitude of the discrepancy even with an animal population chosen for the similarity of its needs to the curve of herbage growth. It follows from this that grazing alone can rarely be an efficient form of harvesting, unless the demand exceeds the supply even at times of maximum grass production. The latter situation can only be sustained by feeding the animals something in addition, to supplement the grazing at times of serious shortage. It is possible to base agricultural systems on this principle but it is more usual to employ an animal population that can be fed by grazing for as long as possible; there are then bound to be periods of surplus pasture production. If these surplus quantities are not removed, the quality of the crop declines and the quantity subsequently grown may also be reduced; in any event the surpluses themselves are wasted.

In order to avoid wastage, herbage is cut and conserved in a variety of ways (Watson and Nash 1960). The processes mainly used are making into hay or silage, with losses up to 30 per cent, or dried grass, which involves more cost but much smaller losses, of about 5 per cent (Alderman 1968). The losses occur in respiration after cutting, in fragmentation of leaf during hay curing operations, and in unwanted fermentation during ensilage. Further losses may occur for all such conserved products during feeding.

The significance of ecological principles to the grass crop

It was concluded early in this chapter that grass treated as a crop was likely to involve greatly simplified plant and animal populations under considerable control. The activities of man not only modify the natural environment but replace those of many of the components of a natural system. Man thus operates to eliminate predators and replaces their activities by planned predation of his own. He may control animal reproduction and, as far as he can, the incidence of disease and disease-producing organisms. The greater the degree of simplification from a natural to a crop-grass situation, the more complex and numerous the activities of the farmer have to be. Problems arise chiefly when the activities required on the part of the farmer are uneconomic or beyond his skill or knowledge. They may be uneconomic if they are required very frequently. Lack of skill may be a deficiency of the individual farmer or represent a more general problem. Lack of knowledge may relate to problems which were not foreseen at all or to which no answer has been found.

If stability in a natural system depends upon variety and complexity of plant and animal species and their interactions, then simplified systems may lack it. Sufficient knowledge of such systems should make it possible to maintain stability at any level of intensity of production, by activities that replace the missing functions. 'Sufficient' knowledge may often be more than is available, however, and even where it exists, it may be costly to obtain and use. The same may be true of the agricultural use of natural grassland and some of the simplification of the grass crop should represent a considerable reduction in the number of possible problems.

It may be the case that any form of monoculture requires increasing control activity the longer it is pursued but if so the grass crop has one major advantage. As a sown crop it does not have to occupy the same land indefinitely. Natural grassland is certainly more varied but in this respect it has the attributes of monoculture, and tends to occupy the same land for longer than any other agriculturally used vegetation.

Indeed, sown grassland, the basis of ley-farming (Stapledon and Davies 1948), has long been used as a break crop between cereals in order to mitigate the effects of monoculture. Although grass has some pests and diseases in common with some cereal crops, for example stem-boring Diptera (Jepson and Heard 1959, Heard and Hopper 1963), the general effect of ploughing and reseeding is beneficial; the effect on weed populations may also be important (Heard 1963). Ploughing itself is an operation of some consequence to all the plant and animal species involved, as well as to soil structure. Its functions have always included the burying of the previous vegetation and the incorporation of its decomposed products in the mixed-up soil. It is laborious, difficult to carry out on many classes of land, and impossible on others. It seems likely to decline now that treatment with herbicides can be used to destroy vegetation just as well as does ploughing (Davies and Jones 1964, Arnott and Clement 1966).

The cost and difficulty of establishing a new grass crop are also relevant to the problem of whether annuals, biennials, or perennials are likely to be most efficient as crop plants. It has been suggested (Woodford 1966) that dual cropping of short-lived annuals might provide the highest biological efficiency.

The use of grass as a crop therefore offers a good deal of flexibility to compensate for the necessary simplification. Rotation of grasses, alternation with other crops, rotation of different kinds of animal on the same grass crop, and alternation of cultural methods, both chemical and physical, are amongst the changes that can be employed.

It follows from this that such grass crops must be in competition with other, quite different, crops as methods of land use, and that the decision to sow grass has to be justified in this context.

References

ALDERMAN, G. (1968) *J. Fmrs' Club*, April, pp. 19–24.
ARNOTT, R. A. and CLEMENT, C. R. (1966) *Weed Res.* **6**, 142–57.
DAVIES, W. and JONES, L. (1964) *Outl. Agric.* **4**, 155–62.
FRYER, J. D. and EVANS, S. A. (1968) *Weed control handbook*, 5th edn. Blackwell, Oxford.

HEARD, A. J. (1963) *Ann. appl. Biol.* **52,** 177–84.
—— and HOPPER, M. J. (1963) *Ann. appl. Biol.* **51,** 301–11.
JEPSON, W. F. and HEARD, A. J. (1959) *Ann. appl. Biol.* **47,** 114–30.
JOBLIN, A. D. H. (1966) *Proc. Ruakura Fmrs' Conf. Wk.,* N.Z., pp. 2–8.
STAPLEDON, R. G. and DAVIES, W. (1948) *Ley farming.* Faber & Faber, London.
WATSON, S. J. and NASH, M. J. (1960) *The conservation of grass and forage crops.*
    Oliver and Boyd, Edinburgh.
WOODFORD, E. K. (1966) *J. Br. Grassld Soc.* **21,** 109–15.

9

The Fauna of Grassland

SINCE grassland may occur in so many forms it is not surprising that the characteristic fauna is extremely variable. It includes microscopic protozoons at the soil surface and very large herbivores like the zebra.

There is little point here in listing the animals that inhabit different grassland types but it is important to appreciate the part that animals may play in the life and death of grassland plants. This is most readily done by considering the characteristic fauna of different parts of the plant's immediate environment and the effect of their activities on the herbage. The most convenient groups concern the fauna of (1) the soil, (2) the soil/plant interface, (3) the vegetation, (4) the whole pasture, and (5) the fauna that live parasitically. Agricultural animals will then be considered in a final section.

The soil

Soil animals are usually small and may be present in enormous numbers. For example, 144 million Collembola (springtails) may be found in a hectare of grassland, and the weight of such small fauna may be of the order of 750 kg/ha. On the other hand, earthworms may weigh between 0·1 and 3·0 g and there may be up to 7 million/ha of grassland, while moles weigh about 85–110 g (males being heavier than females) but are unlikely to exceed forty per hectare. Soil animals that may exert a significant influence on grassland can be described by their activities as follows:

soil movers and burrowers,
those causing decay and decomposition of plant material,
root feeders,
predators on the above.

As Darwin pointed out in 1881, the quantity of soil that a normal earthworm population may move in a year is surprising. An average turnover of soil in England is about 11 tons/acre/year (about 27 000 kg/ha) or 2 cm in depth every 10 years (Lewis and Taylor 1967).

The significance of such earth-moving may lie in its influence on soil structure, affecting aeration, drainage, or root penetration, or it may be in the mixing effect of continually bringing up soil from some depth to the surface where it gradually has organic matter added to it.

Soil movers may also incorporate organic matter into the soil by feeding activities above ground; earthworms do a great deal of this, pulling live and dead leaves and animal excreta into their burrows. Decay and decomposition of dead plant parts is chiefly effected by micro-organisms, such as bacteria, and the important small animals are often chiefly concerned with breaking down detritus and rendering it accessible to attack by bacteria and fungi.

Root feeders include insects that eat whole roots, such as cockchafer (*Melolontha melolontha*) larvae, animals that browse on the root surface, such as eelworms (Banage 1963), and animals that actually live in the root itself.

The effect of all this activity on the plant depends on whether the roots damaged or eaten are active or already dead, and whether they are concerned with nutrient intake or mainly with water uptake. If a useful root system is damaged it is likely that the plant will be placed at a disadvantage compared with adjacent undamaged plants.

The effect of predators depends on the importance of the animals on which they prey.

The soil/grass interface

As Macfadyen (1957) has pointed out, much of the world's living organic matter appears to be concentrated at the boundaries between matter in different phases, such as the air-land boundary.

There is no sharp division between the fauna of the soil and that of the soil surface, however. Both are generally small and feed on vegetation, dead or living, and on other animals. They thus have similar effects on the breakdown of plant material and they may damage roots at or near the surface. They may also feed on the above-ground parts of the plant.

Since the growing-point of grasses usually lies close to the soil surface, there is a considerable risk that the animals of this region may cause damage out of proportion to the amount they consume.

Voles (*Microtus* spp.) are a good example of small mammals that live on the soil surface, making runs and nests in undisturbed herbage and feeding largely on the stem bases of grasses. The predators on this category may not be confined to this region and include birds.

The vegetation

The fauna of the vegetation itself may be small and live on it (for example, leaf-eating insects or nematodes) or feed on vegetation during forays, often nocturnal, from hiding places near the soil surface; the slug *Agriolimax reticulatus* is a good example of these (Newell 1968).

Wolcott (1937) estimated that insects in a pasture in New York consumed 0.94×10^6 g (3.76×10^6 cal) of above-ground vegetation per hectare, during the summer period. As Golley (1960) has pointed out, this could easily make them more important than mice; in fact, in some situations, Wolcott found that the insects ate twice as much as the cows that were present.

Spectacular damage is associated with locusts (Bullen 1966). Grasshoppers in North America, at densities as low as 3/m², on poor grazing land can destroy more than 50 per cent of the vegetation (Anderson and Wright 1962). In the U.S.S.R. one to two grass-hoppers per m² caused an average of 15·6 per cent loss on steppe land in 1958 (Serkova 1961). Many other insects are important pests of grassland; for example, the larvae of the grass moth (*Crambus hortuellus*) in North America (Edwards and Heath 1964). The effect of excluding phytophagous insects for a prolonged period has been little studied (Huffaker 1968).

The larger herbivores may not really live on the vegetation although they may feed on little else. Rabbits (*Oryctolagus cuniculus*, Southern 1940) and hares (*Lepus* spp.) may be considered as marginal examples of vegetation dwellers. They have exerted an enormous influence, nevertheless, on the grasslands of Australia (Fennessy 1962). In a large area of grassland hares may spend their whole lives on the vegetation, eating it as their principal diet and reproducing in a simple nest or 'form' (see Matthews 1962, Burton 1968) within it. Rabbits, however, often make their homes in burrows within adjacent woodland and penetrate into the grassland for feeding. They may, nevertheless, exert considerable influence on botanical composition, as shown in Britain after the outbreak of myxomatosis (Thomas 1960).

Very interesting studies of lemmings (*Lemmus trimucronatus*) have been carried out (Schultz 1964). Most of the forage of the arctic tundra consists of grasses and sedges, and the lemming is the principal herbivore during the 2-month growing season.

The alpine tundra is a good deal more varied (Marr 1964) in both plant (forty-two species) and animal species (pika, *Ochotona princeps*; ptarmigan, *Lagopus lencurus*; deer, *Odocoileus hemionus*; elk, *Cervus canadensis*; mountain sheep, *Ovis canadensis*; coyote, *Canis latrans*; red fox, *Vulpes fulva*; voles, *Microtus* sp.; and, most influential of all, the pocket gopher, *Thomomys talpoides*).

The whole pasture

The fauna here includes the largest grassland animals such as gazelles, zebra, and even elephant, although the last is really a forest animal (Talbot, Payne, Ledger, Verdcourt, and Talbot 1965). Whether they spend most of their time on grassland probably depends on the areas involved. Certainly, the African savannah includes gazelles, wildebeest, impala, and eland amongst its herbivores, lions amongst its predators, and hyaenas amongst its scavengers.

Animals of the whole pasture are usually capable of rapid movement (MacArthur and Connell 1966). Predators are noted for their powers of acceleration, and herbivores for their well-developed senses and capacity for sustained escape. The young of such grazing animals are usually mobile within a remarkably short time of birth. This emphasis on movement, necessary for survival in an environment characterized by little cover and often great visibility, also makes possible considerable migrations, for water or to follow seasonal food supplies. Herbivores are commonly found in herds, and herd-structure is often well developed. The advantages for survival are clear; a predator finds it difficult to catch a whole herd unawares and may be confronted by aggressive males in a defensive ring. The effect on the pasture, however, is that one area is grazed by many more animals than could possibly live on it for long. After a short time, therefore, the herd moves to another area in order to find more food. Thus a form of rotational grazing occurs with all the implications so important in agriculture: alternation of defoliation and a rest period for the plant; avoidance of soiled areas for a period, with its effects on the survival of parasites; heavy treading and trampling for a short period, influencing the establishment of such plants as tree seedlings.

Parasites

Animals themselves represent an environment and parasites are found on and in all of them. Those that are most characteristic of the larger grassland animals are those that spend part of their lives on the herbage itself (see Michel and Ollerenshaw 1963). Parasites in general tend to have simplified lives in many directions, including that of food collection and protection, but they face two major difficulties. These are to avoid killing their host, and to ensure that their offspring find another suitable host animal. External and internal parasites may solve the second problem in somewhat different ways, but many of them take advantage of the fact that other animals eat the same food which may therefore act as a means of transfer from one animal to another.

  It is often assumed that successful parasites do not greatly affect their hosts but two things should be remembered. First, a balance between host and parasite is essentially between species rather than individuals, and secondly, parasites do not operate alone. It is only necessary to consider the interaction with predators to appreciate this point. Predators are often assumed to do relatively little harm to the species they prey upon because they tend to catch the old and sick individuals. In so far as this is all they do, then clearly they make little difference to a herd, since these old and sick individuals would not live for long, and in any case cannot keep up with the herd. A parasitized animal may also be somewhat slower and suffer predation; this means that a degree of parasitism insufficient to cause death directly may still result in it indirectly.

  It is worth noting that predators may also attack females at parturition and destroy the young before they can escape. This can have a considerable effect on the productivity of a herd. When animal populations are cropped by man for his own purposes, the removal of individuals has to be managed to maximize productivity (Nagle and Harris 1966, Passey 1966). Within grassland agriculture it is often possible to exclude other predators; agricultural animals have nevertheless been derived from ancestors evolved in different circumstances and retain many of their behaviour patterns.

Agricultural animals

Relatively few species have been domesticated, and for this and other reasons, the population of animals in agriculturally used grassland shows little of the variety found in natural systems. The animals deliberately kept for their produce include some birds such as geese, but are mostly herbivorous mammals, such as sheep, goats, horses, cattle, buffalo, alpaca, and llamas.

These animals are not generally mixed together to any great extent, so that the main grazing population is usually limited to one or two species.

This does not necessarily reduce the variety of smaller species found within and beneath the vegetation, but many agricultural practices do have this effect. Some of these effects are quite deliberate, as in the use of pesticides to reduce the number of herbage-eating insects or the use of anthelmintic drugs to reduce the number of internal parasites present in the main animal population.

Other practices, the use of fertilizers, herbicides, and cultivations may have considerable effects—not necessarily favourable—on the minor fauna, and these consequences may be very poorly understood.†

Regular and complete defoliation of the pasture will also render the habitat less suitable for other animals (such as hares and partridge), whilst the smaller ones may survive in hedges or in the relatively undisturbed areas adjacent to fences. Voles will often retreat to fence lines in this way.

There are thus direct and indirect effects of agricultural practices on the grassland fauna. In part, agriculture deliberately sets out to control the environment and the fauna, to create a new and different balance of populations, such that the harvest of some product will be increased. In part, however, agriculturalists may not appreciate the complexity of the interactions between fauna, on which their selected productivity depends but which they never see. The soil is especially prone to be considered as simpler than it really is, partly because it is not easy to observe the life within it. It is also easy to ignore nocturnal activities and the consequences of destroying predators are frequently not observed directly.

The balance of nature

A naturally maintained balance between populations is often achieved in undisturbed situations, though the absence of man and his activities

† The recommendations of the 1966 F.A.O./O.I.E. Conference on sheep diseases (Rome) includes the following (p. 134): 'The conference *recognising* the trend to increased use in agriculture of chemicals hazardous to the health of animals and man *recommends* intensification of efforts directed to other means of disease control such as those that affect biological balance.'

is no guarantee of this. Substantial oscillation can occur naturally, and in any event, many balances are the result of accepting vast losses of individuals at a very early stage in their lives (Williams 1964). Agricultural use of an area often changes it greatly, but there is no reason why balanced ecosystems should not be achieved. There is no fundamental difference between agricultural and non-agricultural situations in this respect. The concept of a 'balance of nature' is most easily understood in terms of the relative numbers of predators and their prey, as originally considered by Nicholson (1933). Predator–prey relationships have been much studied (Lotka 1925, Volterra 1931, Gause 1934) and it is possible to visualize man as the major predator in agricultural systems. Within such systems, however, the concept of efficient harvesting or cropping of the agricultural animal population is a relatively simple and straightforward matter.

Two other major concepts of animal ecology must be considered at this point.

Food chains

All animals depend upon plants for their food but, of course, many of them only indirectly. Thus chains can be traced from the plant to the herbivorous animals that feed on it, to the carnivorous animals that feed on the herbivores, and so on (MacArthur and Connell 1966). Most of the food chains have only three or four links, and the main agricultural chains are extremely simple (for example, grass→cow→man). More complex examples are usually present within agricultural systems, and may be of major significance in nutrient cycles (see Chapter 12) or the control of grassland pests.

At each 'trophic level' of a generalized chain, there may be many different species all consuming the same kind of food. A description of these relationships between species and their food is termed a 'food web'.

Pyramid of numbers

There are fewer animals at each successive level of a food chain and they tend to be individually larger; thus a pyramid of numbers (Elton 1935) can be constructed to represent this situation. It is, of course, quite likely that a predator will be larger than its prey but this is by no means invariably so. If a predator species is to survive it must be less numerous than its prey at most times, since sufficient members of the prey species have to survive and reproduce to maintain the population. This is not inevitable, however, if the predator consumes many different species of prey.

In any event, within a given area, it is likely that larger animals will be less abundant than small ones, whether they form part of the same food chain or not.

Many attempts have been made to describe the relationships, of numbers, size, and age, within animal populations, from the logistic equation of Verhulst (1838) to the model of Sinko and Streifer (1967).

Clearly, animal numbers are regulated one way or another, and many mechanisms other than starvation may operate (Solomon 1949, Wynne-Edwards 1962, Williamson 1967).

References

ANDERSON, N. L. and WRIGHT, J. C. (1952) *Tech. Bull. Mont. agric. Exp. Stn.* No. 486.

BANAGE, W. B. (1963) *J. Anim. Ecol.* **32**, 133-40.

BULLEN, F. T. (1966) *J. appl. Ecol.* **3**, 147-68.

BURTON, M. (1968) *Wild animals of the British Isles.* Warne, London.

DARWIN, C. (1881) *Vegetable mould and earthworms.* Murray, London.

EDWARDS, C. A. and HEATH, G. W. (1964) *The principles of agricultural entomology.* Chapman & Hall, London.

ELTON, C. S. (1935) *Animal ecology*, 2nd edn. Methuen, London.

FENNESSY, B. V. (1962) *The simple fleece* (editor A. Barnard), chapter 17. Melbourne University Press.

GAUSE, G. F. (1934) *The struggle for existence.* Williams & Wilkins Co., Baltimore.

GOLLEY, F. B. (1960) *Ecol. Monogr.* **30**, 187-206.

HUFFAKER, C. B. (1968) Part IX of *Productivity of large herbivores* (editors F. B. Golley and H. K. Buechner), *IBP Handbook* No. 7. Blackwell, Oxford.

LEWIS, T. and TAYLOR, L. R. (1967) *Introduction to experimental ecology*, chapter 4, p. 211.

LOTKA, A. J. (1925) *Principles of physical biology.* Williams & Wilkins Co., Baltimore.

MACARTHUR, R. H. and CONNELL, J. H. (1966) *The biology of populations.* Wiley, New York.

MACFADYEN, A. (1957) *Animal ecology.* Pitman, London.

MARR, J. W. (1964) *Grazing in terrestrial and marine environments* (editor D. J. Crisp), pp. 109-18. Blackwell, Oxford.

MATTHEWS, L. H. (1952) *British mammals.* Collins, London.

MICHEL, J. F. and OLLERENSHAW, C. B. (1963) *Animal health, production, and pasture* (editors A. N. Wooden, K. C. Sellers, and D. E. Tribe), chapters 16, 17, and 18. Longmans, London.

NAGLE, J. P. and HARRIS, G. A. (1966) *Proc. Xth int. Grassld Congr.*, Helsinki, pp. 994-7.

NEWELL, P. F. (1968) The measurement of environmental factors in terrestrial ecology, *Br. Ecol. Soc. Symp.* No. 8. pp. 141-6. Blackwell, Oxford.

NICHOLSON, A. J. (1933) *J. Anim. Ecol.* **2**, 132-78.

PASSEY, H. B. (1966) *Proc. Xth int. Grassld Congr.*, Helsinki, pp. 991-4.

SCHULTZ, A. M. (1964) In *Grazing in terrestrial and marine environments* (editor D. J. Crisp), pp. 57–68. Blackwell, Oxford.

SERKOVA, L. G. (1961) Quoted by BULLEN, F. T. (1966) *Trudy Manch-issled Inst. Zashch. Rast. Uralsk* 6, 147–57.

SINKO, J. W. and STREIFER, W. (1967) *Ecology* 48, 910–18.

SOLOMON, M. E. (1949) *J. Anim. Ecol.* 18, 1–35.

SOUTHERN, H. N. (1940) *Ann. appl. Biol.* 27, 509–26.

TALBOT, L. M., PAYNE, W. J. A., LEDGER, H. P., VERDCOURT, L. D. and TALBOT, M. H. (1965) *C.A.B. tech. Commun.* No. 16.

THOMAS, A. S. (1960) *J. Ecol.* 48, 287–306.

VERHULST, P. F. (1838) *Corresp. Mat. Phys.* 10, 113–21.

VOLTERRA, V. (1931) In Appendix to Chapman's *Animal ecology*. McGraw Hill, New York.

WILLIAMS, C. B. (1964) *Patterns in the balance of nature*. Academic Press, New York.

WILLIAMSON, M. H. (1967) *The teaching of ecology*, *Br. Ecol. Soc. Symp.* No. 7, pp. 169–76. Blackwell, Oxford.

WOLCOTT, G. N. (1937) *Ecol. Monogr.* 7, 1–90.

WYNNE-EDWARDS, V. C. (1962) *Animal dispersion in relation to social behaviour*. Oliver & Boyd, Edinburgh.

10

Grass as a Food for Animals— Ruminants

THE ruminants are extremely specialized grass eaters and form the most important group agriculturally. Their nutrition is the subject of extensive research and literature and it is not intended here to attempt a summary, merely to emphasize certain characteristics which are particularly important ecologically.

The nutritional needs of the ruminant

All ruminant animals require water, minerals, certain vitamins, protein, and energy. Water is of great importance; the animal body contains 75–80 per cent of water when very young and about 50 per cent in the mature fat state. The ruminant has a substantial water-storage capacity in its rumen, quite apart from any specialized water-storage tissues.

Ruminants require calcium, phosphorus, potassium, sodium, chlorine, sulphur, magnesium, iron, zinc, copper, manganese, iodine, cobalt, molybdenum, and selenium; they may also need fluorine, bromine, barium, and strontium. Some of these are toxic when taken in excess of requirements, notably copper, selenium, molybdenum, and fluorine (see Underwood 1962).

The functional ruminant does not require certain vitamins in the diet. For example, vitamins of the B complex are synthesized by rumen bacteria, provided that the essential raw materials are present. Vitamin B_{12} deficiency can thus occur due to a shortage of cobalt in the food.

As far as the major components, protein and energy, are concerned, the ruminant is able to derive its needs from very coarse fodders, because of its digestive system, but at the price of a lower efficiency in the utilization of soluble carbohydrates and proteins (Phillipson 1963).

Nutritional physiology of the ruminant

The digestive tract of the functional ruminant is characterized by a stomach divided into four compartments, the reticulum, the rumen, the omasum, and the abomasum. The first two form one large organ in the adult (85 per cent of total stomach capacity in the cow), in which bacterial fermentation of the food takes place. This process is assisted by a continuous flow of saliva (see Phillipson 1963), rhythmic contractions of the rumen walls, regurgitation and cud-chewing, and the presence of vast numbers of bacteria (10^9–10^{10}/ml of rumen contents) and protozoa (10^6/ml, see McDonald, Edwards, and Greenhalgh 1966). Some 70 per cent of the digestible dry matter entering the rumen is converted by these micro-organisms into soluble and gaseous compounds, some of which are absorbed and some lost by eructation (belching).

From the abomasum, in which peptic digestion occurs, onwards, the digestion process is similar for ruminants and non-ruminants.

The nutritional value of herbage

The value of herbage to the ruminant depends upon the physiological state and level of performance of the animal as well as on the composition of the herbage. However small the animal's require-ments for a constituent, an inadequate supply will render that constituent limiting and thus important. The quantity available to the animal is not necessarily equal to that present in the herbage, since not all the herbage eaten is digested or absorbed.

It is necessary therefore to consider first all the main constituents of herbage, even though nutritional value is not usually governed by most of them.

The chemical composition of herbage

This is greatly influenced by (1) the stage of growth of the plants; (2) the botanical composition of the sward; (3) the nutrient status of the soil; (4) the climate; (5) the management of the sward (Tribe, Freer, and Coombe 1963).

In general, therefore, the composition of pasture dry matter is very variable (Ferguson 1963; Tribe, Freer, and Coombe 1963).

Crude protein (nitrogen $\times 6\cdot25$) may vary from 3 to 30 per cent of the dry matter, and crude fibre from 20 to 40 per cent. Water content varies from 65 to 85 per cent, and the total carbohydrate content from 4 to 30 per cent. Cellulose varies within the range 20–30 per cent, and hemicelluloses from 10 to 30 per cent.

The composition of the most important crop grasses and legumes has recently been summarized (see Spedding 1969). Green herbage is exceptionally rich in carotene (up to 550 ppm in the dry matter), the precursor of vitamin A, and the precursor of vitamin D is also usually present.

The mineral content of herbage is illustrated in Tables 10.1 and 10.2. It will be noted that legumes tend to contain more calcium, copper, and cobalt; grasses contain more silica.

TABLE 10.1

The mineral composition of perennial rye-grass (The values quoted are the range of means given in the literature, cited by Whitehead 1966)

Phosphorus	0·26–0·42	% in dry matter
Potassium	1·98–2·50	% in dry matter
Calcium	0·4–1·0	% in dry matter
Magnesium	0·09–0·25	% in dry matter
Sulphur	0·13–0·75	% in dry matter
Sodium	0·10–0·57	% in dry matter
Chlorine	0·39–1·30	% in dry matter
Iron	50–200	ppm in dry matter
Manganese	22–200	ppm in dry matter
Zinc	15–60	ppm in dry matter
Copper	5·4–8·5	ppm in dry matter
Cobalt	0·15–0·16	ppm in dry matter
Iodine	0·22–1·45	ppm in dry matter
Molybdenum	Insufficient data available	
†Selenium	0·1–1·0	ppm in dry matter
†Lead	0·3–3·5	ppm in dry matter
†Fluorine	2–16	ppm in dry matter
Silica	0·6–1·2	% in dry matter

† Values given are for 'herbage' and not specifically for rye-grass.

Most of the minerals required by herbivores are present in herbage and when deficiencies occur they are often due to an excess of something else (such as molybdenum and sulphate in the case of copper deficiency) or to non-availability (often the case with magnesium deficiency). Other common deficiencies are of iodine (Calderbank 1963) and cobalt, and imbalances of calcium and phosphorus may represent a substantial problem (possibly linked to a shortage of vitamin D).

Some animals have special requirements, of course. Many deer shed their antlers annually (for example, stags of the red deer,

TABLE 10.2

The mineral composition of white clover (The values quoted are the range of means given in the literature, cited by Whitehead 1966. In some cases, information is too limited for this)

Phosphorus	0·25–0·40	% in dry matter
Potassium	2·09–3·11	% in dry matter
Calcium	1·36–2·10	% in dry matter
Magnesium	0·18–0·24	% in dry matter
Sulphur	0·24–0·36	% in dry matter
Sodium	0·12–0·41	% in dry matter
Chlorine	0·62–0·91	% in dry matter
Iron	117–291	ppm in dry matter
Manganese	51–87	ppm in dry matter
Zinc	25–29	ppm in dry matter
Copper	7·3–8·7	ppm in dry matter
Cobalt	0·13–0·24	ppm in dry matter
Iodine	0·14–0·44	ppm in dry matter
Molybdenum	0·64	ppm in dry matter
Selenium	0·005–153	ppm in dry matter
Lead	Similar to that of grasses	
Fluorine	Data not available	
Silica	5–10% of that in grasses	

Cervus elephas), and this is said to impose a considerable additional requirement for minerals which may not easily be satisfied by the herbage consumed. This sometimes leads to stags eating cast antlers and old bones (Harrison Matthews 1952).

Other constitutuents of importance include oestrogens (Bickoff 1968) and a variety of substances associated with grasses or the weeds of grassland (Garner 1963).

TABLE 10.3

Protein requirements of cattle and sheep (After Agricultural Research Council 1965) (These values are not absolute but vary with food intake and the concentration of energy in the diet)

Animal	Mean live weight (kg)	Physiological state	Minimum percentage of digestible crude protein needed in dry matter
Cow	500	Maintenance	3·1
Cow	500	Producing 30 kg milk/day	10·7
Ewe	70	Maintenance	4·3
Ewe	70	Producing 1·8 kg milk/day	10·5

Protein

The protein requirements of the ruminant vary with physiological state; they have been summarized recently for cattle and sheep (Agricultural Research Council 1965). In Table 10.3, some of these requirements are given for comparison with characteristic herbage contents. It is generally considered that only animals at the highest levels of performance are likely to obtain insufficient protein from grass cultivated as a crop; legumes supply even more. In many extensive situations, however, the protein content may be well below requirements, as may happen in Australia (Milford 1960).

Energy

In most situations the intake of digestible energy is the factor of greatest importance in the nutrition of the ruminant. The net energy content of herbage depends chiefly on its stage of growth, but the value of digested energy to the animal depends on the amount of energy lost in rumen fermentation and urine excretion, and on the efficiency with which the remaining metabolizable energy can be used.

An illustration of the energy content of herbage compared with animal requirements is given in Table 10.4.

TABLE 10.4

Energy requirements of cattle and sheep (After Agricultural Research Council 1965)

Animal	Mean live weight (kg)	Physiological state	Minimum energy concentration needed in diet (Mcal/kg dry matter)
Dairy cow	500	Maintenance	1·8
Dairy cow	500	Producing 20 kg milk/day	2·6
Dairy cow	500	Producing 30 kg milk/day	3·0
Ewe	70	Maintenance	1·8
Ewe	70	Producing 1·5 kg milk/day	2·2
Ewe	70	Producing 1·8 kg milk/day	2·6
Calorific value of grass dry matter			*c.* 4·25

Digestibility

The most important single measure of the nutritive value of herbage is its digestibility. This is usually measured as the percentage apparent *in vivo* digestibility (*D*), where

$$D = \frac{I-F}{I} \times 100,$$

$$I = \text{food intake, } F = \text{faecal output.}$$

This may be calculated on a dry-matter basis or for any constituent, such as energy. It is possible to use an *in vitro* laboratory technique to estimate digestibility (Shelton and Reid 1960; Tilley, Deriaz, and Terry 1960), a method that can be applied to very small samples and can thus distinguish between different parts of the same plant.

The apparent digestibility of herbage plants varies between species, between varieties, and between parts of the same plant; it declines somewhat as the growing season advances and varies greatly with stage of growth (Raymond, Tilley, Deriaz, and Minson 1960). The interactions between the quantity and quality of herbage production were referred to in earlier chapters. The most important aspects of digestibility at this point are as follows:

1. Digestibility is an index of how much of the ingested food will be retained by the animal.
2. In general, ruminants eat more of more digestible foods (Blaxter 1962) and performance is therefore greatly influenced by digestibility.
3. Herbage plants differ in digestibility, so grazing animals can select more or less nutritious diets to an extent that varies with the grazing behaviour of the animal.
4. Digestibility of plants tends to be higher in the early stages of growth (see Fig. 8.1), so young herbage tends to be more nutritious.

It is of interest that digestibility as measured with sheep differs little from the values obtained with cattle (Blaxter 1964) but red deer have given lower figures for both dry-matter digestibility (53–7 per cent) and cellulose digestibility (14–24 per cent) compared with those of sheep (60–2 and 29–34 per cent respectively) on the same diets (Maloiy, Kay, Goodall, and Topps 1968).

Water buffaloes (*Bos bubalis*) have been found to digest guinea grass (*Panicum maximum*) more efficiently (by 5–7 per cent) than did Holstein cattle (*Bos taurus*, Johnson, Ordoveza, Hardison, and Castillo 1967).

Intake characteristics

However nutritious and digestible the herbage, it remains of little value if animals will not eat it. Ruminants differ from simple-stomached animals, like the pig and man, in the way in which their appetite is regulated. In the monogastric animals, appetite is governed chiefly by the intake of energy as reflected in the blood glucose level. This is also the case with very young ruminants, but in the adult a quite different mechanism operates. The simplest way to visualize the 'bulk theory' of appetite regulation (Campling 1964) is to regard the rumen as a container which the animal will fill to a certain capacity of bulk; it will only eat more if there is room in the container. What regulates intake, therefore, is the rate at which ingesta is removed from the rumen, by digestion, absorption, and onward passage to the omasum and abomasum. This is why there is, in general, a positive relationship between intake and digestibility. Some plant species are consumed by sheep to a greater extent (such as sainfoin) or to a lesser extent (such as timothy) than would be expected from their digestibilities, so there are clearly other factors also (Osbourn, Thomson, and Terry 1966).

In addition to attributes that influence intake by operating in the rather mechanical way described, there are others that make plants unattractive to the animal. Amongst these are the purely physical aspects, such as external spines and hairs, and the structural features, such as deposition of silica and lignification, that may make plants difficult to graze. These features are sometimes grouped under a heading termed 'palatability'. Since this implies some conscious judgement about taste on the part of the animal, whereas we only know that it eats less, it has been suggested (Blaxter, Wainman, and Wilson 1961) that the term should not be used.

There are, however, factors that render herbage unattractive and that have little or nothing to do with the plants themselves. The most common examples relate to soiling with faeces or urine, which will often cause herbivores to reject herbage. It seems reasonable to use the term 'unpalatable' to refer to the effect of such factors.

Advantages and limitations of grass as a feed

The main advantages of herbage as a food for ruminants is that it is a complete diet in a great variety of circumstances. This is, of course, saying very little in relation to animals that have presumably evolved in this direction and are themselves highly specialized to deal with herbage. Agriculturally, however, it is still true that, in a great many circumstances, herbage offers a complete diet. It is when much higher performance (of growth, milk yield, or reproduction) is required that herbage proves inadequate, sometimes in the quantity of a particular mineral, generally in the content of digestible energy. For very young ruminants it is not, and cannot be, the sole diet, and high performance is certainly possible on a combination of milk and pasture. Later on, however, it is rare for pasture to be capable of sustaining the highest growth-rates of which cattle and sheep are capable, and the same is true for lactation.

Thus, agriculturally, some deficiencies are relatively unimportant because the diet will have to be supplemented anyway, and any component not present in adequate amounts can be added.

The main limitations of herbage as a diet are in the irregularity of its supply; this has been referred to in Chapter 3.

Animal residues

A substantial part of the food ingested is excreted in the faeces, some of it relatively unchanged. Faeces also contain dead bacteria and endogenous material such as portions of the lining of the alimentary tract. Other products of metabolism are excreted in the urine. The order of magnitude of these residues is indicated in Tables 10.5 and 10.6: they will be further discussed in Chapter 12 as forming a major part of the nutrient cycle.

TABLE 10.5

Composition of sheep faeces (Percentage content on a dry-matter basis) (Table compiled by E. C. Jones from the literature and from unpublished data at the Grassland Research Institute)

Constituent	Range of values (%)
Ash	8·3–49·7
Nitrogen	1·50–4·64
Cellulose	8·0–34·4
Lignin	9·12–25·9
Ether extract	0·8–10·9
Potassium	0·33–2·04
Sodium	0·05–0·45
Phosphorus	0·82–1·16
Magnesium	0·11–0·41

TABLE 10.6

Composition of sheep urine (Table compiled by E. C. Jones, as in Table 10.5)

Constituent	Range of values
Nitrogen, %	0·22–3·87
Potassium, %	0·7–2·0
Nitrogen as ammonia, mg/100 ml	60–130
Sodium, mg/100 ml	0·95–500
Phosphorus, mg/100 ml	6–14
Magnesium, mg/100 ml	7–113
Calcium, mg/100 ml	5–45

The energy balance of the ruminant

From the foregoing account, it will be clear that of the energy ingested by the ruminant as food, losses occur as methane and ammonia from the rumen, and as energy in faeces and urine; the rest is used to keep the animal warm and maintain its bodily

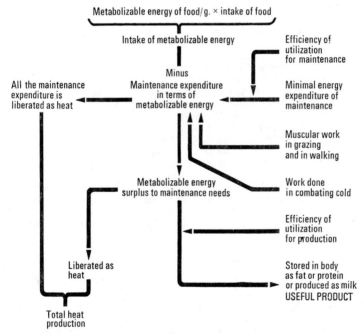

FIG. 10.1. A scheme for relating animal production to food value, which indicates the determinants of production. (From Blaxter 1964*b*.)

functions, to form new tissue or secretions, and to form fat reserves. A diagram relating these processes is shown in Fig. 10.1.

Blaxter (1960) has shown that losses of energy vary with level of feeding. Losses in faeces may be as high as 40 per cent of the gross energy intake of pelleted dried grass, increasing with level of feeding. Losses as methane tend to fall with level of feeding and vary from 5 to 10 per cent of the gross energy intake.

Armstrong (1960) reported values varying from 17·5 to 43·6 per cent for losses in faeces, 3·1 to 7·8 per cent in urine, and 6·5 to 8·4 per cent as methane.

Houpt (1968) measured the heat production of bovine ruminal ingesta and reported the heat of fermentation to be 7–8 per cent of the total daily heat production for a mature, non-lactating cow at maintenance. This fermentation heat (per kg of ingesta) was less than the heat estimated to evolve from average body tissue (per kg of tissue).

References

AGRICULTURAL RESEARCH COUNCIL (1965) *The nutrient requirements of farm livestock*, No. 2. *Ruminants*.
ARMSTRONG, D. G. (1960) *Proc. IXth int. Grassld Congr.*, Reading, pp. 485–9.
BICKOFF, E. M. (1968) *Oestrogenic constituents of forage plants. Rev. Ser.* **1.** Commonwealth Agricultural Bureau.
BLAXTER, K. L. (1960) *Proc. IXth int. Grassld Congr.*, Reading, pp. 479–84.
—— (1962) *The energy metabolism of ruminants.* Hutchinson, London.
—— (1964*a*) *Jl R. agric. Soc.* **125,** 87–99.
—— (1964*b*) *J. Br. Grassld Soc.* **19,** 90–9.
—— WAINMAN, F. W. and WILSON, R. S. (1961) *Anim. Prod.* **3,** 51–61.
CALDERBANK, G. (1963) *Animal health, production, and pasture* (editors A. N. Worden, K. C. Sellers, and D. E. Tribe), chapter 27. Longmans, London.
CAMPLING, R. C. (1964) *J. Br. Grassld Soc.* **19,** 110–18.
FERGUSON, W. S. (1963) *Animal health, production, and pasture* (editors A. N. Worden, K. C. Sellers, and D. E. Tribe), chapter 3. Longmans, London.
GARNER, R. J. (1963) *Animal health, production, and pasture* (editors A. N. Worden, K. C. Sellers, and D. E. Tribe), chapter 28. Longmans, London.
HARRISON MATTHEWS, L. (1952) *British mammals.* Collins, London.
HOUPT, T. R. (1968) *Am. J. Vet. Res.* **29,** 411–19.
JOHNSON, W. L., ORDOVEZA, A. L., HARDISON, W. A. and CASTILLO, L. S. (1967) *J. agric. Sci., Camb.* **69,** 161–70.
MALOIY, G. M. O., KAY, R. N. B., GOODALL, E. D. and TOPPS, J. H. (1968) *Proc. Nutr. Soc.* **27,** 52a–53a.
MCDONALD, P., EDWARDS, R. A. and GREENHALGH, J. F. D. (1966) *Animal nutrition.* Oliver & Boyd, Edinburgh.
MILFORD, R. (1960) *Proc. VIIIth int. Grassld Congr.*, Reading, pp. 474–9.
OSBOURN, D. F., THOMSON, D. J. and TERRY, R. A. (1966) *Proc. Xth int. Grassld Congr.*, Helsinki, pp. 363–7.

PHILLIPSON, A. T. (1963) *Animal health, production, and pasture* (editors A. N. Worden, K. C. Sellers, and D. E. Tribe), chapter 7. Longmans, London.

RAYMOND, W. F., TILLEY, J. M. A., DERIAZ, R. E. and MINSON, D. J. (1960) *Chem. Soc. ind. Monogr.* No. 9, pp. 181–90.

SHELTON, D. C. and REID, R. L. (1960) *Proc. VIIIth int. Grassld Congr.*, Reading, p. 524.

SPEDDING, C. R. W. (1969) *Crop grasses and legumes in British agriculture.* Commonwealth Agricultural Bureau (in press).

TILLEY, J. M. A., DERIAZ, R. E. and TERRY, R. A. (1960) *Proc. VIIIth int. Grassld Congr.*, Reading, p. 533.

TRIBE, D. E., FREER, M. and COOMBE, J. B. (1963) *Animal health, production, and pasture* (editors A. N. Worden, K. C. Sellers, and D. E. Tribe), chapter 4. Longmans, London.

UNDERWOOD, E. J. (1962) *Trace elements in human and animal nutrition*, 2nd edn. Academic Press, New York.

WHITEHEAD, D. C. (1966) *Grassld Res. Inst., tech. Rep.* No. 4.

11

Grass as a Food for Animals—
Non-ruminants

A GREAT many non-ruminant animals eat grassland herbage. Some of them are almost equally specialized in relation to their diet while others do not live entirely on herbage or live on only parts of pasture plants. In this brief account no further mention will be made of animals that feed on relatively small fractions of the plant (such as sap-sucking aphids, seed-eating insects), although they may be of considerable importance as disease vectors, or in terms of the damage they do and the reduction they cause to plant growth.

Of the remaining grass-eaters, some may be classified as agriculturally important producers and others as non-agricultural animals, even though they may be important agricultural pests.

Agricultural animals

Two examples will be taken to illustrate animals that are adapted to a predominantly pasture diet, the horse and the goose; and two examples of non-adapted animals, poultry and pigs.

Horses

The horse has only a simple stomach but possesses a greatly enlarged caecum and colon, both inhabited by micro-organisms that perform the same kind of functions as those present in the rumen. Even vitamins of the B complex are synthesized, and a good deal of cellulose is digested. The difference has been summarized by McDonald, Edwards, and Greenhalgh (1966) as follows: 'In comparison with the ruminant the horse suffers from the disadvantage that the products of microbial digestion have less opportunity of being absorbed and no opportunity of being further broken down by its own digestive enzymes.'

Pasture and dried herbages are thus perfectly satisfactory foods for the horse, even though they may be less efficiently digested and utilized. The efficiency of the horse, however, is a very different topic from that of the meat or milk producer. Horses used for draught purposes require an abundant source of energy, and it has been calculated that the net efficiency of a horse while working is about 24 per cent (the energy of the work done is about 24 per cent of the energy expended in doing that work), and the gross efficiency, as a ratio of the energy of the work done in 9 hours to the energy supplied in the food during 24 hours, is little short of that of a tractor (Sheehy 1955). All this applies to a cart-horse neither gaining nor losing weight. For riding purposes a different type of horse is more efficient, and efficiency in general falls as a horse becomes fatigued.

Geese

Geese are usually regarded as highly efficient grazers. They are certainly capable of extremely close grazing and of living on good-quality herbage alone. Good quality in this case means relatively short, young, leafy material. During winter, while egg-laying, and during the first 6 weeks of life, mash is fed in agricultural systems (Eyles 1963).

The digestive system in poultry differs in several respects from that of the mammal. The main differences are the presence of a storage sac (the crop) joining the oesophagus, and a muscular gizzard between the proventriculus and the ileum, in which food can be ground up with grit. At the junction of the small and large intestines there are two blind sacs (the caeca), and the short large intestine ends in a cloaca from which both urine and faeces are excreted.

Poultry

The digestive systems of poultry (ducks, chickens, and turkeys) are basically as described for geese.

Many reasons have been advanced for keeping poultry on pasture; the main nutritional ones concern the extent to which relatively cheap herbage can replace relatively expensive grain diets, the value of the vitamin A derived from pasture, and the value of non-herbage food obtained under grazing conditions.

Legumes have an advantage of low fibre content which makes them both easy to graze and to digest. Turkey poults over 10 weeks of age can thrive on rations with a 15 per cent crude fibre content, and alfalfa meal has been used to provide 35 per cent of the diet of growing poults without adverse effects on growth or food conversion efficiency (Eyles 1963).

For rapidly growing broilers fresh herbage is of little use because the total nutrient supply is inadequate. Eyles (1963) estimated that the percentage of the daily dry-matter intake that may be supplied as fresh herbage is 5 per cent for chicks and 10 per cent for growing and laying poultry. At the latter rate, very young grass would supply crude fibre as about 17 per cent, crude protein as 24 per cent, calcium as 4 per cent, and phosphorus as 3 per cent of the whole diet. Herbage contributes useful amounts of vitamins of the B complex and of vitamin K, and abundant carotene, in sufficient quantities to meet the vitamin A requirements of all non-ruminants. Other substances carry disadvantages, however. Xanthophylls and other pigments cause a dark yellow pigmentation of the skin and legs of poultry, and of the yolks of eggs (occasionally the fat of pigs is tinged yellow, too).

The most useful pastures for poultry combine 'palatable' legumes (such as white clover, red clover, and lucerne) with persistent grasses that are nevertheless 'palatable' (such as timothy, variety *S.* 50). Of the herbs studied, yarrow seems to be the most favoured.

Herbage can be fed dried and has often been employed in this form solely as a carotene supplement; silage can also be fed to poultry in small quantities.

Leaf-protein extracts have also been used in poultry rations. The object has been to squeeze the juice out of green macerated herbage, and then to filter, dry, and grind the precipitate formed on heating (Pirie 1966). There is no doubt that such methods can reduce the fibre content to a very low level.

It is difficult to manage swards by poultry grazing alone, but there is considerable scope for the integration of grazing by ruminants and non-ruminants.

Additional contributions to the diet under grazing conditions include minerals from the soil, and protein from insect populations. In warm climates the latter may be very numerous.

Pigs

The pig has a relatively simple digestive tract with no special mechanism for dealing with fibrous foods. However, there is extensive microbial activity in the large intestine and caecum, where cellulose is broken down to a certain extent (McDonald, Edwards, and Greenhalgh 1966).

As with poultry, advantages are claimed for grazing in terms of health, especially of breeding stock; in terms of minerals, notably copper and iron frequently derived from the soil; and in terms of a saving of more expensive foods (Sheehy 1955). The contribution of herbage to the diet of the pig may be much greater. Eyles (1963) estimated that the percentage of the daily dry-matter intake that may be provided by fresh herbage is about 10 per cent for weaned pigs and lactating sows, and about 30 per cent for bacon pigs and pregnant sows.

Grass tends to supply an inadequate amount of calcium and phosphorus to pigs, although legumes may contain enough for pigs with low mineral requirement (such as bacon pigs). Bacon pigs and pregnant sows may receive about half their protein needs from herbage, and all the thiamin and niacin that is required. Grazing pigs find legumes palatable and utilize red clover and lucerne well; timothy (variety *S*. 48) is fairly persistent in addition to being palatable. Of the herbs studied, pigs appear to prefer chicory.

Pigs will consume appreciable quantities of silage, provided that it is of low fibre content.

Non-agricultural animals

As mentioned in Chapter 9, a great many non-agricultural species of animal feed on herbage; some of them eat little else, so clearly it provides a satisfactory diet. Herbage is also an adequate food for many agriculturally important animals but for most this is only true at levels of performance that are less than the maximum possible. Increasingly, as higher performance is required, herbage has to be supplemented, although there is much scope for improving the nutritional value of the herbage by plant breeding and management.

For non-agricultural animals in the natural state it may also be true that herbage quality limits performance in terms of growth-rate and reproduction. In this case, it is more logical to look at the question the other way, since the animals only occur on the grassland because it is there. However, this is an oversimplification, especially for animals that are not confined to grassland or to a herbage diet. It is useful to distinguish between those that feed on herbage at particular times, and those that live almost entirely on it. In the former (for example, the pigeon), herbage is selected and only contributes a part of the diet at certain times. Of the animals that may live almost entirely on herbage, there are those that eat only parts of the pasture (for example, voles, slugs and snails, and locusts), and those that may graze whole plants (above ground) but selectively in space (such as the rabbit). These examples will be briefly considered in turn.

Pigeons

Pigeons and many game birds (such as grouse and partridge) certainly consume large quantities of herbage at times. Pigeons often descend on clover early in the spring and may do immense damage at this time, not only in removing leaf and delaying growth, but in severely reducing subsequent growth and total yield.

This is not always so, apparently, and Murton, Isaacson, and Westwood (1966) recorded that subsequent regrowth of clover was *better* after wood pigeons (*Columba palumbus*) had consumed 42 and 57 per cent of clover leaf in two different fields. This was with approximately 2·2–4·8 pigeons per hectare on average, and maximum numbers up to 24·5/ha on one day. The birds fed at the rate of eighty-one pecks per minute, and consumed 30 000 fragments of clover in an 8-hour feeding day. The weight of a full crop was about 43 g.

Presumably, similar considerations apply to these birds as to poultry; the digestive system is similar and nutritional requirements not dissimilar.

Partridges (*Perdix perdix*) change to a vegetable diet after about 2 weeks of age, before which they feed chiefly on insects (Ford, Chitty, and Middleton 1938); they are an example of birds that use grassland vegetation not only for food but also for cover and nesting (Jenkins 1961).

Voles

Voles have been studied extensively (Elton 1942) and their feeding habits recorded in detail. The common vole (*Microtus agrestis*) is primarily a grass eater, although it also eats bark and tree seedlings. It can kill tussocks of *Juncus*, and alter the composition of hill grassland (Tansley 1939). Voles sometimes tunnel just below the surface and eat roots of grasses but leave mosses untouched. The food intake of *Microtus pennsylvanicus* was measured by Golley (1960) as around 12 g dry matter of alfalfa per day for 46-g animals, intake of wet food varying between 61 and 86 per cent of body weight, according to the nature of the diet. The digestibility of energy by *Microtus* fed on lucerne was very high (89·8 per cent). The dry-matter intake of the lemming (*Lemmus trimucronatus*) has been reported as 12 g/day for a 38-g lemming (Schultz 1964).

Slugs and snails

Slugs are important pests of field crops and are most active at night. *Agriolimax reticulatus* (the field slug) is the commonest species on agricultural land in the U.K. (Edwards and Heath 1964). Its weight varies between 0·2 and 0·4 g (Barnes 1949), and it may be extremely abundant (for example, 1 slug per ft² or about 900 cm²). Slugs tend to be indiscriminate feeders and may live partly on decaying vegetation and faeces. Their consumption of vegetation is difficult to estimate, but the account by Barnes (1949) suggests that one slug might eat about 360 g of fresh vegetation per year. It has been suggested (Orraca-Tetteh 1963) that the giant African snail (*Achatina* spp.) should be cultivated as a source of food, though not specially as a grazing animal. It is the largest living land mollusc with a shell up to 200 mm in length, and a foot of about 300 mm. It will live on a variety of vegetation, even in a decaying state.

Locusts

The daily food intake of the desert locust (*Schistocerca gregaria*) varies from 2 g at maximum to around 1 g for the mature insect (Bullen 1966). The capacity of these insects for total crop devastation can be judged from the fact that a swarm may be 10 miles² in area with about thirty locusts per metre²; the mean locust weight of 1·79 g implies a total consumption of 1570 tons (1600 metric tons) of fresh vegetation per day. Such a swarm has been calculated to be able to consume, on natural grazing land, 1000 times the cow-carrying capacity. The digestive efficiency of mature locusts (*Locusta migratoria*) is shown below.

Dry-matter digestibility	49%
Mean live weight of locust	*c.* 2 g (*a*)
Daily food intake (dry matter)	0·6 g (*b*)
Daily rate of growth	*c.* 0·04 g (*c*)
Food conversion ratio (*b/c*)	15
Food conversion efficiency ((*c/b*) × 100)	6·6

(Measured by W. F. Raymond and C. R. W. Spedding at Grassland Research Institute.)

Rabbits and hares

The rabbit (*Oryctolagus cuniculus*) is a widespread pest of grassland, notably in the United Kingdom and Australia. Burrowing rabbits tend to graze near their burrows and create zones of vegetation around them. Parts of the area may be grazed down to a height of about 1 cm; some plant species, including bracken (*Pteridium aquilinum*), are not touched at all, although rabbits eat deadly nightshade (*Atropa belladonna*), being apparently immune to the poisonous alkaloids it contains (Tansley 1939).

The digestive system of the rabbit also includes a capacious caecum in which microbial fermentation takes place, but the most characteristic feature is the habit (refection) of consuming the soft 'night faeces' and thus subjecting material to a second passage down the alimentary tract. Refection was described in 1882, forgotten for some time, and 'rediscovered' in 1939. The consumption of 'night faeces' was observed in domestic rabbits; in the wild rabbit, which is crepuscular, if not wholly nocturnal, refection occurs twice daily, during the day as well as in the middle of the night. It has been estimated that over 80 per cent of the food may be subjected to this process (Harrison Matthews 1952), which provides opportunities for the absorption of B-vitamins as well as of major nutrients. Refection also occurs in the hare (*Lepus* spp.).

The domestic rabbit is a well-established meat-producing animal and has been studied in some detail. It is a very good example of an animal that can obviously live and reproduce on herbage alone but which is unlikely to perform at anything like its maximum rate unless the herbage is of extremely high quality. Dried grass made from young digestible herbage may be good enough, but most hay and silage and much fresh grass will not be.

The requirements of the rabbit for maintenance vary with its weight, from about 100 g clover hay at 1360 g live weight, up to 225 g at a live weight of 5 kg. Total mineral requirement is between 4 and 5 per cent of the ration, and the need for protein varies between 10 per cent for maintenance and 16 per cent for young growing rabbits still receiving milk.

It has been calculated that 1 lb (454 g) of live weight at slaughter can be produced from 2·5 lb (1135 g) of concentrates and 1 lb (454 g) of hay, taking into account the food supply of the doe (Sandford 1966). Modern rabbit production thus uses a good deal of concentrated foodstuffs, but the doe is expected to produce about 73 kg live weight per year (thirty-five progeny in five litters) over an actively productive life of 2½–3 years.

The wild rabbit, by contrast, probably does not live much over a year, and produces about eight progeny to weaning in two litters restricted to a breeding season of less than half the year. The does are, of course, much smaller but the reproductive rate is diminished by regular resorption of embryos before implantation. Thus 60 per cent of litters conceived are stated not to be born (Harrison Matthews 1952). Herbage is a satisfactory diet for the level of performance of the wild rabbit, and at times, especially where grazing is highly selective, could support much more.

The rabbit is thus somewhere between the horse and the ruminant as a digester of grass. It depends on microbial digestion in the lower part of the alimentary tract, but by refection it achieves absorption of the products in the upper part of the tract. The digestibility of herbage by the rabbit is closely related to its fibre content, varying from a digestibility of 40 per cent for a fibre content of 35 per cent in the dry matter, up to nearly 80 for a fibre content of less than 10 per cent (Sandford 1966).

Conclusion

Consideration of wild grass-eaters suggests that the quality of the diet is unlikely to be high enough. Obviously it supports the level of performance characteristic of the wild species that have evolved to use it or that have found it a satisfactory feed during the course of their evolution.

Given herbage with particular attributes, it seems likely that the animals that live most successfully on it are those that are not limited by their own capacity for growth and reproduction. Otherwise, animals that exceeded them in these respects would prove more competitive.

Similarly, it might be argued that the *quantity* of herbage needed by the animal population would exceed that required, on average, and at the times when it supplied the major part of the diet.

Thus it seems probable that more herbage will be grown than the animal population can eat and that, in general, the individual animal could perform better on herbage of higher nutritive value.

If so, it is not surprising that domesticated animals can achieve better performance on better herbage. It may also be the case that maximum performance can only be achieved on the best-quality herbage and even this may need supplementation with more concentrated rations.

References

BARNES, H. F. (1949) *New Biol.* **6,** 29–49.
BULLEN, F. T. (1966) *J. appl. Ecol.* **3,** 147–68.
EDWARDS, C. A. and HEATH, G. W. (1964) *The principles of agricultural entomology.* Chapman & Hall, London.
ELTON, C. S. (1942) *Voles, mice, and lemmings; problems in population dynamics.* Oxford University Press.
EYLES, D. E. (1963) *Animal health, production, and pasture* (editors A. N. Worden, K. C. Sellers, and D. E. Tribe), chapter 12. Longmans, London.
FORD, J., CHITTY, H. and MIDDLETON, A. D. (1938) *J. Anim. Ecol.* **7,** 251–65.
GOLLEY, F. B. (1960) *Ecol. Monogr.* **30,** 187–206.
HARRISON MATTHEWS, L. (1952) *British mammals.* Collins, London.
JENKINS, D. (1961) *J. Anim. Ecol.* **30,** 235–58.
MCDONALD, P., EDWARDS, R. A. and GREENHALGH, J. F. D. (1966). *Animal nutrition.* Oliver & Boyd, Edinburgh.
MURTON, R. K., ISAACSON, A. J. and WESTWOOD, N. J. (1966) *J. appl. Ecol.* **3,** 55–96.
ORRACA-TETTEH, R. (1963) *Inst. Biol. Symp.* No. 10, pp. 53–61.
PIRIE, N. W. (1966) *Science, N.Y.* **152,** 1701.
SANDFORD, J. C. (1966) *The domestic rabbit.* Crosby Lockwood, London.
SCHULTZ, A. M. (1964) *Grazing in terrestrial and marine environments* (editor D. J. Crisp), pp. 57–68. Blackwell, Oxford.
SHEEHY, E. J. (1955) *Animal nutrition.* Macmillan, London.
TANSLEY, A. G. (1939) *The British Islands and their vegetation.* Cambridge University Press.

12

The Nutrient Cycle

THE material incorporated in grassland plants is rarely completely lost to the system. Some constituents are lost in respiration but much of the plant may return to the soil in one form or another. Only where the plant is cut and removed or where it is grazed by an animal that is only visiting the area is the loss complete, and even then this only applies to some of the aerial parts.

Normally, plants senesce and decompose or they are eaten by animals within the area; in the latter case a proportion of the plant is returned to the soil in the excreta of the animal. There are important differences in these two processes, both in the form and distribution of the returned constituents, but there are also similarities and it is not always helpful to separate them. Both usually proceed at the same time and the relative amounts involved vary with a great many factors. In agriculture, a high proportion of the leaf is grazed but the rest of the plant is unaffected.

In both processes the residues may lie on the soil surface, increasing losses by volatilization (see Cooke 1967) and creating an undesirable undecomposed layer, unless they are actively incorporated in the soil by other organisms.

An example of failure to decompose is shown by 'mat' formation in grassland characterized by relatively high carbon to nitrogen ratios, low available nutrient status, low burrowing earthworm biomass, and low soil microbial activity (Kirkwood 1964). 'Mat' formation in this case referred to the accumulation of dead plant material at the soil surface and was associated with 'mat-forming' grass species, such as *Agrostis stolonifera*. This kind of situation not only varies with the soil type (Barratt 1965, 1966) but with such features as the presence of molehills, which are frequently colonized by *Agrostis* spp. (Davies 1966).

Animal faeces may also remain on the soil surface, in the absence of the appropriate fauna, leading to losses by volatilization and a reduction in grass growth on the fouled area. Gillard (1967) found that in South Africa dung beetles of the subfamilies Coprinae and Aphodiinae occur in profusion in the excreta of both domesticated cattle and wild ungulates. These beetles bury and help to decompose faeces very rapidly; their relative absence in Australia is associated with the surface accumulation of dried-out faeces.

Amongst the most important of the agents concerned with the incorporation of organic matter into the soil are the earthworms.

Earthworms

Sears and Evans (1953) and Waters (1955) have shown that the earthworm population under a good pasture may be equal in weight to that of the pasture's carrying capacity of grazing animals. Weight or biomass is often a poor indicator of metabolic activity, however (Macfadyen 1957, Mellanby 1960). The number and species of earthworm vary with the way in which grassland is managed (Heath 1962, Lewis and Taylor 1967) and more worms occur with clover, faeces, and fertilizer nitrogen (Watkin and Wheeler 1966). The latter authors found that *Allolobophora caliginosa* was the main species under pure grass swards, whereas *Lumbricus* species (mainly *L. rubellus*) were dominant under grass/clover swards.

Stockdill (1966) considered that *A. caliginosa* is the most beneficial species in New Zealand and that the effect on pasture production may be very great, an increase of 77 per cent in yield of green pasture being recorded in one experiment.

Stockdill lists the beneficial effects of earthworms as (1) incorporation of applied fertilizers and insecticides, dung, and plant residues, (2) improvement of soil structure, resulting in better moisture-holding capacity and easier root-penetration, and (3) the secretion of plant-growth substances into the soil. There are also some disadvantageous effects, such as possible increase in teeth wear of grazing sheep due to greater ingestion of soil where worms are numerous (Stockdill and Cossens 1966), but these are minor matters.

Earthworms tend to spread rather slowly, and soil conditions must be suitable; moisture is necessary and the soil calcium level must be at least 5 m.e. per cent (Nielson 1951). Where such conditions obtain, introduction of beneficial species is a simple, low-cost, and practicable proposition to areas in which they are not present.

Other soil organisms

Many other organisms play an important part in the incorporation of plant and faecal residues into the soil (see Chapter 9 and Macfadyen 1957). The total biomass, comprising Collembola, Endytraeidae, and tipulid larvae, present in a *Juncus* soil amounted to 75 g/m², of which nematodes, in spite of their numerical abundance, accounted for only 0·53–1·6 g (Banage 1963). In terms of metabolic activity, nematodes have sometimes been ranked as of great importance, and bacteria, fungi, and protozoa are certainly of major importance; probably each group exceeds the metabolic activity of earthworms.

Clearly the pH of the soil and many other factors will influence the rate of decomposition of organic matter. The effect of temperature can be marked, and this may result in greater rates of decomposition in tropical soils.

The nutrients

Any plant constituent may be important but some have greater general significance than others. Trace elements may be of vital importance in some situations and it is startling to realize that selenium, for example, an element that is accumulated by certain plants, is required by the grazing animal in quantities of the order of 1 part in 10 million, yet a dietary intake of 10 times this amount may cause toxicity (Stewart 1965).

The nutrients returned to the soil by plant death and decay are, of course, those contained in the plant or plant part concerned, unless some constituents are withdrawn during senescence. A dying grass leaf gradually loses a substantial part of its carbohydrate by translocation to actively growing parts of the plant. The analysis of plant material returning to the soil may thus differ considerably from that of the growing plant.

Herbage that is eaten by herbivores is digested to a variable extent, and a variable proportion is absorbed by the animal. The residue is excreted in the faeces along with waste products of the animal's metabolism. Typical analyses from the faeces of sheep were given in Table 10.5. Many herbivores also excrete waste products as urine.

The nutrient cycle is thus a dynamic process of circulation of all these elements within and between soil, plants, and animals. The rate at which this circulation occurs is important and so are the gains and losses which are associated with different parts of the cycle. The main gains and losses can be grouped as follows:

Gains

1. Nitrogen fixation by legumes (and fertilizer application in agriculture).
2. Elevation of elements from the subsoil by plants.
3. Water and minor additions of nitrogen and some other minerals in rainfall (or, locally, in flood water).
4. Oxygen and carbon dioxide in respiration and photosynthesis respectively.

Losses

1. Erosion and leaching from the soil.
2. Animal bodies not returned to the system.
3. Volatilization from excreta.
4. Carbon dioxide in respiration.

Two of these processes require further discussion: the significance of excreta, and the nitrogen cycle.

The significance of excreta

The importance of excreta depends on the amounts of useful plant nutrients contained and the proportion lost to the system or rendered unavailable (Maclusky and Holmes 1963).

In general, plant nutrients become much more available as a result of their passage through the animal, especially in the urine fraction, which contains some 70–80 per cent of the excreted nitrogen, sulphur, and potassium. Since faeces are rich in phosphorus (Gunary 1968), much of it transformed into the inorganic form, and calcium and magnesium, multiple soil deficiencies may be exaggerated, except where both faeces and urine are deposited together (Hilder 1966*a*).

Soluble constituents may be lost by leaching, and losses by volatilization may also be high. Doak (1952) recorded up to 12 per cent loss of nitrogen from urine.

A major factor in determining whether nutrients are genuinely available for further plant growth is the distribution of excreta (Barrow 1967).

With sheep in Australia, for example, it has been found that their habit of concentrating in camps (night camps or tree shade) may effectively remove from the main pasture a large proportion of the excreta deposited. Hilder (1966b) found that about one-third of the total faecal output was deposited on less than 5 per cent of the area of grazed paddocks. Judging from soil potassium content, he concluded that urine was distributed in a similar pattern to that of faeces.

Quite apart from camps, faeces and urine are deposited unevenly over the whole area. MacLusky (1960) estimated that with cattle the area covered by faeces was 7·3 ft² per cow per day (about 6600 cm²), and the area affected by urine was similar. Peterson, Lucas, and Woodhouse (1956) concluded that after 10 cow years about 6–7 per cent of the pasture would have received no faecal return, yet about 15 per cent would have received four excretions in the same period. The quantity of faeces and urine excreted daily by cattle and sheep vary with the size and physiological state of the animals; typical examples are given in Table 12.1.

TABLE 12.1

An illustration of the quantities of faeces and urine produced daily by cattle and sheep

	Urine		Faeces			
	Volume litres	Dry matter (g)	Dry matter per unit of body weight (g/kg day)	Wet weight (kg)	Dry matter (kg)	Dry matter per unit of body weight (g/kg day)
Sheep (70 kg)	1–5	100–500	1·4–7·2	1·8	0·58	8·3
Cattle (350 kg)	10–25	1000–2500	2·8–7·2	34	5·78	16·4

Many animals, such as the horse, exhibit marked and characteristic behaviour patterns in relation to the deposition of faeces and urine (Hafez 1962). So characteristic are these patterns that they differ consistently even between mares and stallions. Both defaecate in a special area but stallions back up to it whilst mares face it; the result is a steady extension of the fouled area in the latter case but not in the former (Hammond 1944). Rabbits also use latrines or earth closets (Hafez 1962).

Where faeces and urine are actually deposited they may smother the herbage or render it unpalatable to the grazing animal; the significance to the recycling of nutrients is much affected by the fact that patchy distribution may result in more or less of any nutrient being present than is required. Amongst the most important of these nutrients is always nitrogen, although others, such as potassium, may be of great importance in some circumstances.

Mundy (1961) found that the effect of sheep urine on production and botanical composition of a grass/clover sward was due almost entirely to its content of nitrogen and potassium; water and indole acetic acid content, for example, had no effect.

The nitrogen cycle

Nitrogen in the faeces and urine represents a high proportion of what was in the plant. For sheep and cattle, faecal excretion of nitrogen tends to be constant at about 0·8 g nitrogen/100 g dry matter consumed (Blaxter and Mitchell 1948, Barrow and Lambourne 1962). Nitrogen in the feed in excess of this amount is excreted in the urine. Losses may be quite different from faeces and urine and will thus vary with the nitrogen content of the feed.

The effect on herbage growth of adding faeces and urine has been studied by several workers. Green and Cowling (1960) concluded that the effects of excreta were small; nevertheless, it is thought that 25–30 per cent of excreta nitrogen may be recovered in subsequent grass growth (Herriott and Wells 1963). Cowling (1966) found that recovery of nitrogen applied as fertilizer varied from 50 to 70 per cent but pointed out that this was in the harvested grass, not in the whole plant.

In a theoretical analysis of the nitrogen economy of soil/plant/animal systems, Davidson (1964) emphasized the need to distinguish between the initial build-up of nitrogen in circulation and the long-term maintenance of a nitrogen level providing maximum recovery of fertilizer nitrogen.

He postulated that, with about 80 per cent of herbage nitrogen returned as excreta, of which 25 per cent would be recovered in grasses in the first season and 25 per cent in the second season, applying 33 kg nitrogen per hectare annually (after an initial heavy dressing) would provide higher percentage recoveries of nitrogen than applying 66 kg nitrogen per hectare annually. In 5 years of grazing experiments, involving continuous cattle grazing of *Eragrostis*, *Cynodon*, and *Paspalum* species without legumes on poor soils in South Africa, the apparent recoveries of fertilizer nitrogen in animal liveweight were 22·4 and 11·6 per cent, respectively, for the 33 kg and 66 kg nitrogen levels.

The circulation of nitrogen in the non-harvested parts of the plant should not be ignored.

Grass roots, for example, may contain 1·5 per cent nitrogen in their dry matter, and they may live for only a few days in some circumstances, although several months would be a reasonable estimate for grasses in Britain (Garwood 1967a). It is worth recalling that these same grasses may have a total root weight in the 0–15 cm horizon of 5500–7700 kg of ash-free dry matter per hectare (Garwood 1967b).

This brings us to the role of the legume in incorporating atmospheric nitrogen into the soil and thus into the nitrogen cycle.

It is well known that the presence of legumes in nitrogen-deficient soils results in greatly increased herbage production, not only from their own growth but also from that of associated grasses. It is not always easy to quantify the nitrogen contributed by the legume.

In East Africa, Jones (1967) found that *Glycine javanica* added 176 kg nitrogen/ha/year over the first 5 years, and 110 kg nitrogen/ha/year over the last 4 years. Henzell (1962), also studying tropical legumes, recorded nitrogen fixation at levels varying from 35–85 per cent, relative to that of white clover, by *Stylosanthes boferi* and *Indigofera spicata*, respectively.

Bryan (1962) recorded annual accumulations of 111 and 258 kg nitrogen/ha for these same two species, over a period of 4 years in southern Queensland. Moore (1962) reported that *Centrosema pubescens*, in a pasture with African star grass (*Cynodon plectostadyum*), accumulated 275 kg nitrogen/ha/year more than the grass alone.

In the United Kingdom, Cowling and Lockyer (1967) reported that the quantities of nitrogen (in kg/ha) in various grass species that could be ascribed to benefit from clover varied from 25 to 51, but these figures represent only a part of the nitrogen fixed by the legumes.

Walker, Orchiston, and Adams (1954) constructed a model of the nitrogen economy of grass/legume swards. This took the form of the following equation:

$$G_n = bC_n + cF_n + K,$$

where G_n = yield of nitrogen in the grass,
$\quad C_n$ = yield of nitrogen in the clover,
$\quad F_n$ = applied fertilizer nitrogen,
and $\quad K$ = a constant related to soil nitrogen.

From this they produced a general equation:

$$G_n = 0.67 (C_n + F_n) + K$$

where K varied from sward to sward.

Without clover, as Cowling, Green, and Green (1964) pointed out, this becomes

$$G_n = 0.67 F_n + K;$$

an apparent recovery of 67 per cent of applied nitrogen.

Without added nitrogen, the equation becomes

$$G_n = 0.67 C_n + K;$$

thus the contribution of nitrogen to the grass by clover should be about 0.67 kg for every kg of nitrogen harvested in the clover.

Cowling, Green, and Green (1964) discussed the usefulness of the model and concluded that the use of pure grass swards in conjunction with mixed swards gave better estimates of the recovery of fertilizer nitrogen and of the transfer of nitrogen from clover to grass.

Their findings as to the ratio of extra nitrogen in the grass ascribed to clover, and to the nitrogen harvested in the clover, were not dissimilar to 0.67, over a 3-year period. They varied a good deal with the level of fertilizer nitrogen used, and tended to increase with time, suggesting that the effect of clover occurs mainly through decay of clover roots and/or nodules. Recirculation of nitrogen through the animal is also regarded as an important means of nitrogen transfer from clover to grass (Wolton 1963).

Three other ways in which legumes release nitrogen for possible transfer to an associated grass have been investigated by Whitney and Kanehiro (1967), using *Desmodium intortum*, *D. canum*, and *Centrosema pubescens* as the legumes, and *Digitaria decumbens* as the grass.

They found that loss of nitrogen by leaching from leaves during storms was of the order of less than 0.1 kg nitrogen/ha per storm; a similar loss was recorded by release from the root system after each defoliation of the top growth. By contrast, the estimated amount of nitrogen available due to leaf fall was 0.2 kg nitrogen/ha/week.

In an experiment involving *Lolium perenne* and *Trifolium repens*, Bland (1967) found that underground nitrogen transference, of about 33 kg nitrogen/ha, could only be demonstrated in the third year. This work was carried out on plots in Scotland with the species both segregated and non-segregated underground.

The high rate at which nitrogen can be recirculated in grassland is determined by the relatively short time for which it is incorporated in plant material and the relatively small proportion that remains incorporated in animal bodies. The latter may not return to the soil for long periods, depending on the longevity of the animal, but in no circumstances, natural or agricultural, does this account for very much of the nitrogen involved.

Indeed, considering the importance for plant growth of the nitrogen in circulation, it is surprising to find that the quantity involved is very small relative to the total soil nitrogen commonly found under grassland. This may easily amount to 0·3 per cent nitrogen in the dry soil to a depth of 5 cm (Williams and Clement 1966). The problem of nitrogen in relation to productivity, therefore, is much more a question of a relatively small increase in the amount circulating than of relatively large additions to the system.

References

BANAGE, W. B. (1963) *J. Anim. Ecol.* **32**, 133–40.
BARRATT, B. C. (1965) *Pl. Soil* **23**, 265–9.
—— (1966) *Proc. N.Z. ecol. Soc.* **13**, 24–9.
BARROW, N. J. (1967) *J. Aust. Inst. agric. Sci.* **33**, 254–62.
—— and LAMBOURNE, L. J. (1962) *Aust. J. agric. Res.* **13**, 461–71.
BLAND, B. F. (1967) *J. agric. Sci., Camb.* **69**, 391–7.
BLAXTER, K. L. and MITCHELL, H. H. (1948) *J. Anim. Sci.* **17**, 351–72.
BRYAN, W. W. (1962) *Bull. Commonw. Bur. Past. Fld Crops* **46**, 147–60.
COOKE, G. W. (1967) *The control of soil fertility.* Crosby Lockwood, London.
COWLING, D. W. (1966) *Proc. Xth int. Grassld Congr.,* Helsinki, pp. 204–9.
—— GREEN, J. O. and GREEN, S. M. (1964) *J. Br. Grassld Soc.* **19**, 419–24.
—— and LOCKYER, D. R. (1967) *J. Br. Grassld Soc.* **22**, 53–61.
DAVIDSON, R. L. (1964) *J. Br. Grassld Soc.* **19**, 273–80.
DAVIES, H. (1966) *J. Br. Grassld Soc.* **21**, 148–9.
DOAK, B. W. (1952) *J. agric. Sci.* **42**, 162–71.
GARWOOD, E. A. (1967a) *J. Br. Grassld Soc.* **22**, 121–30.
—— (1967b) *J. Br. Grassld Soc.* **22**, 176–81.
GILLARD, P. (1967) *J. Aust. Inst. agric. Sci.* **33**, 30–4.
GREEN, J. O. and COWLING, D. W. (1960) *Proc. VIIIth int. Grassld Congr.,* Reading, pp. 126–9.
GUNARY, D. (1968) *J. agric. Sci., Camb.* **70**, 33–8.
HAFEZ, E. S. E. (1962) *The behaviour of domestic animals.* Baillière, Tindall, & Cox, London.
HAMMOND, J. (1944) Discussion in *Proc. Br. Soc. Anim. Prod.,* p. 103.
HEATH, G. W. (1962) *J. Br. Grassld Soc.* **17**, 237–44.
HENZELL, E. F. (1962) *Aust. J. exp. Agric. Anim. Husb.* **2**, 132
HERRIOTT, J. B. D. and WELLS, D. A. (1963) *J. agric. Sci.* **61**, 89–99.
HILDER, E. J. (1966a) *Wool Technol. Sheep Breed.* **13**, 11–16.
—— (1966b) *Proc. Xth int. Grassld Congr.,* Helsinki, pp. 977–81.

JONES, G. H. J. (1967) Quoted in *Rur. Res.—C.S.I.R.O.* **59**, 29–32.

KIRKWOOD, R. C. (1964) *J. Br. Grassld Soc.* **19**, 387–95.

LEWIS, T. and TAYLOR, L. R. (1967) *Introduction to experimental ecology.* Academic Press, London and New York.

MACFADYEN, A. (1957) *Animal ecology.* Pitman, London.

MACLUSKY, D. S. (1960) *J. Br. Grassld Soc.* **15**, 181–8.

—— and HOLMES, W. (1963) *Animal health, production, and pasture* (editors A. N. Worden, K. C. Sellers, and D. E. Tribe), chapter 2. Longmans, London.

MELLANBY, K. (1960) *Soils Fertil.* **23**, 8–9.

MOORE, A. W. (1962) *Emp. J. exp. Agric.* **30**, 239–48.

MUNDY, E. J. (1961) *J. Br. Grassld Soc.* **16**, 100–5.

NIELSON, R. L. (1951) *N.Z. Jl Agric.* **83**, 433–5.

PETERSON, R. G., LUCAS, H. L., and WOODHOUSE, W. W. (1956) *Pl. Agron. J.* **48**, 440–4.

SEARS, P. D. and EVANS, L. T. (1953) *N.Z. Jl Sci. Tech.* No. 1. **35**, Suppl. 1, 42–52.

STEWART, A. B. (1965) *Advmt Sci., Lond.* **22**, 1965–6.

STOCKDILL, S. M. J. (1966) *Proc. N.Z. ecol. Sci.* **13**, 68–75.

—— and COSSENS, G. G. (1966) *Proc. N.Z. Grassld Ass.* 168–83.

WALKER, T. W., ORCHISTON, H. D. and ADAMS, A. F. R. (1954) *J. Br. Grassld Soc.* **9**, 249–74.

WATERS, R. A. S. (1955) *N.Z. Jl Sci. Tech.* No. 1. **36**, 516–26.

WATKIN, B. R. and WHEELER, J. L. (1966) *J. Br. Grassld Soc.* **21**, 14–20.

WHITNEY, A. S. and KANEHIRO, Y. (1967) *Agron. J.* **59**, 585–8.

WILLIAMS, T. E. and CLEMENT, C. R. (1966) *Proc. 1st gen. Meet. Eur. Grassld Fed.*, Wageningen, 1965, pp. 39–45.

WOLTON, K. M. (1963) *J. Br. Grassld Soc.* **18**, 213–19.

13

Grazing

THE word 'grazing' has been defined in several ways, varying from the familiar feeding on grass by cows to the less familiar feeding of copepod crustacea on marine algae (Cushing 1964). There is probably no 'correct' definition but the most useful, in relation to grassland, involves the partial defoliation of grassland herbage by the animal itself. Harvesting by machine is clearly not grazing and the complete removal of entire plants can hardly be described in this way. It is customary to use the term for larger animals only, but there is no reason why the feeding of slugs should not be so described. It differs from 'browsing' (see Flook 1964) chiefly in that it is generally applied to the above-ground parts of relatively short plants (grasses, legumes, and herbs), whilst browsing generally refers to feeding on parts of shrubs and trees. It then so happens that browsing tends to remove stems as well as leaves, but grazing frequently affects only leaves.

Agriculturally, grazing differs from mechanical defoliation in several ways but chiefly in that the animal is present during grazing and will therefore trample and soil the herbage as well as eat it. Even agricultural animals are not necessarily present the whole time, however; they may be housed at night or for whole seasons, usually in the winter. Their activities are not necessarily all that different from those of wild animals which spend only part of the time grazing on grassland. Slugs and rabbits are both present on the herbage for only a part of each day, and many animals that graze predominantly during the spring and summer may feed on other materials during the winter.

The most important part of a useful definition of grazing concerns the fact that only a part, perhaps a very small part, of the plant is removed at any one time. This, incidentally, is very similar to the way in which the word is used in non-technical language; a 'graze' is essentially a superficial injury.

This method of feeding has important implications and consequences for both the animal and the plant.

The effect on the animal

This is of very great consequence to agricultural animals, in terms of (1) the amount of food eaten, (2) the nature of the diet, and (3) the incidence of disease.

1. An animal that has to collect its own food by grazing must devote a long time each day to this activity (see Table 13.1). This is especially so if plants are small, if they are sparsely distributed, and

TABLE 13.1

Time spent in grazing

Species		Reference	Hours spent grazing/day	Comments
Cattle		Hafez (1962)	4–9	
	Fulani cattle (Nigeria)	Haggar (1968)	5·26	Dry season
			6·74	Wet season
	Aberdeen Angus ⎱ Herefords ⎰	Johnstone Wallace (1969)	7·53	2·47 of this at night
	Calves	Roy, Shillam, and Palmer (1955)	7·57	Good pasture
			9·28	Poor pasture
	Dairy cows	Waite, MacDonald, and Holmes (1951)	9·9	Close folding
			9·1	Rotational system
Sheep	Texel	⎫	2·3	
	Fleisch merino	⎬ Sharafeldin and Shafie	2·6	
	Caucasian merino	⎪ (1965)	2·6	
	Ossimi	⎭	4·5	
	Sheep and goats	Hafez (1962)	9–11	
	Sheep	England (1954)	9·60	Good pasture
			12·18	Bare pasture
	Merino	Arnold (1963)	10·0	Maximum
Eland		After Littlejohn (1968)	6·0	
Roe deer		Bubenik (1960)	6·0–7·0	Spring/summer– autumn/winter

if the animal is large and requires a great deal of food (Waite 1963). As mentioned in Chapter 10, larger animals need more food, but there are many other factors that also influence food requirement.

The ability of the larger grazing animal to collect enough depends on the quantity present per unit area of land, the amount the animal can ingest in one bite, and the rate at which it can bite. When there is very little herbage per unit area, a sheep will increase both the rate at which it eats and also the time spent in grazing, but there are, of course, limits to both of these (Arnold and Dudzinski 1966).

The larger grazing animals are active creatures capable of ranging over considerable distances (see Table 13.2).

TABLE 13.2

Distance walked daily

Species	Distance (miles)	Reference
Cattle	2–3	Hafez and Schein (1962)
Sheep	3–8	Hafez and Schein (1962)

2. The fact that grazing involves the removal of only a part of the plant means that the grazing animal can be selective. It can graze preferentially those plant parts that are more attractive, more nutritious, or more easily apprehended, and avoid those which are unpleasant, injurious, soiled, or difficult to obtain. The ability to graze selectively can be exploited agriculturally, and varies with the relative sizes of animal and plant and with the method of grazing. Sheep are considered to be more selective than cattle in this sense; in avoiding soiled *areas*, however, cattle are often more particular than sheep. In this connection, it has been suggested that it is the dung itself that causes rejection of soiled areas by cattle, rather than some feature (such as phosphorus/nitrogen imbalance) of the herbage grown on the area (Marten and Donker 1966).

Sheep bite off plant leaves, severing them between the lower incisors and the horny pad of the upper jaw. Cattle, on the other hand, use their tongues to grasp a bunch of grass leaves which they pull off in a plucking action. Such vigorous defoliation will uproot plants that are not firmly rooted. Rabbits graze by cutting the leaves between upper and lower incisors, and geese pluck with a sideways motion of the beak.

The same concept of selectivity can hardly be applied to much smaller herbage eaters. The grazing snail is free to feed selectively but could not in any case consume the whole plant unless this was very small. In the latter case, which might involve a seedling plant, the whole plant is not grazed but destroyed. The sheep could destroy a whole plant but generally does not, unless food is very scarce.

Since grazing usually involves plants that are close to the ground, this method of feeding often leads to the ingestion of other materials which may markedly influence the nature of the diet. During close grazing by sheep, for example, quite remarkable quantities of soil may be ingested; Healy (1967) quotes intakes of up to 400 g soil/ sheep per day. The abrasive action of such soil may effect the rate at which teeth wear out (Healy and Ludwig 1965; Cutress and Healy 1965; Ludwig, Healy, and Cutress 1966; Healy, Cutress, and Michie 1967) to such an extent that it is of economic importance in pastoral systems. Similarly, cattle have been found to ingest large quantities of soil; Healy (1968) reported intakes of up to 450 kg/cow per year.

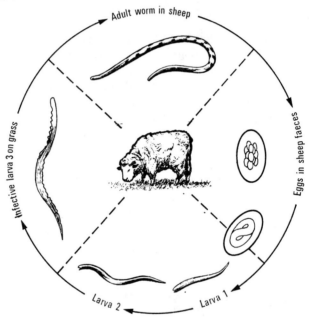

FIG. 13.1. Diagrammatic representation of the life history of *Haemonchus contortus*, the large stomach worm of the sheep. (After Michel and Ollerenshaw 1963.)

3. The diseases especially related to the act of grazing are those caused by parasites which depend on this feeding process for transfer to a new host. Some, like the keds (*Melophagus ovinus*) that parasitize sheep externally, simply make physical contact and attach themselves to a new host. This could happen without actual grazing. Others, such as the roundworms (nematodes) parasitic in the alimentary tract of the sheep, have a free-living phase in their life-cycle (Fig. 13.1). This is spent as a microscopic infective larva

wriggling or resting in the surface moisture on the herbage. These larvae are ingested with the herbage and establish themselves as adults in the stomach or intestines of their new host. Many parasites of agricultural importance behave in this way, and in some cases, the same species of lungworms (*Dictyocaulus* sp.) and intestinal nematodes (for example, *Trichostrongylus* spp.) occur in both wild animals (such as deer and rabbits) and domesticated species (such as cattle and sheep). Other parasites, such as the common liver fluke (*Fasciola hepatica*), require a secondary host (the snail *Limnaea truncatula* which becomes active when the average soil temperature reaches 10 °C, Attfield 1968). This may involve an even closer relationship with grazing, since the snails often live in the muddy depressions where cattle have trodden and the infective fluke larvae are most numerous on the herbage, near water, most readily available in drought.

Energy used in grazing

In addition to the foregoing effects on the animal, there is an energy cost of grazing. Langlands, Corbett, McDonald, and Reid (1963) found that the daily maintenance requirement of grazing sheep (approximately 463 g digestible organic matter for a 45-kg sheep) was 24 per cent higher than that for housed sheep. Similarly, assessments for a 1000-lb (450 kg) dairy cow (7·1 lb or 3·2 kg digestible organic matter daily), reported by Corbett, Langlands, and Boyne (1961), were considered to be 18 per cent higher than estimates for housed cattle. It has been suggested (Blaxter 1960, Clapperton 1961) that the energy cost of locomotion would only increase the maintenance requirement by about 10 per cent. There are, of course, other differences between the housed situation and the grazing environment, and Lambourne (1961) has postulated a differential energy cost of grazing related to the quality of the herbage.

The effect on the plant

The presence of the animal, coincidental with grazing, has important effects on the plant population, mainly due to physical damage other than by defoliation and the deposition of excreta. These will be briefly considered before discussing the major factor, defoliation, itself.

Excreta

The effect of faeces and urine on the plant, in terms of a nutrient cycle, was considered in Chapter 12. Since deposition may be extremely patchy, it is possible for particular plants to receive toxic quantities of urine or an excessive quantity of faeces. Either can have deleterious effects and produce dead patches of herbage.

Physical damage

Grazing animals frequently sit, lie, scratch, and paw on the pasture in addition to walking, running, and jumping on it. The former activities may damage plants, usually in a patchy manner, but are not generally of major significance.

Treading, however, can certainly influence both the growth and botanical composition of grassland (Edmond 1964, 1966). Serious damage is more likely with heavy animals, especially when running, and it is more likely to occur when the soil is wet. The degree of damage varies with the structure of the sward, in particular whether it has a 'mat' or not; it also varies with the nature of the soil, and some plant species are more susceptible than others.

It is not difficult to demonstrate the possibility of severe damage experimentally, and a casual examination of gateways, areas near to feeding or watering places, or the tracks made by animals, shows quite clearly that plant growth may be almost entirely suppressed. It is much more difficult to assess the significance of normal treading dispersed over the main grazing area.

'Poaching' is generally worse during the winter and, at high stocking rates of grazing sheep, a choice has to be made between allowing them access to the entire area or incurring severe damage on a part of it. In Ireland, Conway (1968) found that when sheep were wintered on one-twelfth of the area, there was a loss in subsequent dry-matter output of 25 per cent on that twelfth, but this was equal to only 2 per cent of the whole dry-matter output.

Two effects may be distinguished, a short-term direct physical damage to the plant by crushing and tearing, and a longer-term effect on plant growth due to the 'puddling' or 'poaching' effect of treading on the soil surface.

Clearly, the extent to which treading is dispersed or concentrated will be important and will vary with the tendency of a species to flock or herd, to make and follow well-established tracks, and the speed and weight of the animals involved. Both kinds of damage, to plant and soil, are probably greatly increased when the animal has hooves and when it is accelerating. Hooves not only possess sharp cutting edges but they carry the weight of the animal on a very small surface area (see Table 13.3); this results in surprisingly high downward pressures when ungulates walk, and quite powerful horizontal forces when they run or accelerate.

TABLE 13.3

Hoof areas and pressures (examples measured on individual animals)

	Total hoof area (cm²/animal) (a)	Weight of animal† (kg) (b)	Pressure (b/a) (g/cm²)
Sheep			
(Kerry Hill)	92·4	74·3–87·5	800–950
	79·8	59·0–73·5	740–920
Cattle			
(South Devon)	350	500–560	1430–1600
(Jersey)	250	320–365	1280–1460

† The range given is the annual variation in the live weight of the individual.

Defoliation

As has been mentioned earlier (see Chapters 5 and 8), the pattern of defoliation can influence the amount of herbage grown and the amount harvested. The component factors may be listed as follows:

severity,
frequency,
patchiness,
selectivity,
heterogeneity.

The first two also apply to defoliation by cutting; the last three are especially characteristic of grazing.

1. *Severity.* This may refer to the proportion of the herbage present that is removed. Consider two swards of equal height and density; the one that has a higher proportion removed may be described as more severely defoliated.

In the case of swards differing in height and density, severity is better described in terms of the absolute amount left after defoliation. Complete removal of all green parts clearly places a stress on the plant, but a vital consideration is whether or not the growing point is damaged. It is a characteristic of typical grasses that the growing point lies below the height at which the large animals graze, and it is a characteristic of grazing that a small enough proportion is removed at any one time to allow survival and regrowth of the plant.

A particular feature of grazing is that many animals (certainly from the size of a sheep downwards) can defoliate, when necessary, more severely than can cutting by normal agricultural machinery.

2. *Frequency.* The importance of frequency varies with severity. If very little is removed each time, frequency is unimportant, but if most of the plant is removed, long intervals are required for the plant to recover.

Morley (1968) has used a computer examination of a mathematical model of pasture growth to compare variations in the number of subdivisions within a rotational grazing system. He found the optimum number to be less than ten, but considered that the optimum lengths of intervals between grazings and of grazing periods were not sharply defined. Systems of grazing management, he concluded, may therefore vary within fairly wide limits, without serious loss of pasture production, provided pasture stability and animal welfare are not jeopardized.

Grazing is often less controlled than cutting in agricultural practice and may occur too frequently.

Continuous grazing has often been considered disadvantageous because it has been supposed that plants would be grazed both frequently and severely. It has been suggested that this is most unlikely, unless there is overstocking (Spedding 1965), and it has since been demonstrated that (*a*) whole plants may only rarely be entirely defoliated under continuous grazing, and (*b*) sheep, at least, defoliate tillers at intervals of 7–36 days depending upon the grazing pressure (Hodgson 1966, Morris 1968).

Morris (1968) studied sheep grazing *S.* 37 cocksfoot maintained at three levels of leaf-area index by adjusting the stocking rate. The lambs removed approximately 25 per cent of the leaf present, and their growth was linearly related to the leaf-area index.

The grazing interval was recorded for small areas and found to be related to the leaf-area index, as shown below.

	Leaf-area index		
	3·0	4·5	6·0
Mean grazing interval (days)	19	24	36

Wild animals, however, may deliberately graze the same plants frequently because the herbage is less woody, more succulent, or more nutritious.

3. *Patchiness* of defoliation must occur unless the number of

animals and their food requirement is close to that which the herbage can support. Patches are often the result of minor initial preferences being perpetuated or the result of avoiding soiled areas.

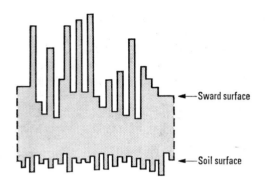

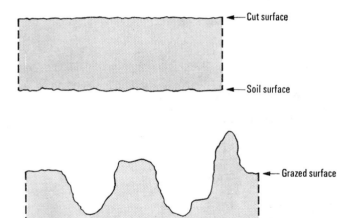

FIG. 13.2. Diagrammatic representations of sward profiles to illustrate the kind of heterogeneity found at the surface of both soil and sward.

Where extensive management allows, the behaviour of the animal often determines what areas are grazed and to what extent. Sheep grazing a hill pasture will even split themselves into sub-flocks composed of families, restricted to different areas (Hunter 1964).

Similarly, in the Soay sheep of Hirta, the range of each individual ewe is small and well defined (Jewell 1966*a*, 1966*b*).

4. *Selectivity* in defoliation influences plant as well as animal growth (Arnold 1964) but all depends upon whether the selection is against one plant species or another, or whether it is towards more or less vital plant tissues. In one study (Martin 1964), lambs selected substantially the same diet as their ewes.

5. *Heterogeneity.* The grazing process is, in several ways, a more variable form of defoliation than cutting. It is never quite accurate, even with careful cutting, to visualize a uniform layer of herbage, because the soil surface is uneven (see Fig. 13.2). Grazing usually results in greater unevenness in height of plants and leaves left after defoliation. This may also mean that even when some areas of the pasture are closely grazed, few plants are wholly defoliated. This has consequences to the mean leaf area present and to the extent to which completely defoliated areas can grow again (see Smith 1968). The importance of the heterogeneity of grazing varies with the relative sizes of the plant units (for example, the tillers) and of the grazing animal.

References

ARNOLD, G. W. (1963) *Wool Technol. Sheep Breed.* **10**, 17–19.
—— (1964) *Grazing in terrestrial and marine environments* (editor D. J. Crisp), pp. 133–54. Blackwell, Oxford.
—— and DUDZINSKI, M. L. (1966) *Proc. Xth int. Grassld Congr.*, Helsinki, pp. 367–70.
ATTFIELD, J. G. (1968) *Span* **11**, 23.
BLAXTER, K. L. (1960) *Proc. VIIIth int. Grassld Congr.*, Reading, p. 479.
BUBENIK, A. B. (1960) *Mammalia* **24**, 277–85.
CLAPPERTON, J. L. (1961) *Proc. Nutr. Soc.* **20**, xxxi.
CONWAY, A. (1968) *Span* **11**, 47–9.
CORBETT, J. L., LANGLANDS, J. P. and BOYNE, A. W. (1961) *Proc. VIIIth int. Congr. Anim. Prod.* **3**, 245.
CUSHING, D. H. (1964) *Grazing in terrestrial and marine environments* (editor D. J. Crisp), pp. 207–25. Blackwell, Oxford.
CUTRESS, T. W. and HEALY, W. B. (1965) *N.Z. Jl agric. Res.* **8**, 753–62.
EDMOND, D. B. (1964) *N.Z. Jl agric. Res.* **7**, 1–16.
—— (1966) *Proc. Xth int. Grassld Congr.*, Helsinki, pp. 453–7.
ENGLAND, G. J. (1954) *Br. J. Anim. Behav.* **2**, 56.
FLOOK, D. R. (1964) *Grazing in terrestrial and marine environments* (editor D. J. Crisp), pp. 119–128. Blackwell, Oxford.
HAFEZ, E. S. E. (editor) (1962) *The behaviour of domestic animals*. Baillière, Tindall, & Cox, London.

HAFEZ, E. S. E. and SCHEIN, M. W. (1962) *The behaviour of domestic animals* (editor E. S. E. Hafez) chapter 10. Baillière, Tindall, & Cox, London.
—— and SCOTT, J. P. (1962) *The behaviour of domestic animals* (editor E. S. E. Hafez) chapter 11. Baillière, Tindall, & Cox, London.
HAGGAR, R. J. (1968) *Tropical agriculture.* Butterworths, London.
HEALY, W. B. (1967) *Proc. N.Z. Soc. Anim. Prod.* 27, 109–20.
—— (1968) *N.Z. agric. Res.* 11, 487–99.
—— CUTRESS, T. W. and MICHIE, C. (1967) *N.Z. Jl agric. Res.* 10, 201–9.
—— and LUDWIG, T. G. (1965) *N.Z. Jl agric. Res.* 8, 737–52.
HODGSON, J. (1966) *J. Br. Grassld Soc.* 21, 258–63.
HUNTER, R. F. (1964) *Grazing in terrestrial and marine environments* (editor D. J. Crisp), pp. 155–71. Blackwell, Oxford.
JEWELL, P. A. (1966a) *Comparative biology and reproduction in mammals* (editor I. W. Rowlands), pp. 89–116. Academic Press, New York.
—— (1966b) *Symp. zool. Soc. Lond.* 18, 85–109.
JOHNSTONE WALLACE (1969) See Jones, J. L. (1969) *Fmrs' Wkly*, 10 January, v.
LAMBOURNE, L. J. (1961) *Proc. N.Z. Soc. Anim. Prod.* 21, 92.
LANGLANDS, J. P., CORBETT, J. L., MCDONALD, I. and REID, G. W. (1963) *Anim. Prod.* 5, 11–16.
LITTLEJOHN, A. (1968) *Br. vet. J.* 124, 335.
LUDWIG, T. G., HEALY, W. B. and CUTRESS, T. W. (1966) *N.Z. Jl agric. Res.* 9, 157–64.
MARTEN, G. C. and DONKER, J. D. (1966) *Proc. Xth int. Grassld Congr.*, Helsinki, pp. 359–63.
MARTIN, D. J. (1964) *Grazing in terrestrial and marine environments* (editor D. J. Crisp), pp. 173–88. Blackwell, Oxford.
MICHEL, J. F. and OLLERENSHAW, C. B. (1963) *Animal health, production, and pasture* (editors A. N. Worden, K. C. Sellers, and D. E. Tribe), chapter 16, p. 446. Longmans, London.
MORLEY, F. H. W. (1968) *Aust. J. exp. Agric. Anim. Husb.* 8, 40–5.
MORRIS, R. M. (1968) Pasture growth in relation to pattern of defoliation by sheep. Ph.D. thesis, Reading University.
ROY, J. H. B., SHILLAM, K. W. G. and PALMER, J. (1955) *J. Diary Res.* 22, 252–69.
SHARAFELDIN, M. A. and SHAFIE, M. M. (1965) *Neth. J. agric. Sci.* 13, 239–47.
SMITH, A. (1968) *J. Br. Grassld Soc.* 23, 294–8.
SPEDDING, C. R. W. (1965) *J. Br. Grassld Soc.* 20, 7–14.
WAITE, R. (1963) *Animal health, production, and pasture* (editors A. N. Worden, K. C. Sellers, and D. E. Tribe), chapter 9. Longmans, London.
—— MACDONALD, W. B. and HOLMES, W. (1951) *J. agric. Sci.* 41, 163–73.

14

Factors Affecting the Efficiency of Utilization

UTILIZATION, in a grassland context, refers to the proportion of herbage present that is harvested. It is therefore primarily an agricultural concept, representing the herbage production or yield relative to the amount grown or present. It is not without relevance to biological productivity but is perhaps better treated separately in its restricted agricultural sense, as in this chapter, and in its general biological sense, as in Chapter 15.

Agriculturally, it embodies an obvious and common-sense notion about how much of the plant material is successfully harvested by machine or by farm stock. So obvious is the general notion that it rather obscures the considerable difficulty of more precise definition.

There is no problem in defining one of the parameters; this is the quantity harvested by whatever process is being considered. The terms in which the quantity is expressed may vary (for example, dry matter, fresh herbage, digestible organic matter, energy) but there is no problem if this is done consistently.

The chief difficulty lies in defining of what the yield is a proportion; whether it is the amount present or the amount grown, for example. Clearly there may be a big difference between the two. If grassland were harvested only once or twice a year, the amount present at the time of harvest would be much less than the amount grown per annum or since the previous harvest. Since there seems little point in computing efficiency against an unattainable standard, at least two separate issues must be involved.

1. Utilization by a harvesting method (such as grazing by a particular kind of animal at a given stocking density) can be assessed on one harvesting occasion as the ratio of

$$\frac{\text{amount harvested} (= \text{removed})}{\begin{array}{c} \text{amount present at the beginning} \\ \text{of the harvesting period} \end{array}}. \tag{A}$$

This implies a definite harvesting period and a defined commodity, such as leaf, above-ground herbage, or herbage above some arbitrary height.

Efficiency in this process is simply the extent to which the total quantity of this commodity, present at one point in time, is harvested.

2. The second aspect includes both time and the quantity of commodity grown in a time interval. Any interval can be selected; a year is a directly useful one and very instructive. During this interval, both growth and senescence will occur and, if the former exceeds the latter, the commodity will accumulate and may then be subjected to periodic harvests, each of which can be treated as in (1) above.

Harvesting frequency must now also become important and the effect of frequency will vary with climatic factors (such as temperature and light), especially with those that influence rates of growth and senescence.

As well as harvesting methods, harvesting *patterns* may therefore be considered, involving different sequences of frequency and severity. The efficiency of these patterns can be judged either by the proportion harvested of what is grown or by the proportion harvested of what could have been grown. If the pattern adopted harvests nearly everything but results in very low crop production, it can hardly be regarded as efficient over a period of time. In other words, a crop growth potential is envisaged and the problem is how to maximize the amount harvested. Since harvesting patterns do affect the amount grown, it appears necessary to take this into account, but it sounds illogical to talk of utilizing something that may not be there. This suggests that this second aspect of utilization is really concerned not with utilizing the crop but with utilizing the land and other resources employed. Once this is accepted, then it becomes more sensible to consider the two main bases of the assessment separately. The following ratios may then be used:

$$\frac{\text{Utilization of crop}}{\text{over a period of time}} = \frac{\text{total amount harvested}}{\text{total actually grown}} \tag{B}$$

$$\frac{\text{Utilization of crop}}{\text{potential}} = \frac{\text{total amount harvested}}{\text{potential growth}}. \tag{C}$$

Both calculations relate only to the resources actually employed (sunlight received and fertilizers actually used); they differ in that the effect of the harvesting pattern on plant growth is treated in the same way as these other factors in (B) but is regarded as a component of efficiency in (C).

It is better to consider the factors affecting the efficiency of each type of utilization separately.

(A) This is the simplest case, in which time is relatively unimportant. An efficiency of 100 per cent is represented by total removal of all the above-ground parts or whatever is the commodity. For many plant species this may be markedly deleterious; clearly, a major question is likely to concern the level of efficiency of crop utilization below which no significant deleterious effects occur.

The factors affecting efficiency are those which determine severity of harvesting. For cutting methods, the main factor is the height of cutting above the soil surface. For grazing, the main factor is essentially the same, the closeness of grazing, but many other factors influence this. Characteristics of the animal and its behaviour, such as those mentioned in Chapter 13, may have a considerable influence. These interact with characteristics of the plant species. An upright species like cocksfoot (*Dactylis glomerata*) can be almost completely defoliated, even by cattle. Species with a rosette-like habit of growth, such as *Plantago media*, are difficult for even smaller animals to graze completely.

In purely quantitative terms, grassland plants may be more or less available to the grazing animal. A distinction may be made between plants that are *accessible*, that is, it is physically possible for an animal to seize the plant, and those that are *available* to a greater or lesser extent. Plants are less available if so dispersed that an animal would have to travel great distances to collect enough to eat. They are also less available if they are so short and close to the ground that collection would be so time-consuming as to restrict an animal's daily food intake.

The major factor affecting the efficiency of grazing utilization, is the relationship between the amount of plant material available and the requirement of the animal population. This relationship is referred to as the *grazing pressure*, but there is no standard way of expressing it. It is influenced by the *stocking rate* (the number of animals per unit area over a period of time), by the *stocking density* (the number of animals per unit area at a point in time), by the food requirement of each individual animal (depending on its size and physiological state, see Table 14.1), as well as by the quantity of herbage available. It is as well to note that when matching animal requirement and herbage supply, a form of expression must be used that takes nutritive value into account. One of the most useful agriculturally is the amount of digestible organic matter per unit area of land (see Holmes and Jones 1964).

TABLE 14.1

Variation in the food requirements of cattle and sheep, related to size and physiological state (kg dry matter required daily on a diet with an energy concentration of 3·0 Mcal/kg of dry matter) (From Agricultural Research Council 1965)

	Physiological state	Live weight (kg)	Food requirement
Cow	Dry, non-pregnant	500	3·4
	Pregnant, carrying a 40 kg calf	500	5·3
	Producing 30 kg milk/day	500	16·4
Ewe	Dry, non-pregnant	70	0·6
	Producing 1.8 kg milk/day	70	1·90
Sheep	Growing at 100 g live weight gain/day	40	0·74
	Growing at 300 g live weight gain/day	40	1·41

Expressions for grazing pressure that employ animal numbers are only suitable when comparing different grazing pressures for the same kind of animal. It is better to use a direct statement of the food requirement of the animals present or a good index of this, such as metabolic size, calculated for adult cattle and sheep as ΣW^x, where $W =$ the live weight of each individual and x is an exponential with a value of 0·73–0·75.

There are therefore two useful expressions for grazing pressure:

(1) $$\frac{\text{herbage actually consumed per day}}{\text{herbage available (or present) per day}};$$

(2) $$\frac{\text{herbage required per day}}{\text{herbage available (or present) per day}}.$$

The second may indicate the pressure of grazing (how hard animals will seek herbage and how hard they will work to obtain it even when the requirement is not actually satisfied). The first expression is the same as the second when requirements are met. It is possible, however, to have the same value for (1) from different situations in which requirement is and is not being met. This may represent a considerable weakness, since the various situations in which a given number of adequately fed animals consume the same amount as twice as many under-fed animals may be completely different. Similarly, situations in which animals differ in size as well as number may be quite different even though the total food requirement is the same.

If this total is less than the herbage available, the efficiency of utilization cannot be 100 per cent; if the food requirement cannot be met, utilization could theoretically be this high. It should be noted that, in this case, the same animals probably cannot be fed on the same area the next day. The problem in animal production is to achieve this kind of efficient utilization without reducing the food intake of the individual animal and thus depressing its performance (see Chapter 15).

(B) Both (B) and (C) involve the efficiency of harvesting discussed in (A) and are thus influenced by the same factors. They are, in addition, affected by those factors that influence plant growth and sward structure.

Within category (B), the total amount of herbage grown is unimportant unless it affects utilization efficiency at one time, that is, of type (A). This can, in fact, occur. The simplest case is illustrated by the following example.

Suppose adult cattle graze a pasture of upright plants of a height of 20 cm. Suppose there are sufficient cattle to graze most of the herbage, so that efficiency of utilization is high (for example, 80 per cent). If the pattern of harvesting, of which this one harvest is a part, reduces the rate of plant growth, next time the same cattle graze this same area there may be much less herbage present. If the same absolute quantity remains unharvested as on the first occasion (because it is not so readily available), the part removed will this time represent a much smaller proportion of that present. Efficiency of utilization may therefore be lower, for example, 50 per cent (see Fig. 14.1 for an example involving cutting). Thus, where a low crop growth-rate leads to less efficient harvesting, the effect of the pattern of utilization on crop growth-rate will have an influence on over-all utilization efficiency, even when calculated as in (B).

The other main aspect of assessing efficiency over a period of time is that the structure and botanical composition of the sward may change with time. Again, efficiency of harvesting at one time may influence that possible on subsequent occasions. Similarly,

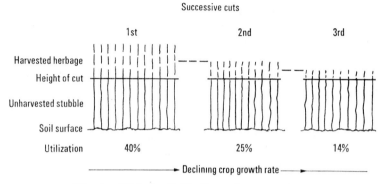

FIG. 14.1. Efficiency of utilization and crop growth-rate.

the frequency of harvesting may change both structure and species composition, and influence the efficiency of utilization with any given harvesting method. This is illustrated, for the simplest case of successive cuts at the same height, in Fig. 14.2.

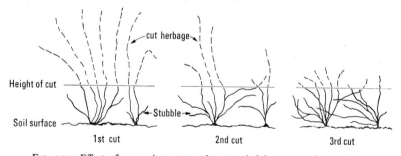

FIG. 14.2. Effect of successive cuts at the same height on sward structure.

(C) It seems obvious that what is required for agricultural purposes is both efficient utilization in sense (A), and very high crop production. Thus (C) would appear to be the most useful expression. To some extent this is so, and it is legitimate to ask at what percentage values for (A) and (B) is (C) maximized for different animals, pastures, and harvesting patterns.

The problem would be easier to investigate if the climatic factors governing crop growth-rate were constant. They are not, and the result, as shown in Chapter 5, is a marked seasonality in plant growth and production.

It is unlikely, therefore, that a constant harvesting severity or frequency will result in maximum efficiency of utilization in the (C) sense. Animals do not remain constant either, in size or physiological state, and some of the relevant populations (such as ewes and lambs; mixed grazing with sheep and cattle) involve mixtures of age, size, and species. It is not surprising that situations of such complexity are difficult to study experimentally, or that sensible recommendations may be extremely difficult to apply in farm practice (see Morley 1968). Quite apart from economic considerations of the cost of increasing efficiency relative to the value of the increment harvested, the information necessary for such management may not be available in practice. There is therefore a strong incentive to simplify situations in order to achieve simple methods which are practicable and relevant. This is quite different from applying simple methods to complex situations just because no others can be used; the latter represents an attempt to oversimplify by ignoring the complexity. The genuine simplification sought in agriculture has to result from real simplification of the situation. Common trends in this direction are a reduction in the number of plant species grown together (see Chapter 8) and in the number of kinds of animal kept together (see Chapter 15).

One of the simplest situations is where harvesting is carried out entirely by machine. It is much easier to work out harvesting patterns based on cutting that will give maximum efficiency in sense (C). As examples, two contrasting herbage species may be taken; (1) lucerne (*Medicago sativa*), and (2) perennial rye-grass (*Lolium perenne*).

1. Greater yields are obtained when lucerne is cut infrequently, less severely, or later (Leach 1968). In general, the species is severely damaged and may be completely killed out by frequent severe cutting.

2. Perennial rye-grass also yields more dry matter when harvested infrequently, and its yield may be reduced by harvesting frequently, severely, or too early. The yield of digestible organic matter, however, is much less affected by variations in harvesting frequency over quite a wide range.

Furthermore, it is quite difficult to kill a rye-grass sward by severe or frequent harvesting; this is largely due to its ability to adopt an extremely prostrate form of growth.

Patterns of harvesting for some species may therefore be specified to maximize production but, as indicated in Chapter 5, it remains possible that alternative patterns of harvesting may exist that do not differ markedly in efficiency of utilization.

The relative efficiency of cutting and grazing

Few experiments have been carried out specifically to compare cutting and grazing in terms of utilization efficiency. Frame (1966) found little difference between the two, obtaining values of 50–60 per cent (amount of herbage digestible organic matter removed as a percentage of the digestible organic matter available) for both cutting and sheep grazing of perennial rye-grass/white clover swards. Similar results, on a dry-matter basis, have been obtained by other workers (Sears 1953; Sears, Lambert, and Thurston 1953; Taylor, Washko, and Blaser 1960; Wolton 1963).

In many grazing situations where animal production is of some importance, the values recorded may be much less. Campbell (1966) found values ranging from 15 to 30 per cent, with an average for all years and treatments of 25 per cent, using dairy cows in New Zealand. Similar figures have been obtained in southern England using sheep (Spedding, Betts, Large, Wilson, and Penning 1967; Spedding 1967).

References

AGRICULTURAL RESEARCH COUNCIL (1965) *The nutrient requirements of farm livestock*, No. 2. *Ruminants.* Agricultural Research Council, London.

CAMPBELL, A. G. (1966) *Proc. Xth int. Grassld Congr.*, Helsinki, pp. 458–63.

FRAME, J. (1966) *Proc. Xth int. Grassld Congr.*, Helsinki, pp. 291–7.

HOLMES, W. and JONES, J. G. W. (1964) *J. Br. Grassld Soc.* **19**, 119–29.

LEACH, G. J. (1968) *Aust. J. agric. Res.* **19**, 517–30.

MORLEY, F. H. W. (1968) *Aust. J. exp. Agric. Anim. Husb.* **8**, 40–5.

SEARS, P. D. (1953) *N.Z. Jl Sci. Technol.* **35A** (Suppl. 1), 1–29.

—— LAMBERT, J. P. and THURSTON, W. G. (1953) *N.Z. Jl Sci. Technol.* **35A**, 199–220.

SPEDDING, C. R. W. (1967) *Proc. IXth int. Congr. Anim. Prod.*, Edinburgh, pp. 174–87.

—— BETTS, J. E., LARGE, R. V., WILSON, I. A. N. and PENNING, P. D. (1967) *J. agric. Sci.* **69**, 47–69.

TAYLOR, T. H., WASHKO, J. B. and BLASER, R. E. (1960) *Agron. J.* **52**, 217–20.

WOLTON, K. M. (1963) *J. Br. Grassld Soc.* **18**, 213–19.

15

Concepts of Efficiency in Secondary Production

THE same considerations apply here, as in Chapter 4, to the meaning of efficiency. It must refer to the quantity of some output per unit of resources employed, and both inputs and outputs may be numerous. Agricultural and natural ecosystems will differ chiefly in the *rate* of production, and thus the scale of resource use, since man can import inputs to a system in great quantities. Natural systems may be more complex and may also involve a greater number of different inputs (see Macfadyen 1948, for a discussion of the meaning of productivity in biological systems).

The same difficulty occurs in expressing the efficiency of secondary production as with that of primary production, that many ratios can be used and inputs can only be combined if they can sensibly be expressed in common terms. The chief difference is that the efficiency of secondary production can be based on the use made of primary production; the latter in this context acts as a summary of the inputs that influence it. This is very useful in comparing the efficiency of secondary production based on the same flora but will not serve for comparisons in which the plant species differ or where the quantity of primary production is greatly influenced by the form of secondary production considered.

The basic concept, therefore, is again

$$E \text{ (efficiency)} = \frac{P \text{ (production)}}{R \text{ (resources)}}.$$

The problems lie chiefly in deciding on the most useful expressions of P and R.

Production

Secondary production may refer to the amount of one selected product, such as meat, over a given period of time or from a given area of land, or it may refer to the total quantity of animal matter produced. In the first case, it is clear that the amount of product is that present at the end of the period; in the second case, since nothing may ever be removed or harvested, it can be the *increase* present at the end of a period, compared with what was present at the beginning, or it may be the total animal matter that was produced during the period, whether present at the end or not.

Comparisons of growth increments cannot always be validly made over a standard period of time; it is often better to assess food-conversion efficiency of an individual over a standard weight gain (Taylor 1968) or for a given quantity of food. Different species or breeds have different mature weights and differ in growth-rate for this reason. Taylor (1965) has found that the time taken to reach a particular degree of maturity (that is, any fraction of mature weight) tends to be directly proportional to the mature weight raised to the 0·27th power. Thus when age from conception is divided by the 0·27th power of the mature weight, a 'metabolic age' is derived that is independent of mature weight.

Even with a selected product like meat, a situation may often arise in which animals gain weight during one part of the year which they lose at another. Cattle and sheep in agricultural systems commonly do this; sometimes it is a sensible use of fat reserves deposited when food is plentiful and drawn upon when food is scarce. The effect of growth-rate and pattern on efficiency will be considered in the next chapter, but it is bound to be much affected by the way in which production is computed.

Agriculturally, the situation is plain; a product can be defined, and production is the amount that can be removed at the end of the period that was not removable at the beginning.

Non-agricultural assessments are entirely different. It is not difficult to adopt the view that an increment must be involved, that productivity must be represented by an increase in the animal mass present, or of the total biomass, or of the organic content of the environment. Over short periods this will generally occur but over longer periods some balance will tend to be reached. When the total animal population is as large as can be supported, no further increment can occur. This may be associated with a situation of great biological activity and the *rate* of this activity may also be accepted as a measure of productivity. The most useful expression of this aspect of productivity is energy and the rate at which energy flows through a system has become a major concept (Macfadyen 1964).

The main products then are those characteristic of agriculture (such as meat, milk, wool and hides, and breeding stock), similar selected aspects of special biological interest (accumulation of organic matter, population increase of a particular species), and energy.

Resources

Primary production is clearly a major resource and will often be the most relevant to expressions of efficiency. Secondary production can also be expressed in terms of any of the resources involved in primary production or of additional inputs, which affect the animal population directly (such as pesticides, shelter, and supplementary food).

Time may be a major resource, and features in many agricultural calculations because of its direct economic importance. For example, suppose that within one year the same total output of meat could be obtained from the same number of animals but growing at different rates. Ignoring any differences in the amounts of food required, the different periods of time for which money (representing the value of the animals at least) was invested, to obtain the same return, would be of great economic significance.

The other major resources in agriculture are land, animals, buildings and equipment, foodstuffs, chemicals, fertilizers, labour, and money (in which all the others can be expressed).

The major resources involved in the biological productivity of natural grassland are those required by the plant population: sunlight; carbon dioxide, oxygen, and nitrogen in gaseous form; and water and minerals in solution.

The choice of resources for any consideration of efficiency must depend upon the purpose of the calculation, and the use of each resource may be of interest for different reasons. In general, however, there will be more interest in the use made of those resources that are costly or in short supply. The efficiency with which plants use carbon dioxide or oxygen is normally of less consequence because there is no over-all shortage of these gases; there may nevertheless be a local shortage of carbon dioxide within a grass canopy. Similarly, efficiency of water use by a grass crop is of great importance in arid situations but not where rainfall is both high and well distributed. In short, where a resource is unlimited the efficiency with which it is used is of less consequence, provided that its availability is not limited in some other way. In the case of water, it is quite possible to have a plentiful supply at a depth in the soil to which only a few roots penetrate. The efficiency of these roots or of the use made of such water as they obtain may be important, even though more roots would avoid any water shortage, since the number of functional roots may be affected by soil structure, the activity of pests, or even the way in which the above-ground parts are being treated.

Agriculturally, primary production is usually expressed in terms of its food value to the particular animal considered. Energy and nitrogen (or protein) are most used because these are the major constituents usually limiting animal production. The resources employed in primary production may have monetary values quite unrelated to their capacity to increase such production, however. Land, for example, is a major agricultural resource and, although its agricultural value is related to its potential for primary production, including the amount of sunlight that falls on it, many other factors also influence land values.

Light may not always be a limiting factor in agriculture but it is one of the inputs that cannot be manipulated, except at very great cost. The efficiency with which it is used by grass species is of agricultural importance, but it is not often used in the calculation of efficiency in secondary production. This is chiefly because it is included with other factors when primary production is the base, or because it has no cost other than that part of the cost of land that derives from its light-receiving potential. In this connection it will be recalled (Chapter 5) that the slope of the land must be a major factor.

Methods of expressing efficiency

It will be obvious that a great many ways of calculating efficiency in secondary production are perfectly legitimate, and it may seem a simple matter to choose which are most appropriate to a particular purpose. The problems arise mostly from the difficulty of distinguishing clearly what the purpose really is and exactly what is being calculated. This is most readily illustrated by a simple agricultural example.

Consider a hectare of grassland producing h kg of herbage dry matter (in a harvestable as well as a nutritious form) per year; this may be taken as the major resource. Suppose that meat (as kg of carcass/ha/year) is the major output and it is desired to compare the relative efficiencies of cattle and sheep. Cattle rarely produce meat within 1 year, most cattle being slaughtered at ages between 1 and 2 years. For simplicity, however, we will imagine calves on grassland from birth to slaughter at 1 year old. For some weeks they cannot live on herbage alone and they will therefore require milk and other foods. Suppose that this hectare will support for 1 year x calves and that each provides a carcass of y kg. Efficiency is thus $xy/h \times 100$ (per cent).

The same area would support x^e ewes producing x^l lambs, each providing y^l kg of carcass. Efficiency is thus $(x^l y^l)/h \times 100$ (per cent). There is nothing wrong with these calculations but it is essential to realize that each is based on the *introduction* of animals at the outset; animals which differ in size, shape, and number in the two cases and have to be replaced annually, totally in the case of cattle and partially in the case of sheep. Quite apart from additional food-stuffs and the difficulty of taking them into account, we have in effect selected a year out of context and the results only apply to this 1-year situation.

There are two ways of looking at this. One is to insist that the situation must be self-perpetuating and complete. Thus the resources used would have to include all the food required to maintain the necessary breeding population for a year, and to sustain whatever annual replacement rate was required, as well as all the food used directly by the carcass-producers. This is another way of saying that the calculation should cover a period of years, long enough to encompass the life span of the breeding animals.

The other way is to regard each as a useful calculation but to accept that the initial 'capital', whether expressed in monetary terms or not, can include livestock. This appears more sensible in agriculture but is by no means obvious in all cases. For example, the cost of seed may only occur in one year out of several for sown grassland, and a period of temporary grassland may be followed by a quite different crop. It is always possible to add in to the calculation the additional resources required to produce the initial animals or seed, and in some cases this can be expressed in the same terms as the other resources. It should be noted that this is not the same problem as ensuring that the product represents a genuine increment. The weight gained by a calf still depends on having the calf to begin with; subtracting the initial weight of the calf from the final weight is not the same as adding in the food required to produce the calf in the first place. It is not always easy to be sure that the increment gained has not been at the expense of something other than the measured resources. Growth of suckling lambs is often accompanied by a loss of weight in the ewe, and the output of lamb carcasses may be misleading if this is not taken into account. Thus if a product is selected as the output, increments in other directions may be counted as additional products (by-products of the main process) but all losses from the system must be considered as resources used.

Efficiency in animal production in agriculture may thus be calculated as follows.

1. *For the individual animal* over any period (t),

$E = P/R$ for any product and any resource.

The most useful expression to take as an example is the efficiency of food conversion to meat where

P = carcass or liveweight increment during t, and
R = food consumed in period t.

2. *For an animal population* over one reproductive cycle.
The most useful expression is for one reproductive unit in a meat-producing process.

P = carcass output ($=$ carcass wt $C \times$ number of progeny N),
R = the sum of the food required by the dam during pregnancy (D_p), lactation (D_l), and the non-pregnant, non-lactating period (D), and the food required by each of the progeny (Y).

Thus $E = \dfrac{N \times C}{D_p + D_l + D + (N \times Y)}$.

For simplicity the adult male has so far been omitted.

3. *For a self-contained population.* The product is diminished by the progeny needed for maintaining the population of breeding females and males. In agricultural animals, relatively few males are required (for sheep, for example, one ram is kept for thirty to forty ewes) so this component of the calculation is small. The simplest procedure is to reduce the numerator by the number of progeny (n) required to replace the breeding stock, and to increase the denominator by the additional food required to rear them to breeding age (this may be more than one year but adding in the total is simpler

than accounting separately for the breeding stock replacements of various ages).

$$\text{Thus } E = \frac{(N-n)C}{D_p + D_1 + D + Y(N-n) + n B} \quad ,$$

where B = the additional food required by each breeding replacement animal.

It is possible to substitute other products, such as milk or wool, in these calculations and to substitute other resources, such as land. In the latter case, variations in primary production would be accepted, whether due to the land and its environment or to the animal population.

In many cases by-products may be large but it may be impossible to disentangle the resources used for them. In meat-producing sheep, for example, it is not possible to subtract the food used for wool growth. Similarly, it makes little biological sense to subtract from the food consumed by a milk-producing cow, the food used above maintenance during pregnancy (that is, in the production of the new-born calf). Where all the products can be used as human food, it is possible to combine them as calories or protein. Where one product is food and another clothing, only monetary terms can be used to combine them in one figure.

Efficiency of non-agricultural secondary production

When it is possible to identify a product within a biological system, it is also possible to measure its rate of production, or productivity. The difficulty arises when it is desired to measure the production of entire communities. As is well known, chemical elements may circulate quite rapidly within an ecosystem and thus be used more than once. It is not easy, therefore, to use these elements as indices of productivity. Macfadyen (1957) has pointed out that energy is one measurable entity which does not recirculate in the community; it can therefore be used as an index of the 'activity' of a community (see also Lindemann 1942, Slobodkin 1959, Phillipson 1966). Since this concept of 'energy flow' is of such value for this purpose and has been widely discussed, it is worth examining it in some detail.

Suppose that nitrogen had been chosen as the indicator, and 'nitrogen-flow' used to measure activity. All organisms contain nitrogen and it may be used as a better index of the quantity of active protoplasm present than is obtained by using biomass (which includes, for example, shells, and, in many animal bodies, a great deal of water). The difficulty lies primarily in the fact that a unit of nitrogen may 'circulate', or move from one trophic level to another, in any direction. Furthermore, its rate of circulation may vary greatly with the species in which it occurs, depending on both longevity and rate of release after death.

Now the energy derived from solar radiation is intercepted by the earth and a proportion is used by plants, for their own metabolism and in the construction of new organic matter.

If a plant simply dies and decays, all this stored energy is dissipated; it is not generally usable by other plants. There are, however, exceptions to this. For example, parasitic plants such as *Cuscuta trifolii* (a dodder) derive their energy from clovers, and many bacteria and fungi are involved in the processes of decay. However, the energy cannot be re-used by the same kind of plant. Some of the energy present in herbage is consumed by herbivorous animals; these also use a part of their energy intake for metabolic purposes and a part is stored in animal tissues, often as fat. These fat stores may be subcutaneous and serve also to insulate the animal, or intermuscular (and intra-muscular), or may be deposited in special reserves (as depot fat, in a hump, in the tail, or round the kidneys) of very great significance in enabling animals to survive during seasons of poor food supply.

The energy equations for an individual animal have been expressed by Southwood (1966) as follows:

gross energy or energy intake (ingestion)	=	digestible energy (assimilation) + faecal waste ↓	=	metabolizable energy + urinary waste ↓	=	resting energy + activity + growth + reproduction

(where only the upper term partakes in the equation to its right).

Just as with nitrogen, stored energy remains for varying periods within different animal bodies before it is liberated by the animal itself (for example, as heat), by death and decay (again involving bacteria), or by consumption by another animal. In the last case, the energy may be said to be transformed to another trophic level (predators) at a higher point in the food chain. However, the animal and its energy may be consumed by an omnivorous animal or, when dead, by scavenging beetles, which in their turn may be consumed by herbivores during grazing. In any event, recycling of the energy may occur within a trophic level when predators eat other predators. Of course, some energy is lost at each transfer, but this may commonly be the case with nitrogen also.

TABLE 15.1

Energy relationships for native and sown pasture ecosystems (kcal/m²/ year; solar radiation = 1 672 000), for Australian conditions of sheep grazing (From Moule 1968)

	Pastures	
Energy transactions	Native	Sown
Accumulation		
New energy production		
Tops	1880	5600
Roots	500	1400
Total	2380	7000
Expenditure		
Food	300†	1880‡
Excreta	130	790
Respiration	180	1090
	610	3760
Wool	5	40
Total	615	3800
Availability		
For other primary consumers and decomposers		
Tops	1265	1800
Roots	500	1400
Excreta	130	790
Total	1895	3990
	(80 per cent of net production)	(57 per cent of net production)

† One sheep per acre at maintenance.
‡ Four sheep per acre at maintenance for 5 months, above maintenance for 4 months, and below it for 3 months.

This discussion may be summarized by saying that energy-flow is a unifying concept, making it possible to describe the pattern of activity, its rate and distribution, within an ecosystem. It is unifying in the sense that all the different organisms within the system can be described in this way more usefully than in any other. Good examples are given by Moule (1968; see Table 15.1), by Macfadyen (1964) for a meadow grazed by beef cattle, and by Mann (1967) for a meadow in southern England. Biomass, as a sum of the weights of all organisms present, may indicate neither activity nor even living matter. The biggest deficiency in an expression of biomass is that it takes no account of the differences between animals of different weights. Two small animals may weigh the same as one big one, but their respiratory activity is more related to their surface area than to their weight. This particular difficulty has been met in several ways, notably by Brody (1945) who defined a more useful description, termed 'metabolic size', as $W^{0.73}$, where $W =$ live weight in kg (see also Kleiber 1947, Colburn and Evans 1968). The fact is, however, that no statement of 'mass' necessarily indicates 'activity'. This also applies to energy. A large fat cow may represent a large quantity of energy, but it could be eating very little and simply maintaining its weight. A small thin calf, by contrast, could be eating a great deal more per unit of weight or size, and could be depositing fat and other tissues at a rate of 1 kg/day. A slightly different calf could weigh the same but be much fatter and thus represent a greater quantity of energy.

Energy flow is therefore most useful because it describes both where the energy is and the rate at which it is being transformed within a system. It may be an enormous task to achieve such a description but it is a useful picture of biological activity.

It is not always clear, however, what significance should be attached to a greater or lesser activity. Obviously, great activity may involve diversity and may therefore be difficult to associate with the production of any *one* product. On the other hand, a situation of great biological activity clearly represents a great potential for the productivity of *some* products.

References

BRODY, S. (1945) *Bioenergetics and growth*. Reinhold, New York.
COLBURN, M. W. and EVANS, J. L. (1968) *J. Dairy Sci.* **51**, 1073–6.
KLEIBER, M. (1947) *Physiol. Rev.* **27**, 511.
LINDEMANN, R. L. (1942) *Ecology* **23**, 399–418.
MACFADYEN, A. (1948) *J. Anim. Ecol.* **17**, 75–80.
—— (1957) *Animal ecology*. Pitman, London.
—— (1964) *Grazing in terrestrial and marine environments* (editor D. J. Crisp), pp. 3–20. Blackwell, Oxford.

MANN, K. H. (1967) The teaching of ecology. *Br. Ecol. Soc. Symp.* No. 7, pp. 103–11.

MOULE, G. R. (1968) *Wld Rev. Anim. Prod.* **4**, 46–58.

PHILLIPSON, J. (1966) *Ecological energetics.* Arnold, London.

SLOBODKIN, L. B. (1959) *Ecology* **40**, 232–43.

SOUTHWOOD, T. R. E. (1966) *Ecological methods.* Methuen, London.

TAYLOR, ST. C. S. (1965) *Anim. Prod.* **7**, 203–20.

—— (1968) In *Growth and development of mammals* (editors G. A. Lodge and G. E. Lamming). Butterworths, London.

16

Factors Affecting the Efficiency of Secondary Production

THE efficiency of secondary production may be expressed in terms of basic resources, in which case the factors affecting primary production (see Chapter 5) also apply. These factors will only be discussed here if they have, in addition, an independent influence on secondary production. Where the efficiency of secondary production is assessed in terms of the proportion of the primary production that is transferred, the factors affecting primary production can be more or less ignored. It cannot be assumed, however, that the secondary production processes will have no effect on the amount of primary production. On the contrary, this interaction may well be of the greatest importance. The simplest way to consider the factors affecting efficiency is therefore to identify those which influence the components of the various expressions of efficiency (see Chapter 15). The great merit of this approach is that it is then absolutely clear to what definition of efficiency the factors apply, and that the most important factors tend to be considered first. Lines of factors of decreasing importance to (or at least of increasing remoteness from) the main process may be visualized as radiating outwards (see Fig. 16.1).

Taking the simplest example, of meat production from an individual growing animal (see p. 133), E (efficiency) $= P/R$ (where P is the quantity of meat produced and R is the quantity of food consumed in the same period), and the factors affecting E are those which affect P and R.

The most important for P are:

(1) body weight gain,
(2) proportion of 'meat' in the body weight gain;

and for *R*:

(1) food used for maintenance,
(2) food used for body weight gain.

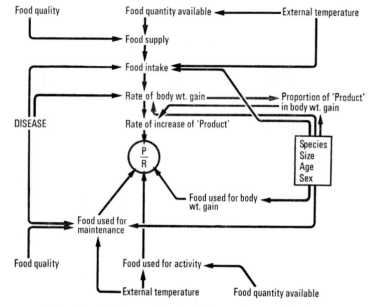

Fig. 16.1. The factors affecting efficiency of meat production.

These can easily be expanded, for a period of *d* days, as follows:

P. (1) Live weight gain per day multiplied by *d*, where growth-rate is affected by

(*a*) species, age, size, and sex,†
(*b*) external temperature,
(*c*) food intake per day (quality and quantity),
(*d*) health or disease.

(2) Body composition, which is affected by

(*a*) species, age, size, and sex,
(*b*) growth-rate.

R. (1) *d* × body weight × maintenance requirement per unit of body weight, which is affected by

† It should be noted that sex can be modified (Bradford and Spurlock 1964) and that nearly half of the sheep and cattle kept for meat are castrated.

(*a*) species, age, size, and body composition,
(*b*) external temperature,
(*c*) food quality,
(*d*) health or disease.

(2) Food for production $= d$ (total food intake per day minus maintenance requirement per day) and is thus affected by

(*a*) food supply available,
(*b*) factors given in $R(1)$, above.

Several features are immediately apparent. First, the rapidity with which the number of factors increases; secondly, the complexity of each apparently simple factor; thirdly, the fact that the same factors begin to appear at different points on each expanding line, and in particular, that many factors are common to both P and R.

It is, of course, essential in ecological studies to recognize the complexity of biological systems, but it is also essential that attempts at understanding are neither deterred nor defeated by it. The complexity in this instance is not greatly diminished by the fact that factors are repeated, for this represents a network of interconnecting components with important interactions. Radiating lines represent the situation very poorly, and a network is more appropriate.

This can be described as a 'flow diagram' and is very often the first step in describing a complex biological system before giving the description mathematical expression (see Appendix). The sheer physical complexity of putting these descriptions on paper is sufficient to explain the need for mathematical symbols; they are, at the very least, an essential shorthand language.

In this particular example, if the animal and its food are specified the situation is greatly simplified. Imagine that the species, age, size, etc. of the animal are known, and that the food is all of one kind and of known quality. Disease may be of great importance but a reasonably healthy animal may be envisaged without difficulty. The external temperatures may be imagined to stay within a range which leaves the animal relatively unaffected.

Importance of growth rate

Efficiency (E) is then governed chiefly by the rate of growth allowed by the food supply (both potential growth-rate and maintenance requirement are largely inherent in the description of the animal). In other words, the amount of food consumed each day in excess of the quantity required to maintain the animal at constant weight, chiefly governs the rate at which the product is produced. The higher the proportion of the total food intake that is devoted to production, the more efficient is the process (Blaxter 1964*a*).

Thus, in time *t*,

$$E = \frac{\text{product grown daily } (p) \times t}{\text{daily maintenance requirement } (M) \times t + (\text{food for } p) \times t}$$

$$= \frac{p \times t}{t(M + \text{food for } p)} = \frac{p}{M + fp}$$

and, if *M* remains constant, *E* increases with increasing *p*. The effect may be very marked, especially if *M* is large (see part of Table 16.1 relating to the lamb only); the extreme example is where there is no growth and $E = 0$. Clearly *E* always lies between 0 and 1 for normal expressions of meat and food, since the quantity of product will never equal or exceed the quantity of food used. *E* is often conveniently expressed as a percentage in consequence.

It cannot, in fact, be assumed that *M* is independent of growth rate, but it is generally increased by a relatively small amount as growth rate increases.

TABLE 16.1

Effect of lamb growth rate on efficiency (E) $\left(\dfrac{\text{kg carcass} \times 100}{\text{kg digestible organic matter}}\right)$

(From Spedding 1969)

Lamb growth rate		Lamb only	Ewe plus lamb
Low	live weight gain (g/day)	162	162
	kg carcass gained	14·8	
	kg carcass produced		17·0
	kg digestible organic matter consumed	87·6	387·6
	E	16·9	4·4
High	live weight gain (g/day)	256	256
	kg carcass gained	14·9	
	kg carcass produced		17·3
	kg digestible organic matter consumed	69·8	369·8
	E	21·3	4·7
	Improvement in E due to increased growth rate	26% (4·4 units)	6·8% (0·3 units)

This whole concept is of great importance in agriculture and has been fully discussed by Brody (1945). Blaxter (1964*a*) pointed out that although maintenance needs and voluntary intake vary from individual to individual (by about 10–15 per cent or so), the size of differences in efficiency of feed conversion is likely to be less than this.

This same general argument can be applied to the production of milk or wool.

A cow of a given size will require so much food each day to maintain its weight. This represents a substantial annual input of food, and if the cow neither calves nor lactates, all for nothing. The efficiency of production will clearly rise with milk yield, simply because the maintenance cost is being diluted by the greater production, or expressed another way, the maintenance 'overhead' cost is spread over a greater quantity of product.

Now the value of E will thus vary from one stage of lactation to another, and cows must be compared at the same stage or, better, over the whole lactation. The same applies to all production processes, and short-term assessments of E tend to be dominated by the rate of production.

As was pointed out in Chapter 15, E may be most usefully calculated for a whole animal population over one reproductive cycle, or, better still, over an appreciable period of time, long enough for lifetime performance to be taken into account.

The formulae for E in these circumstances can readily be expanded in the same way as for an individual animal. The resulting number of factors is even greater and their relative importance changes. The situation has been worked out in some detail for the sheep (see Spedding 1965, Large 1969).

The main additional factors of importance are:

(1) the reproductive rate per breeding female,
(2) the length of the breeding life,
(3) the age at which breeding begins,
(4) the proportion of males in the population,
(5) the size of the final product,
(6) the size of the dam.

Agriculturally, many of these factors are under control. The proportion of males is kept to the essential minimum but the *size* of the sire can then be much greater; this allows the (cross-bred) product size to be increased without increasing the size of the dam. By good nutrition and efficient disease control, (2) can be maximized and (3) minimized, although the latter is more difficult in a seasonal breeder. A ewe lamb has to be grown very rapidly, so that it is sufficiently developed physiologically to respond to shortening day length in its first autumn if it is to lamb at 1 year of age instead of the normal 2.

In general, however, the reproductive rate and the size of dam and product are the most important factors in such a system. Before examining this further, it is informative to consider the importance of growth rate again.

The reason why growth rate was important, in the case of the individual animal, was that it greatly influenced the amount of food required to gain a given amount of weight. Within a whole population, however, the food consumed by the growing animal is only a part of the total and in lamb production it happens to be a relatively small part. The different effect of an increase in lamb growth rate on the value of E calculated for the lamb itself and for the ewe/lamb unit, is also shown in Table 16.1.

Size of product

There is also a big difference in the relative importance of product size in these two circumstances.

Bearing in mind that efficiency of production depends upon growth rate and the amount of food required for maintenance, it is clear that larger animals may be less efficient unless they also grow faster. Between species larger animals do tend to grow faster, but within a species, during early growth for example, this is not generally the case. Indeed, the typical growth curve for young mammals flattens out as the animal grows larger (see Fig. 16.2). Thus, as the lamb grows larger, it eats much more but grows less rapidly. It is true that the calorific value of the food is usually higher in early life, and the calorific content of the body weight gained may be higher at heavier weights; nevertheless, efficiency tends to decline with increasing age and weight. Agriculturally, it would seem that animals should be slaughtered very early in life, but there are other factors to be taken into account, both economic and biological.

Biologically, the new-born animal has already cost a great deal of food, represented by the food consumed by its dam during some previous period. When the calculation is made for the whole population, it is immediately apparent that the size of the product may have a very large effect. This is illustrated in Fig. 16.3.

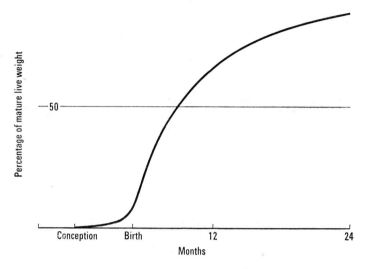

Fig. 16.2. Characteristic sigmoid shape of the mammalian growth curve. Based on a 70 kg sheep; actual growth-rates depend upon nutrition.

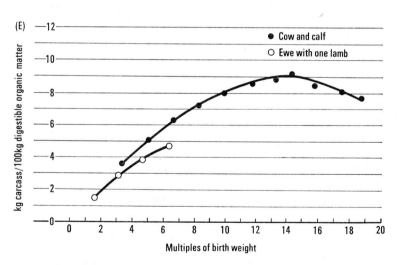

Fig. 16.3. Effect of product size (expressed as multiples of birth weight) on efficiency (E).

In fact, if the food supply allows, it is biologically efficient to produce almost the largest product size that can be achieved, provided that rapid growth can be maintained.

Size of the dam

This is important for two main reasons. First, it has some influence on the potential size of the product produced by the progeny. Secondly, it largely determines the food required to maintain the population of breeding females. The effect of this component depends on the proportion of the total food consumed that it represents. In

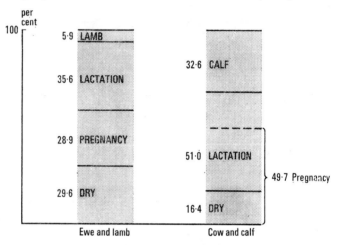

FIG. 16.4. Distribution of annual food consumption.

sheep, it is relatively large because the lamb normally lives for only a part of the year (about 4–5 months) and rarely attains the size of the ewe. Where replacements are reared the situation is quite different, so ewe size matters rather less in breeding than it does in lamb meat production, and the situation is further modified by the reproductive rate.

In cattle the size of the cow may have less effect, because the progeny take much longer to reach slaughter weight and their food consumption is therefore a higher proportion of the total than with sheep (see Fig. 16.4).

There is another aspect of size that is well illustrated by cattle. Consider two dry cows of different sizes; for example, a Jersey weighing 350 kg and a Friesian weighing 550 kg. The former will consume about 8·0 kg dry matter daily and the latter about 12·6 kg. Now suppose that each cow requires a similar additional quantity of food to produce a gallon of milk. Then the total quantities of food required per gallon will become increasingly close as the two cows give more milk. In fact, the Jersey, giving richer milk, will require rather more food per gallon than the Friesian. The size of the dam may thus be less important when rates of performance are high.

This applies particularly to the reproductive rate.

The reproductive rate

The importance of this factor is well illustrated by the sheep and the rabbit (see Figs. 16.5 and 16.6; Gregory 1932; and Hammond 1941).

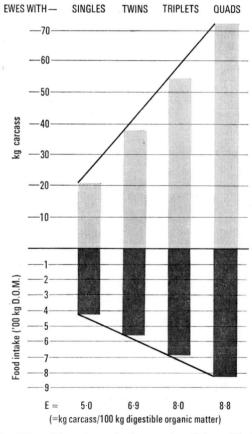

FIG. 16.5. Effect of litter size on food conversion efficiency (*E*) of sheep.

Efficiency increases with litter size and breeding frequency, provided that the progeny can be reared satisfactorily. This will normally depend on the whole environment as well as on the milking ability of the dam. Agriculturally, there are excellent methods available for rearing both lambs and calves from birth; this makes it possible to

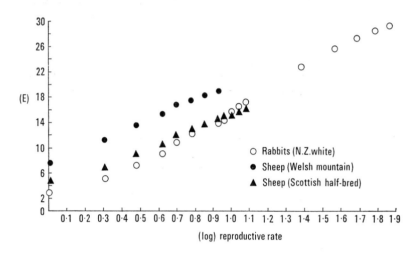

FIG. 16.6 Effect of increasing reproductive rate on food conversion efficiency for sheep and rabbits.

Sheep. Based on data for lambs artificially reared on milk substitute (4 weeks) and then fed lucerne nuts. Constant carcass weight at slaughter assumed to be 12·5 kg. Growth rate = 256 g/day.

Rabbits (New Zealand white). Theoretical calculation assuming a maximum litter size of twelve. Conception is assumed to occur only when the previous lactation is complete giving a maximum of six litters per year. Proportionately more food has been allocated to the doe during pregnancy and lactation as the litter size increases. Young rabbits with six or fewer siblings are assumed to eat 2·63 kg of solid food from weaning to slaughter and those with seven or more to eat 3·5 kg (dry matter).

operate efficiently at much higher reproductive rates (especially at higher litter sizes in sheep) than would otherwise be possible. The situation may be quite different in non-agricultural systems (Lack 1948).

The essential differences between litter size and breeding frequency, as methods of increasing the number of progeny per dam per year, are the number of pregnancies, during which extra food is consumed, and the average size of the progeny at birth.

During pregnancy the dam eats more than when non-pregnant, but the quantity is in proportion to the total foetal weight (Russel, Doney, and Reid 1967) rather than to the foetal number, and it is limited by the capacity of the dam to consume food and to carry a foetal burden. Larger litters therefore tend to require more food up to a point, beyond which the food requirement remains relatively constant because the total foetal weight does so too.

The essence of all this is that efficiency is dominated by the proportion of the food that is devoted to production relative to maintenance, just as it was for the individual animal. But in the case of a reproducing population, the maintenance requirement is governed more by the size of the dam, and the production potential is largely determined by the reproductive rate.

Longevity

As already mentioned, the length of time for which the breeding female (especially) continues to reproduce influences efficiency, because the resources used to reach breeding age are a smaller proportion of the total when longevity is increased. Where animals are harvested, as in agriculture, longevity and reproductive rate operate in a combined fashion. Thus, both factors have to be taken into account in calculating, for example, a 'replacement rate' for sheep. The following formula has been quoted by Mattner and Moule (1965) for the calculation of the number of females that must be retained for breeding in order to maintain a constant flock size.

The percentage (*S*) of young ewes to be selected can be calculated from

$$S = \frac{2\,000\,000}{MN(100-d)}$$

where M = mean percentage of lambs marked to ewes mustered at marking,

N = average number of times that a ewe is mated during her lifetime, and

d = average death-rate (per cent) in the young ewes prior to mating age.

The same approach can be adopted for any controlled population, and a not dissimilar one for natural populations.

The environment

Clearly, any aspect of the environment, including other animals, may directly affect those very components that have been discussed in this chapter as of greatest importance in determining the efficiency of secondary production.

Disease is a good example. It may reduce animal growth rate or result in death; it may reduce the reproductive rate by decreasing fertility or fecundity, and by increasing neonatal mortality. Disease may be caused by infectious organisms, such as viruses or bacteria, by parasites, such as nematodes, or by nutritional imbalance, such as deficiency or toxicity.

Climatic factors may act directly on the animal population and the effects of wind, rain, extreme temperatures, and too much or too little sunshine can be considerable, especially if combined with undernourishment. Warm-blooded animals are able to prevent serious change in deep body temperature (this is known as homeo-thermy), and the air temperature below which an animal must increase its heat production by shivering, thus diverting energy to an unproductive channel, is called the 'critical temperature'. It can be expressed by the following equation (from Blaxter 1964b):

critical temperature (°C) = $C_T = T_R - (H - E_M)(WI_T + I_F + I_E)$,
or $C_T = T_R - H(I_T + I_F + I_A) + E_M(I_F + I_A)$,

where T_R = deep body temp.,

H = thermoneutral heat production (Mcal/m² per day),

I_T = tissue insulation under cold conditions,

I_F = coat insulation,   (°C/Mcal/

I_A = air interface insulation,   m²/day)

E_M = minimal loss of heat by vaporizing moisture from the skin and respiratory passages (Mcal/m²/day), and

W = weighting term ($H/H - E_M$) for tissue insulation.

Obviously, animals can be drowned or frozen, or suffer heat stress; less obviously, their maintenance requirement may be increased, their activity reduced, or their behaviour altered in ways which increase the risk of predation, decrease their productivity, and reduce their food intake, their chances of effective mating, or their chances or survival during parturition (Hafez 1967) or immediately after birth (Moule 1962).

A cow walking 1 mile may produce approximately 330 kcal/450 kg live weight. In the tropics, the animals may have three times this amount of heat added by solar radiation, all to be dissipated by radiation, evaporation, conduction, and convection. For adult cattle, at 30 °C, vaporization from the skin accounts for 75 per cent and respiration 25 per cent of the heat loss. At 10 °C the respiratory loss is 10 per cent, skin vaporization 25 per cent, and losses by radiation and convection amount to about 65 per cent. Thus as temperature increases, so evaporative heat loss becomes more important (Findlay 1959). Breeds differ in their behavioural reactions to temperature. When Aberdeen Angus and Brahman cattle were exposed to a temperature of 35 °C, the former spent 54 per cent of their time grazing and rested in the shade, while the Brahman grazed for 71 per cent of their time and rested in the sun.

Nutrition

A major effect of climate is expressed through the nutrition of the animal. At the beginning of this chapter it was pointed out that the level and efficiency of primary production would also influence the level and efficiency of secondary production.

Quite apart from the total primary production, however, there are important matters of quality and distribution. The total primary production may not be available for a particular form of secondary production; some parts of it (such as deposits of silica within grasses) may be rendered unavailable to all forms of secondary production for hundreds of years. The nutritive value of herbage was discussed in Chapters 10 and 11, and it will be clear that more herbage, in terms of fresh or dry weight, does not necessarily mean more animal production, even when it is all consumed; much will depend upon the usefulness of the herbage to the animal consuming it and this will vary with the physiological state of the plant material. It will also be recalled, from Chapters 3 and 4, that grassland primary production is distributed non-uniformly in time, and to a lesser extent in space. The consequences of this to the animal population are considerable.

This is a convenient point at which to stress the extent to which the discussion in this chapter has been related, for purposes of simplicity and clarity, to mammals. One characteristic of mammals is that they are homeothermic and thus their food requirements for maintenance are relatively high and relatively constant. Their pattern of food requirement therefore differs markedly from the extremely seasonal distribution of the food supply from grassland. This is illustrated for individual cattle and for a flock of sheep in Fig. 16.7.

Agriculturally, the discrepancies have to be met chiefly by supplementary feeding of food imported into the area, and by conservation of surplus herbage as hay, silage, or dried grass.

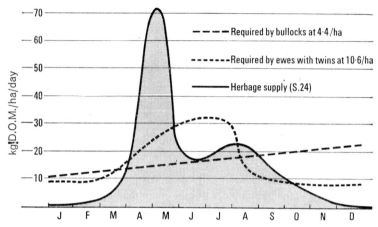

FIG. 16.7. Balanced total supply and demand (5800 kg digestible organic matter/ha/year).

In some situations, such as mountain sheep farming, much of the winter food shortage is met by drawing upon the animal's own fat reserves. In non-agricultural systems this is widespread. Grazing mammals do not store food (other than in their bodies) for times of food shortage; indeed it would only be possible in the case of seed-eaters. In time of drought or very low temperatures, such animals have to live on herbage remaining from previous growth (and this may be present in substantial quantities) or on their fat reserves, unless they are able to change to a non-herbage diet. Fat reserves may be localized in fat depots, varying with species and environment (see Table 16.2). The only other possibility is to reduce the requirement, either by fluctuations in population size or by reducing the individual's need. The second possibility may be achieved by ensuring that periods of high food requirement (for example, during lactation) coincide with periods of herbage growth or by such extreme solutions as hibernation.

Local shortages may be met by migration. Shortages due to drought may be solved in this way, and so may direct water shortage, but shortages due to low temperature are rarely localized. Even so, some migration may occur to lower altitudes at such times.

TABLE 16.2

Fat reserves of grazing animals in relation to environment (From Mason 1967, Talbot, Payne, Ledger, Verdcourt, and Talbot 1965, Blake 1967)

Species	Site and nature of fat reserve	Environmental stress when fat reserves are used
Anatolian fat-tailed sheep (Red Karaman) (1)	Tail: 44 cm long and 31 cm broad; weight about 6 kg but up to 12 kg; represents up to 25% of carcass wt.	Very hot, dry summers and very cold winters (Turkey)
Wildebeest (*Connochaetes* spp.), and wild herbivores in Africa generally (2)	Relatively constant, very low fat content (2–5% in the carcass)	Savanna: seasonal migrations to meet the dry-season food shortages
Domestic cattle (mature beef animal: carcass weight 189 kg) (3)	Fat = 34·5% of carcass, distributed as follows: subcutaneous = 10·7% intermuscular = 17·7% kidney = 6·1%	Cold winters and hot dry summers
Sheep (adult female: carcass weight 32 kg) (3)	Fat = 47% of carcass, distributed as follows: subcutaneous = 24·5% intermuscular = 16·5% kidney = 5·8%	Cold winters and hot dry summers

(1) Mason, I. L. (1967) *The sheep breeds of the Mediterranean.* C.A.B.
(2) Talbot, L. M., Payne, W. J. A., Ledger, H. P., Verdcourt, L. D. and Talbot, M. H. (1965) The meat production potential of wild animals in Africa. *Tech. Commun.* No. 16. C.A.B.
(3) Blake, C. D. (editor) (1967) *Fundamentals of modern agriculture.* Sydney University Press.

Distribution of primary production in space presents a different problem. The simplest example is where the pasture is extremely short, due to the growth habit of the predominant species. Much of the herbage may then be unavailable to some herbivores (as discussed in Chapter 14).

For non-mammals the situation may be quite different. In insects, for example, the generation interval may be much shorter than the seasonal periods; it is then possible for the population size to fluctuate enormously. This, coupled with the capacity of some individuals to overwinter, which is associated with the fact that the metabolic rate of poikilotherms is linked to the ambient temperature, means that the food requirement of the population can vary as greatly as does the pasture supply. This is illustrated for slugs in Table 16.3.

TABLE 16.3

Seasonal variation in the food requirement of the slug Agriolimax reticulatus (Daily dry-matter requirement expressed as a percentage of the weight of the slug (100 mg) and based on a daily mean temperature) (After Hunter 1968)

Jan.	Feb.	Mar.	April	May	June	July	Aug.	Sept.	Oct.	Nov.	Dec.
4 °C	6 °C	7 °C	8 °C	11 °C	14 °C	17 °C	16 °C	14 °C	11 °C	6 °C	4 °C
0·45	0·68	0·70	0·73	0·77	0·77	0·80	0·80	0·77	0·77	0·68	0·45

It should be noted that periods of slow growth or of maintenance do not have the same implications to efficiency of food conversion in the case of poikilotherms as they do for homeotherms.

Much of the foregoing is really concerned with the extent to which animals are adapted to their whole environment.

Adaptation to the environment

Adaptation may be related to any part of the environment and may be chiefly a matter of the individual animal or it may involve the entire population. Sheep are the most widespread and populous of the domesticated ruminants and are represented by about two hundred breeds in eighty-three countries from the Arctic circle to the southern tip of South America (Moule 1968).

An individual animal must be able to tolerate the ranges of climatic conditions that are characteristic of the environment, or it must be able to avoid or circumvent harmful conditions. The means adopted by different species of animal are extremely varied and represent one of the most fascinating fields of study within ecology. Indeed, the whole question of adaptation is central to ecological thinking, provided that it is not regarded as simply a matter of how well an individual can tolerate the environment in which it lives. This same individual must be adapted, not only to the climate, but also to the other organisms inhabiting the same environment. These vary from animals of the same species and competitors for the same food, to predators, parasites, and the plant populations.

Some of the most important adaptations are related to suscepti-bility and resistance to endemic disease. Differences of this kind have been a major factor in determining whether wild animals are better able to exploit natural environments than the common domesticated species (Crawford 1968). They are rarely the only important features, however.

It is often assumed that exotic cattle in East Africa are best suited to conditions of good nutrition and absence of climatic stress whereas the indigenous animals can manage better in poor nutritional and climatic conditions. Rogerson, Ledger, and Freeman (1968) have demonstrated that the exotic cattle have higher food and water intakes, relative to maintenance, than indigenous cattle. This leads to much greater efficiency in food conversion. Since water intake is related to dry matter intake, part of the greater need for water is due to the greater food intake.

The adaptation of a species is as much or more concerned with the way in which the whole population fits in with its food supply and with the other animal and plant populations (McDowell 1968). This is frequently dominated by the distribution of food supply and with the climatic and other factors responsible for the pattern of distribution. In the arid areas of Australia, for example, the red kangaroo (*Megaleia rufa*), probably the largest of all living marsupials, appears to be so well adapted that it has been suggested (Sharman 1967) that farming in much of the rough grazings of inland Australia might be better based on it, rather than on domesticated ruminants.

The yak (*Bos grunniens*) and the crosses with mountain cattle (called tsauri), on the other hand, are adapted to life over 2400 m above sea level; they are used for milk production and as pack and draught animals (von Schulthess 1967). The buffalo (*Bubalus bubalis*) is also used for milk production (in the United Arab Republic, the Phillipines, Pakistan, and India) and for milling in India, pulling carts in Java, logging in Burma, as pack animals in Pakistan, riding in Borneo, and artillery hauling in Turkey; it was used in the cavalry of ancient Thailand (Cockrill 1967). It is thus extremely versatile and occurs in twenty-three countries; the world population is about 110 millions, half of which are in India.

Clearly, the advantages of adaptation are greatest where there is no control of the environment. Shade can be provided, but very high temperatures demand an animal that can tolerate them. In tropical areas, Zebu type cattle (*Bos indicus*) have advantages over European breeds (*Bos taurus*), due to their superior thermo-regulatory ability (Dowling 1965), but the extent of the advantage depends upon the severity of the heat stress and on the accompanying non-climatic

factors (see Bianca 1965). Where the total environment is uncontrol-
led by man, it tends to support a great variety of plant species, and
in these circumstances, secondary productivity may be higher
(indeed is likely to be higher) when the animal population also consists of a variety of species. Thus the biomass of wild ungulates
supported by the savanna lands of Africa may be from two to fifteen
times higher than that of domestic livestock (Talbot 1964). In particular, wild animals may have special advantages in terms of
protein production from natural environments (Maloiy 1965;
Ledger, Sachs, and Smith 1967; Crawford 1968; Talbot, Payne,
Ledger, Verdcourt, and Talbot 1965). The eland (*Taurotragus oryx*),
especially, has been studied from this point of view and is considered
to have two main biological advantages over domestic animals in
Africa: first it is reported as having a higher reproductive rate, and
secondly it is better adapted both physiologically and behaviourally
(Skinner 1967). It voids faeces of low moisture content and it has
been estimated that 4 l water/100 kg body weight/day is available
to the eland from food and metabolic sources. Grant's gazelle
(*Gazelle granti*) is stated to live through the dry season without
drinking water (Jewell 1968) and it is possible that the hygroscopic
nature of its food could be of importance in its ability to survive
drought (Taylor 1968). McCulloch and Talbot (1965) have demonstrated that wild ungulates lay down little fat (content from 0 to 6
per cent of body weight) even when food is plentiful. The following
data show the difference between cattle and Thomson's gazelle in this
respect.

	Percentage of cold carcass	
	Lean	*Fat*
Bos taurus	56	28
Bos indicus	61	19
Thomson's gazelle	80	1.6

Clearly, adaptation to the environment must influence the efficiency
of any particular form of secondary production. It may be assumed
that in a natural ecosystem of long standing, all the populations are
more or less adapted and that the efficiency of production is as high
as the climatic and edaphic conditions will allow. It follows from
this that the factors influencing the efficiency of total secondary
production in natural ecosystems are those contributing to, or de-
tracting from, this 'balance of nature'. Any interference may thus

reduce total productivity, although the result may be greater production in a particular direction (the object of agricultural interference).

Such a balance, however, may only apply over long periods and may include violent fluctuations involving great inefficiency of resource use. The balance finally achieved may be marked by considerable stability but it may also be marked by a rather low level of productivity. It remains an interesting and important question as to whether it is lower than it need be or whether it can only be raised by substantial additional inputs.

References

BIANCA, W. (1965) *Rev. Prog. Dairy Sci.*, Section A, Physiology.
BLAKE, C. D. (1967) *Fundamentals of modern agriculture.* Sydney, Australia.
BLAXTER, K. L. (1964*a*) *J. R. agric. Soc.* **125**, 87–99.
—— (1964*b*) The biological significance of climatic changes in Britain (editors C. G. Johnson and L. P. Smith). *Inst. Biol. Symp.* No. 14, pp. 157–68.
BRADFORD, G. E. and SPURLOCK, G. M. (1964) *Anim. Prod.* **6**, 291–9.
BRODY, S. (1945) *Bioenergetics and growth.* Reinhold, New York.
COCKRILL, W. R. (1967) *Wld Rev. Anim. Prod.* **3**, No. 13, 98–107.
CRAWFORD, M. A. (1968) *Vet. Rec.* **82**, 305–14.
DOWLING, D. F. (1965) *Aust. Vet. J.* **41**, 57–61.
FINDLAY, J. D. (1959) *Agric. Prog.* **34**, 74–7.
GREGORY, P. W. (1932) *J. exp. Zool.* **62**, 271–85.
HAFEZ, E. S. E. (1967) *Wld Rev. Anim. Prod.* **3**, No. 14, 22–37.
HAMMOND, J. (1941) *Biol. Rev.* **16**, 165–90.
HUNTER, P. J. (1968) *Malacologia* **6**, 391–9.
JEWELL, P. A. (1968) *Nature, Lond.* **218**, 993–4.
LACK, D. (1948) *J. Anim. Ecol.* **17**, 45–50.
LARGE, R. V. (1969) *Anim. Prod.* (In press).
LEDGER, H. P., SACHS, R. and SMITH, N. S. (1967) *Wld Rev. Anim. Prod.* **3**, No. 11, 13–37.
McCULLOCH, J. S. G. and TALBOT, L. M. (1965) *J. appl. Ecol.* **2**, 59–69.
McDOWELL, R. E. (1968) *Climate versus man and his animals.* Cornell University, New York.
MALOIY, G. M. O. (1965) *Nutr. Abstr. Rev.* **35**, 903–8.
MASON, I. L. (1967) *The sheep breeds of the Mediterranean.* Commonwealth Agricultural Bureau.
MATTNER, P. E. and MOULE, G. R. (1965) *Field investigations with sheep—a manual of techniques* (editor G. R. Moule), pp. 11–17.
MOULE, G. R. (1962) *The simple fleece* (editor A. Barnard), chapter 7. Melbourne University Press.
—— (1968) *Span* **11**, 36–9.
ROGERSON, A., LEDGER, H. P. and FREEMAN, G. H. (1968) *Anim. Prod.* **10**, 373–80.
RUSSEL, A. J. F., DONEY, J. M. and REID, R. L. (1967) *J. agric. Sci., Camb.* **68**, 359–63.

SHARMAN, G. B. (1967) *Sci. J.*, March, pp. 53–60.
SKINNER, J. D. (1967) *Anim. Breed. Abstr.* **35**, 177–86.
SPEDDING, C. R. W. (1965) *Sheep production and grazing management.* Baillière, Tindall, & Cox, London.
TALBOT, L. M. (1964) The biological productivity of the tropical savanna ecosystem. *IUCN Publ., new Ser.* No. 4, p. 2.
—— PAYNE, W. J. A., LEDGER, H. P., VERDCOURT, L. D., and TALBOT, M. H. (1965) *C.A.B. tech. Commun.* No. 16.
TAYLOR, C. R. (1968) *Nature, Lond.* **219**, 181–2.
SCHULTHESS, VON, W. (1967) *Wld Rev. Anim. Prod.* **3**, No. 13, 88–97.

17

Animal Production from Grassland—Milk

MILK is a watery secretion of the mammary gland; it is the only source of nutrients for the progeny of mammals for a short period after birth, and the main source until weaning.

The composition of milk varies with the species of animal (see Table 17.1) and changes to a variable extent during lactation. The secretion immediately after parturition (called colostrum) is more concentrated and contains antibodies which can be absorbed by the suckling young shortly after birth and which have a protective value, for a time, against diseases to which the dam has been exposed.

Milk is produced at a rapidly increasing rate from birth until a peak quite early in lactation, thereafter the yield declines steadily, resulting in the characteristic lactation curves shown in Fig. 17.1.

Much of the milk produced by domesticated mammals is used in the rearing of their progeny; this double processing, of herbage to milk and then milk to meat, is often considered to be inefficient. This is certainly so when the progeny could grow at the same rate without it, but the situation is quite different during the early phase of growth when the young must have milk. An example of the effect of double conversion on the food-conversion efficiency of sheep is shown in Fig. 17.2.

In some primitive agricultural situations, the milk is partly used to suckle the young and partly removed for human consumption. The idea is that the young do not require all the milk produced but must have some, that the dam may produce more and give it more readily if young are suckled, and that the young can actually remove more than can normal milking procedures. It may be that the full advantages of such multiple use have not yet been exploited in improved agricultural systems.

TABLE 17.1

The variation in milk composition between species (From Kon and Cowie 1961 except where as stated below)

Constituent	Units	Indian buffalo	Guinea-pig	Friesian cow	Sheep	Goat	Llama	Horse	Reindeer	Yak	Rabbit	Ass
Fat	g/100 g	7·45	3·9 g/100 ml (F)	3·50	7·50	4·50	3·20	1·60	22·50	7·00	16·00 (D)	1·50
Non-fatty acids	(Nitrogen × 6·38) g/100 g	9·32		8·60	10·90	8·70	10·80	8·50	14·20	10·90	8·60	8·60
Protein	g/100 g	3·78	8·1 g/100 ml (F)	3·25	5·60	3·30	3·90	2·20	10·30 (D)	5·20	9·20 (D)	2·10
Casein	g/100 g	3·20		2·60	4·20	2·50	—	1·00	8·30 (D)	—	—	—
Lactose (anhydrous)	g/100 g	4·90	3·00 (A)	4·60	4·40	4·40	5·30	6·00	2·40	4·60	2·00 (D)	6·20
Ash	g/100 g	0·78	0·82 g/100 ml (F)	0·75 (F)	0·87	0·80	0·80 (A)	0·40	1·40 (D)	—	2·20 (D)	0·40
Potassium	g/100 g	—		0·15 (E)	0·19	0·17		0·07				—
Sodium	g/100 g	—		0·05 (E)	0·046 (B)	0·034 (C)		—				
Calcium	g/100 g	0·18		0·12 (E)	0·19	0·14		0·10				0·09
Magnesium	g/100 g	—		0·01	0·015 (B)	0·02		0·01				
Chlorine	g/100 g	0·06		0·11 (E)	0·14	0·15		0·02				0·04
Phosphorus	g/100 g	0·12		0·10 (E)	0·15	0·12		0·06				0·05
Iron	mg/100 ml				0·77 ppm (B)	0·2 mg/100 g (C)					0·12	
Gross energy	kcal/100 g	100	94 cals/100 ml (F)	62	105	71	65	47	250	100	264 (A)	46

A dash denotes lack of reliable information.

Sources other than Kon and Cowie: (A) Abrams 1961, (B) Ashton and Yousef 1966, (C) Diem 1962, (D) Hammond 1957, (E) Maynard 1951, (F) Mitchell 1962.

Where milk is a major product it is removed once, twice, or three times daily, by hand- or machine-milking, from females that are housed or pastured; they may be milked where they are or taken at

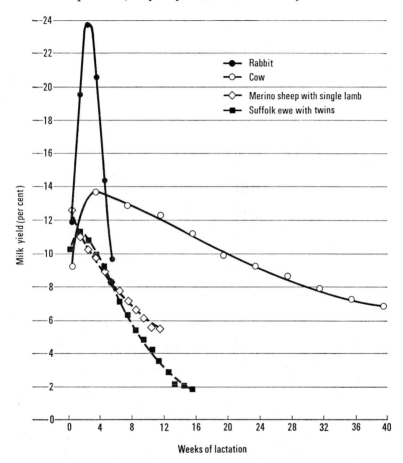

FIG. 17.1. Lactation curves of milk yield (g/day) expressed as a percentage of total milk yield.

intervals to a milking parlour. These practices may have marked effects on grazing behaviour, the amount of damage done to pastures by treading, and the ease and accuracy with which dietary additions can be made.

The nature of the product makes it relatively easy to describe and measure, but the quantity may still be expressed in several different ways. The simplest is the weight or volume of whole milk but, where the composition varies, it may be better to describe the quantity of total solids, butter-fat, protein, or solids-not-fat (S.N.F.).

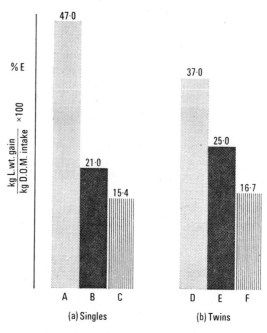

FIG. 17.2. The effect of 'double conversion' on food conversion efficiency in sheep (for ewes weighing 75–80 kg, fed on dried grass or lucerne nuts). The figures illustrate only two examples, (*a*) for ewes with single lambs, and (*b*) for ewes with twins, between the ages of 8 and 16 weeks. A, lamb only. B, lamb+ewe at maintenance. C, suckled lamb+its ewe. D, lambs only. E, twin lambs+ ewe at maintenance. F, suckled twins+their ewe. (From an expt. by R. V. Large and J. M. Walsingham.)

Milk is not necessarily the only output of a lactating animal. The female animal may herself gain or lose weight, and contain more or less fat and protein; she may be pregnant towards the end of a lactation and part of her food then goes to the developing foetus; and she may be growing a coat, hide, or fleece representing a quite separate product. For such reasons it may not be possible to separate out strictly the efficiency of milk production.

Efficiency in milk production

The efficiency with which an individual female produces milk, even without the complications of pregnancy, weight change, or coat growth, varies with the stage of lactation.

A cow giving no milk still requires a large quantity of food, and a cow will need more than a goat. If both animals produce the same quantity of milk, whether they require exactly the same additional quantities of food or not, the goat will be the more efficient at over-all food conversion. Similarly, the cow at the peak of lactation will tend to be more efficient than when giving less milk. Comparisons must be made with care, therefore, especially between species.

Recent findings by W. P. Flatt at Beltsville (see Corley 1968) have stressed the great importance of high milk yield in determining efficiency. He found that very high yielding individuals (*c.* 45 kg milk daily) eat a great deal of food; although the high level of food intake leads to decreased digestibility, less energy is lost in urine and methane. Such cows also show a phenomenal capacity to mobilize body fat to sustain production demands and are able to convert efficiently large amounts of varying rations to milk. They replace body fat efficiently in late lactation and it appears that use of fat, in circumstances where this is necessary to achieve a higher milk yield, is not as inefficient energetically as had been thought, and leads to enhanced over-all efficiency.

As indicated in Chapters 15 and 16, efficiency can also be expressed over a whole lactation, on an annual basis, per unit of land, or for a whole reproducing population over a substantial period.

Using land as the basis of calculation allows the effect of the animal on primary production to be taken into account and this could be of considerable importance.

Taking into account the whole reproducing population has obvious advantages but it is difficult to compare the value of the different numbers and kinds of progeny inevitably produced, even if they are regarded as merely by-products. The full implications are not even realized if these progeny are simply considered as they appear at birth, but to do otherwise is to determine the efficiency of whole agricultural systems, not just lactation.

The most useful single assessment of the efficiency of milk production is therefore the quantity of milk produced per unit of total food used over the period of one successful mating to the next. This efficiency (E) then takes into account the food required to maintain the animal (F_m) during lactation and until the next lactation begins, the food required to support the pregnancy prior to lactation (F_p), and the additional food needed during lactation (F_1). For a total output of product ($P = x$ kg milk), therefore,

$$\%E = \frac{P \times 100}{F_m + F_p + F_1}.$$

This is satisfactory for animals like the sheep, in which lactation and pregnancy do not overlap; the most relevant pregnancy is then the one prior to the lactation considered because it may affect the amount of milk produced. In the cow, where pregnancy and lactation do overlap, it is more sensible to include the pregnancy that occurs during the lactation studied, if only because of the difficulty of calculation in any other way.

The efficiency thus assessed would be better based on more than one lactation, unless different lactations are being compared, and if species comparisons are made, the data should be collected from many animals. The calculation by-passes the question of differences in animal size, since it deals directly with the main important consequences of size, the food consumed and the milk produced. It is solely concerned with the efficiency of food use for milk production, however, and the progeny must be included in any wider (including any financial) calculation.

Estimates of efficiency are given for some of the main milk-producing domesticated animals in Table 17.2, together with the milk yields taken as representative and used in the calculations.

TABLE 17.2

Percentage efficiency for milk (kg milk/100 kg digestible organic matter consumed per year)

Dam	Progeny	Percentage efficiency	Milk yield (kg)	Reference
Cow	Single	162	3640	Spedding (1969)
Goat	Twins	155	1141	Spedding (1969)
Sheep	Twins	59·6	212·6	after Wallace (1948)
Sheep	Single	41·2	131·7	after Wallace (1948)

Working with the weight or volume of whole milk is clearly misleading where there are large differences in composition. The quantity of water present has no great nutritional significance to the consumer, whether this be man or the animal's own progeny.

There are good reasons for calculating efficiency in terms of energy, fat, protein, or even minerals. Table 17.3 shows the results for the

same data as shown in Table 17.2, but expressed as total energy and
as protein.

TABLE 17.3

Percentage efficiency for milk energy and protein (Results are for the same
data as in Table 17.2 but expressed as total energy and protein, using
conversion values from Table 17.1)

Dam	Progeny	Crude protein	Energy
Cow	Single	34·2	14·8
Goat	Twins	34·2	15·0
Sheep	Twins	19·7	8·4
Sheep	Single	13·6	5·8

There are a great many subsidiary calculations that can usefully
be made to improve our understanding of the whole milk production
process. The length of lactation is obviously an important factor in
over-all efficiency and will differ greatly, between species, in absolute
terms. One way to make helpful comparisons would be to express
lactation length as a proportion of the period between one parturition
and the next; another would be to express the total time lactating
as a proportion of the animal's lifetime.

In all this, the male is regarded as of negligible consequence; for
the species mentioned this is a reasonable assumption but in other
circumstances it might not be so.

The importance of the peak yield suggests that this, too, might usefully be compared between animals and species; this might best be done
by expressing the peak yield as a fraction of the mature body weight of
the female or of some derived value (such as $W^{0.73}$, see pp. 123, 137).

Examples of the differences in lactation length and peak yield
between species are given in Table 17.4.

TABLE 17.4

Differences in lactation length and peak yield between species

Species	Lactation length (days)	Peak yield (g/kg day)	Source
Eland, Rhodesian, first lactation	213–65	6·5	Skinner (1967)
Eland, Russian, second lactation	290	8·5	Crawford (1968)
Sheep, Préalpes ewes, milked	175	22·7	Ricordeau and Denamur (1962)
Cow, Africander	238	30·0	Skinner (1967)
Cow, Friesian heifer	305	30·9	Wood (1967)
Sheep, Scottish half-bred, with twins	112	48·3	Mitchell (1962)
Cow, Mature shorthorn	300	43–9	Maynard (1951)
Rabbit	40–50	66·6	Lebas (1968)
Goat	280	133·4	Newman (1967)

Agriculturally, many workers have devised expressions for efficiency of milk production in the cow (Brody 1945, Johansson 1961). Gross efficiency has been used as equal to the

$$\frac{\text{energy in the product}}{\text{T.D.N. (total digestible nutrients) energy in the feed}}$$

and net efficiency has been defined as gross efficiency minus the energy required for maintenance. Expressions of these kinds have been mostly concerned with the relationships between milk yield and a body measurement or between milk production and the food required above maintenance. Examples of these are given in Table 17.5.

TABLE 17.5

Examples of expressions of efficiency

Gross efficiency (Johansson 1961)	$= \dfrac{\text{energy in products}}{\text{T.D.N. energy in feed}}$
Net efficiency (Johansson 1961)	$=$ gross efficiency minus energy required for maintenance (usually calculated from $W^{0.7}$)
Efficiency of protein conversion Wilson (1968)	$= \dfrac{\text{annual crude protein yield}}{\text{annual crude protein consumed}}$
Index of economic production (Horn 1967)	$= \dfrac{F+R}{2}$ where F is the butter-fat production of a cow and R is the value calculated on fat-corrected milk per unit live weight (expressed in girth or height of withers)

No firm conclusions are yet possible as to the optimum cow size for milk production, and it may be that no single answer will satisfy all economic criteria. Furthermore, it cannot be assumed that different animals must be developed for milk and meat production. 'Dual-purpose' cattle may thus be of great importance and these may be produced by cross-breeding for the cow or for its progeny. Recently, Horn (1967) has proposed an 'index of economic production', for dual-purpose breeds, to be compared with the production of a standard cow. The latter, he suggests, could be a cow of 650 kg live weight, producing 4000 kg milk with a fat content of 4 per cent, or 615 kg of fat-corrected milk (F.C.M.) per 100 kg live weight.

The 'index of economic production' (E) could then be calculated from the formula

$$E = (F+R)/2$$

where F is the butter-fat production of a cow and R is the value of fat-corrected milk per unit of live weight or size (expressed in girth or height of withers). The index of economic production would be expressed as a percentage of the value for the standard cow.

Very high output per hectare can be achieved with the dairy cow. Campbell (1968) gives outputs of 660 kg of butter-fat per hectare in New Zealand, entirely from pasture. In other parts of the world high yields from pasture have to be supported by a good deal of supplementary feeding.

References

ABRAMS, J. T. (1961) *Animal nutrition and veterinary dietetics*. Green, Edinburgh.
ASHTON, W. M. and YOUSEF, I. M. (1966) *J. agric. Sci.* **67**, 77–80.
BRODY, S. (1945) *Bioenergetics and growth*. Reinhold, New York.
CAMPBELL, A. G. (1968) *Span* **11**, 50–3.
CORLEY, E. L. (1968) *Span* **11**, 28–31.
CRAWFORD, M. A. (1968) *Vet. Rec.* **82**, 305–18.
DIEM, K. (1962) *Scientific tables*. Geigy Pharmaceutical Co.
HAMMOND, J. (1957) *Progress in the physiology of farm animals*, vol. 3. Butterworths, London.
HORN, A. (1967) *Wld Rev. Anim. Prod.* **3**, 35–45.
JOHANSSON, I. (1961) *Genetic aspects of dairy cattle breeding*. Oliver & Boyd, Edinburgh.
KON, S. K. and COWIE, A. T. (1961) *Milk: the mammary gland and its secretion*, vol. 2. Academic Press, New York.
LEBAS, F. (1968) *Annls. Zootech.* **17**, 169–82.
MAYNARD, L. A. (1951) *Animal nutrition*, 3rd edn. McGraw Hill, New York.
MITCHELL, H. H. (1962) *Comparative nutrition of man and domestic animals*, vol. 1. Academic Press, New York.
NEWMAN, G. A. (1967) Personal communication.
RICORDEAU, G. and DENAMUR, R. (1962) *Annls Zootech.* **11**, 5–38.
SKINNER, J. D. (1967) *Anim. Breed. Abstr.* **35**, 177–86.
SPEDDING, C. R. W. (1969) *Agric. Prog.* **44**, 7–23.
WALLACE, L. R. (1948) *J. agric. Sci.* **38**, 93–153.
WILSON, P. N. (1968) *Chemy Ind.* 899–902.
WOOD, P. D. P. (1967) *Nature, Lond.* **216**, 164.

18

Animal Production from Grassland—Meat

MEAT is a more variable product than milk and is also much more difficult to describe. In Chapters 15 and 16 these problems were largely ignored, and meat output was expressed as the weight of carcass. The latter has some validity, since it is frequently what the farmer is paid for, and it is a better index of edible meat than is the live weight of the animal. The proportion of carcass in the live weight is usually termed the dressing- or killing-out percentage (D.O. or K.O. percentage); it varies with species, age, rate of growth, and above all, fatness (see Seebeck and Tulloh 1966). The carcass is a somewhat arbitrary fraction, however; it includes much inedible bone and excludes edible portions (notably the offal). A statement of the most desirable composition of meat is difficult to arrive at.

To a large extent, meat is primarily a source of protein, but it also contains many other valuable elements. Its fat content greatly influences its calorific value and may be of great importance in cooking, as well as affecting tenderness and taste. Mention of these aspects serves to emphasize the extent to which meat is a luxury in the diet of mankind. Where hunger is greatest, meat represents a relatively small proportion of the diet. It is, however, one major way in which herbage can be rendered useful to man, and a vast area of the world grows such herbage and may not be capable of supporting crops of direct usefulness.

Examples of the chemical composition of carcass meat are given in Table 18.1, and the differences in composition characteristic of different meat-producing grassland animals are illustrated in Table 18.2. Meat tends to have a relatively constant protein and amino-acid content (Fauconneau 1967) and the nutritive value of lean meat is also relatively constant.

TABLE 18.1

The chemical composition of carcass meat (boneless) (After King Wilson 1959)

Animal		Water (%)	Protein (%)	Fat (%)	Minerals (%)
Rabbit	Young	..	20·7	3·8	1·5
	Adult	65	20·9	6·2	1·3
Cattle	Forequarter	..	18·3	18·9	0·9
	Hindquarter	62	19·3	18·3	0·9
Sheep	Shoulder	..	15·6	30·9	0·9
	Leg	62 (derived)	18·7	17·5	1·0

TABLE 18.2

Carcass composition

Species	Details	Fat†	Lean†	Bone†	Reference
Cattle					
Friesian	510 ⎫	14·7	70·9	14·3	⎫
Hereford × shorthorn	490 ⎬ kg at slaughter	21·1	66·8	12·1	⎬ Carroll and
Aberdeen Angus × shorthorn	450 ⎭	22·3	66·1	11·8	⎭ Coniffe (1968)
Sheep Suffolk	19·1 kg carcass weight	31·0	56·0	13·0	Hammond (1955)
Bulls	⎫ side of carcass from	21·8	61·2	17·0	⎫ Robertson,
	⎬ live weight of 428 kg				⎬ Wilson, and
Steers	⎭	29·9	53·3	16·7	⎭ Morris (1967)
Buffalo	male	5·6	74·4	20·0‡	⎫
Eland	male	4·2	79·0	16·8‡	
Gazelle, Grant's	male	2·8	79·6	17·6‡	
Gazelle, Thomson's	male	2·0	82·0	16·0‡	⎬ Ledger, Sachs,
Gerenuk	male	2·0	80·6	17·4‡	and Smith
Impala	male	1·9	81·4	16·7‡	(1967)
Zebra	male	2·5	78·5	19·0‡	
Zebu cows	Fat	32·9	53·6	13·5‡	
Zebu cows	Thin	13·4	64·7	21·9‡	⎭

† Percentage of carcass weight at slaughter.
‡ Derived from 100 minus (fat + lean), as percentage.

Meat production obviously involves reproduction, and the efficiency of the whole process is much influenced by the reproductive rate (see Chapter 16). Thus efficiency has to be calculated over a period long enough to take into account all phases of the animal's life. The growth of the progeny results finally in a carcass but this is not necessarily the only product. Both male and female breeding animals, at the end of their useful breeding lives, may also contribute a sizeable quantity to the total output; this comes chiefly from the females since they are generally much more numerous, and meat from the entire male often has undesirable characteristics of taste and toughness. The growth of the progeny begins, of course, at conception and frequently the period of pregnancy equals, or even exceeds, the period of growth after birth. In the sheep, for example, gestation lasts about 147 days and many lambs are slaughtered at ages of less than 120 days. The actual quantities grown are not in proportion to these periods, and only about 15 per cent of the final weight is gained during pregnancy (it should be noted that this figure is affected by the fact that lambs are commonly slaughtered at light weights, much less than their mature size). For further information on the length of gestation periods, see Kenneth and Ritchie (1953).

The contributions to the total meat output that are provided from mature animals and by younger progeny are illustrated for sheep and cattle in Table 18.3. It will be noted that where the progeny are killed at an early age, it may take many of them to equal the weight of the dam; conversely, the direct contribution of the dam to meat output is proportionately less when the reproductive rate is high.

Table 18.3

Proportion of meat from progeny and culled breeding females for:

Cattle, with one calf per year producing a carcass of 225 kg, mature cows weighing 450 kg (carcass = 250 kg);

Sheep, with a replacement rate of 20 per cent per year, ewes weighing 70 kg (carcass = 36 kg), lambs producing carcasses of 18 kg;

Assuming that replacements are purchased, not reared within the herd or flock;

Meat production expressed as kg carcass per year from progeny (P) or culled breeding females (C), all of which are usable for meat

Cattle	Replacement rate (%)		
	20	30	40
P	225	225	225
C	50	75	100
Percentage $\dfrac{P}{P+C}$	82	75	69
Sheep	Number of lambs per ewe per year		
	1	2	3
P	18	36	54
C	7	7	7
Percentage $\dfrac{P}{P+C}$	72	84	88

The main meat-producing herbivores of the world have not been subjected to equal intensities of selective breeding, and it is as well to remember this when comparing species; the same point may be made in relation to comparisons between meat production and, for example, milk production.

Since an output of 660 kg of butter-fat per hectare in New Zealand was referred to in the previous chapter, it is worth noting that the comparable figure for carcass meat per hectare was given as 495 kg (Campbell 1968). Under Irish conditions, Conway (1968) has recorded an output of 352 kg carcass plus 42 kg wool from 16·8 ewes and their lambs per hectare.

In Chapter 16 the main factors influencing the efficiency of meat production were discussed. When comparing the importance of, say, litter size and lambing frequency, as determinants of efficiency, it is fairly safe to calculate on the basis of the weight of carcass produced. In comparisons of efficiency between species or with other production processes, this is clearly not satisfactory. Those concerned with profitability must express the output in financial terms, and the weight of carcass will be a component of the calculation. For all other purposes it is necessary to measure the output of human food. This does not, of course, eliminate the difficulty; bones are not normally consumed (although they may make some contribution), fat consumption varies between people and regions, losses in cutting, cooking, and on the plate vary greatly, and the variation that exists in the consumption of particular parts, sometimes regarded as 'delicacies', is legendary.

Efficiency of meat production

Probably the two most important expressions of efficiency are:

(1) the quantity of edible protein produced per unit of food energy or protein consumed,

(2) the quantity of edible energy produced per unit of food energy consumed.

The information required to make these calculations is not available for many species of herbivores, and is incomplete even for the common domesticated animals. In addition, it will be clear from Chapter 16 that there is not just one answer for each species.

Protein production

An example of this calculation is given in Table 18.4 for sheep, cattle, and rabbits, at high levels of performance. Efficiency has been

calculated in terms of protein output per unit of protein (nitrogen ×
6·25) consumed.

TABLE 18.4

*The efficiency of nitrogen production on an annual basis for sheep, cattle,
and rabbits* (After Wilson 1968)

Species	Details	Annual yield (kg N) (a)	Annual consumption (kg N) (b)	Percentage efficiency (a/b)
Cattle (beef)	Steer producing 295 kg carcass	5·45	90·90	6
Sheep	2 litters of 3 producing 15·9 kg carcasses	1·75	20·00	9
Rabbit	4 litters of 10 producing 1·36 kg carcasses	1·31	7·64	17
Cattle (milk)	1500 gal at 3·25 per cent protein	34·90	9·19	38

Similar calculations based on the consumption of food energy
are given in Table 18.5.

TABLE 18.5

Efficiency of protein production per unit of food energy

$$\text{(Efficiency} = \frac{\text{g N in annual protein yield}}{\text{Mcal in annual food intake}} \text{ for sheep)}$$

Breed	Litter size	Efficiency†
Devon longwool	1	0·12
,,	2	0·17
Kerry hill	1	0·16
,,	2	0·20
Welsh mountain	1	0·20
,,	2	0·26

† The percentage of protein in the annual
carcass yield is based on values from Wallace
(1955).

Energy production

It would be of interest to see how much of the total energy ingested
appears in the 'harvested' animals, that is, in the whole bodies of
both mature and 'progeny' products. The energy fixed for the use of
man cannot exceed this figure.

Accepting the normal proportions of the whole body output that
are regarded at the present time as edible, for each of the species
considered, the efficiency of edible energy produced per unit of
energy consumed can be calculated (see Table 18.6 for sheep).

TABLE 18.6

Efficiency of energy conversion by sheep

$$\text{Efficiency} = \frac{\text{edible carcass output of progeny (kcal/year)}}{\text{food consumed by dam and progeny (kcal/year)}} \times 100$$

assuming that 85 per cent of the carcass is edible and that edible meat contains 4·4 kcal/g)

Breed	Litter size	Efficiency
Devon longwool	1	2·4
,,	2	3·5
Kerry hill	1	3·2
,,	2	4·1
Welsh mountain	1	3·7
,,	2	4·8

The figures for entire populations, maintaining themselves over a substantial period of time, can be converted to efficiency estimates based on energy input per unit of land, simply by multiplying by the efficiencies of (*a*) energy fixation by the plant populations and (*b*) utilization by the animal of what is produced by the plant population. Alternatively, efficiencies can be calculated from actual output data.

TABLE 18.7

Efficiency of meat production per unit of usable light energy received, for sheep production in southern England: mean for 5 years and 48 ewes each year (From Spedding *et al.* 1967)

	kg/ha per year	Mcal/ha per year
Meat production, carcass (*P*)	170	636†
Herbage production, dry matter (*H*)	6020	25 585
Usable incident solar radiation (*R*)	..	35×10^5

† energy in the boneless carcass (= 85 per cent of carcass).
% efficiency $(P \times 100)/H = 2·5$ Mcal
$(H \times 100)/R = 0·73$ Mcal
$(P \times 100)/R = 0·02$ Mcal.

Examples of these calculations and their results are given in Table 18. 7. It is obvious that the result of multiplying one value by another ignores any interaction and assumes that the efficiency of the animals is independent of the efficiency of the plants. In fact, of course, both may be influenced by such factors as the amount of crop grown per unit area of land.

In considering such figures, however, it should never be forgotten that maximum efficiency, in any useful sense, will never be 100 per cent.

These calculations based on populations are generally the most relevant but they suffer somewhat from the fact that they are associated with particular animals, at particular reproductive rates, or using particular foods, in particular conditions. They may not indicate very well the extent to which they may be improved by better breeding or nutrition. Although the efficiency associated with the individual growing animal is only a part of the whole picture, it does, in fact, more nearly indicate one kind of potential.

The efficiency of the individual animal

The most efficient population imaginable would have properties, such as an extremely high reproductive rate and a small mature female body size relative to the size of the progeny, that minimized the proportion of the total food intake required for the maintenance of the breeding population. The maximum efficiency of a population approaches, but cannot equal, the efficiency of an individual. Such a figure therefore indicates both the order of magnitude of the potential and a maximum value that cannot be exceeded. This is of considerable help in looking to the future; it enables assessment of the following form: no matter what improvements take place in either species *A* or *B*, the efficiency of *A* can never exceed that of the potential for *B* if the individual potential of *A* is lower, unless the improvements are concerned with individual efficiency.

The latter, it will be recalled, does vary with species and breed, and also with rate of growth. There is thus further scope for improvement, and the best assessment of potential will be derived from calculations based on the maximum growth rate that can fairly be associated with an individual of the species considered. Growth rate can be manipulated in non-nutritional ways, such as implantation of hormones or synthetic compounds with oestrogenic activity, for example, stilboestrol, or hexoestrol (El-Shazly 1967).

It is worth remembering that lean-meat distribution in lambs is hardly affected by breed, plane of nutrition, or slaughter weight (Carroll 1967). The composition of the fat-free, boneless carcass is constant when the fat content of the carcass reaches more than 18 per cent (referred to as 'chemical maturity').

Values for potential efficiency are shown in Table 18.8 for some meat-producing species on which adequate information is available. Even in the special case of maximum growth rate in an individual, efficiency is likely to change as the animal grows larger. The efficiency of the growth process therefore varies with the period over which it is calculated, and in species comparisons care must be taken that comparable periods are selected. It is of little use to take the same period of time, since this might cover the whole growth of some species and only the early phases for others; nor is the problem solved by taking the periods occupied by the same absolute weight change. The latter is, however, a very sensible way of making comparisons *within* a species and may therefore be of some help. Clearly, in some fashion, the growth measured must represent the same proportion of the whole growth period. Taylor (1965) has shown that the time a species takes to reach a given fraction of its mature weight tends to be proportional to its mature weight raised to the 0·27th power.

TABLE 18.8

Potential efficiency of individual animals from birth to slaughter

$$\text{Efficiency} = \frac{\text{kcal carcass meat†}}{\text{kcal food‡}} \times 100$$

	Breed		Efficiency	Multiple of birth weight represented by slaughter weight
Sheep	Devon longwool	(9)	6·10	3·8
	Kerry hill	(10)	7·20	3·8
	Welsh mountain	(10)	7·30	3·8
Cattle	South Devon	(2)	2·90	5·2
	Welsh black	(7)	3·00	6·0
	Jersey	(2)	3·60	9·2

† (Callow 1948) For both cattle and sheep the energy value of boneless meat is given by:

$$9·01 \ FT/C + 27 \text{ kcal}/100 \text{ g carcass}$$

where $FT/C =$ 40 for sheep at slaughter
14 for sheep at birth
25 for calves at slaughter
10 for calves at birth.

‡ Solid plus milk (or solid needed to provide milk) consumed by an individual from birth to slaughter.

( ) Number of animals on which the calculation is based.

Killing-out percentage at birth is assumed to be 66 per cent for calves and 50 per cent for lambs.

The simplest relevant calculation then is the increment of product (weight, energy, or protein) per unit of food (similarly expressed) from birth (or some comparable starting-point) until a given percentage of the gain possible (from birth to mature size) has been achieved.

From an agricultural point of view, the choice of period must take into account the nature of the product that is desired or can be sold.

Implications of efficiency comparisons

In some senses, milk and meat production are alternative ways of producing human food, although neither process can easily be separated entirely from the other. They can be compared in terms of the efficiency with which protein or energy are produced, and when the other resources used are taken into account and the by-products added in, implications as to which process man should employ may be deduced. This will be further considered in Chapter 20, but it is worth pointing out here that any such implications must also take into account four major factors. These are the environment, alternative animals, alternative crops, and alternative human foods.

The environment

Milk and meat cannot necessarily be produced in the same environment, and maximum efficiency in the two processes may demand more or less of the environment, at more or less cost. The same applies to the following possibilities.

Alternative animals

The possibility must be recognized that better meat-producing species of animals already exist that have not yet been explored or exploited and that could be domesticated. This is perhaps less likely to be true of the grazing animal than of meat-producing animals in general. It is true, of course, that herbivores in agriculture will not necessarily remain grazing animals; this would also separate the animal and the diet from the environment in which the latter is grown.

One interesting consequence of the conclusion that the efficiency of the growing individual represents a figure that the efficiency of the population cannot exceed, is that the number of starting-points to the growth process that can be derived from one individual needs to be extremely high.

In mammals, this is so for the male but of limited possibility in the female. The mammal thus suffers from the following disadvantages:

(1) A high maintenance requirement because it is warm-blooded;
(2) The dam has a limited capacity to carry progeny in pregnancy;

(3) The progeny are dependent on milk (or a liquid substitute) for some part of their lives.

These disadvantages of the mammal are not incidental, they are characteristic; a definition of the mammal would include both warm-bloodedness and the great dependence of the young on the dam.

Birds, on the other hand, although certainly warm-blooded, differ in the other respects. Geese, for example, can produce eighty progeny per breeding female per year (compared with one to six for sheep and one to two for cattle), and there is no nutritional dependence of the progeny on the dam at all.

Alternative crops

In thinking about the efficiency of meat production, the possibility of improvement in the food of grazing animals must not be ignored, although this is unlikely to influence the general conclusions already reached.

In considering the wider implications, however, the possibility of human food being based on crops rather than on meat must be faced. As already mentioned, relatively few humans can afford meat on any scale, and there are many reasons why a reduction in meat consumption might occur even where it is now consumed at a high level.

Alternative human foods

The final possibility exists that wholly synthetic diets may be acceptable in due course (Blount 1968); they would certainly be acceptable to the hungry. It may even be thought that this is ultimately certain and that the real question relates only to the time scale. To the applied biologist, to the agriculturalist, and to the research that should be encouraged, the question of this time scale is of immense consequence. It does not relate only to meat production, however.

References

BLOUNT, W. P. (editor) (1968) *Intensive livestock farming.* Heinemann, London.
CALLOW, E. H. (1948) *J. agric. Sci.* **38**, 174–99.
CAMPBELL, A. G. (1968) *Span* **11**, 50–3.
CARROLL, M. A. (1967) *Proc. C.I.C.R.A. Conf.*, Dublin, pp. 81–5.
—— and CONIFFE, D. (1968) *Growth and development of mammals* (editors G. C. Lodge and G. E. Lamming), chapter 7. Butterworths, London.

CONWAY, A. (1968) *Span* **11**, 47–9.

EL-SHAZLY, K. (1967) *Wld Rev. Anim. Prod.* **3**, No. 11, 45–56.

FAUCONNEAU, G. (1967) *Proc. C.I.C.R.A. Conf.*, Dublin, pp. 1–20.

HAMMOND, J. (1955) Anatomy of meat animals: lecture given to the Institute of Meat Teachers' Conference, Cambridge.

KENNETH, J. H. and RITCHIE, G. R. (1953) Gestation periods: a table and bibliography. *Commonw. Bur. Anim. Breed. Genet., tech. Commun.* No. 5. Commonwealth Agricultural Bureau.

KING WILSON, W. (1959) Modern rabbit keeping. *M.A.F.F. Bull.* No. 50. H.M.S.O., London.

LEDGER, H. P., SACHS, R. and SMITH, N. S. (1967) *Wld Rev. Anim. Prod.* **3**, 13–36.

ROBERTSON, I. S., WILSON, J. C. and MORRIS, P. G. D. (1967) *Vet. Rec.* **81**, 88–103.

SEEBECK, R. M. and TULLOH, N. M. (1966) *Anim. Prod.* **8**, 281–8.

SPEDDING, C. R. W., BETTS, J. E., LARGE, R. V., WILSON, I. A. N. and PENNING, P. D. (1967) *J. agric. Sci.* **69**, 47–69.

TAYLOR, ST. C. S. (1965) *Anim. Prod.* **7**, 203–20.

WALLACE, L. R. (1955) *Proc. Nutr. Soc.* **14**, 7–13.

WILSON, P. N. (1968) *Chemy Ind.*, pp. 899–902.

19

Animal Production from Grassland—Wool and Hides

WOOL and hides are the two principal contributions to man's clothing but there are some others of importance. While all these products may be only secondary to a meat-producing enterprise, in some cases it is entirely the other way round.

Wool

The emphasis on wool production varies greatly with the situation. In Britain, the monetary contribution of wool to a sheep farmer's income varies from about 15 per cent in the lowlands to about 40 per cent in mountain regions. Wool is thus secondary, and consideration of efficiency in its production is extremely complicated. In Australia, by contrast, sheep are commonly kept primarily for wool production and the national importance of the product has naturally led to much detailed study of all aspects of the process. An excellent picture of the Australian wool industry is available (Barnard 1962), which brings together information from all the contributory disciplines as a background to a discussion on the future for wool. Ryder and Stephenson (1968) have recently summarized the world position for wool production.

The fleece of the sheep consists of wool fibres, each of which is a cylindrical structure (the diameter of a fine wool fibre is about 20 μm) composed of dead cells that are filled with a fibrous protein called keratin (distinguished by its high content of sulphur, in the form of the amino-acid cystine). The outer cuticle of the fibre is formed of flattened scale cells; these overlap and their edges protrude. Fibres vary in length and waviness (crimp), and the weight (W) of a clean fleece may be described by the formula

$$W = L \times A \times N \times D \times S \text{ (Ryder 1963/4)},$$

where L = the average length of the wool fibres,
A = their average cross-sectional area,
N = the average number of fibres per unit area of skin (that is, the fibre density),
D = the density of the wool substance (equals its specific gravity, relatively constant at 1·31),
S = the total area of the skin surface bearing wool.

The quantity of wool grown varies greatly with the breed of sheep (1 to 2 kg from a Welsh mountain ewe but up to 8·5 kg for a Lincoln in 1 year), and also varies with season, nutrition, and reproduction (Ross 1965, McFarlane 1964, Doney 1966). The *yield* is what is clipped and may be affected by losses due to shedding and by the frequency of shearing (Lightfoot 1967). The maximum rates of wool growth observed during a favourable season are considered to approach the limit (1·6–1·8 mg clean wool/cm² day) of which sheep are capable (Schinkel 1963).

Wool is a more complex subject than at first appears and the fleece provides a habitat for many micro-organisms, some of which cause damage (Mulcock 1965). Fleece wool, as it comes from the sheep, also contains associated substances, some natural and some impurities (dust, seeds, and other vegetable matter). The general character of the raw fleece is shown in Table 19.1.

TABLE 19.1

The general character of the fleece (From Carter 1961)

			Per cent	
Raw or greasy fleece	⎧ Moisture		5–20	⎫
	+ Foreign matter	⎧ organic (vegetable matter)	0·5–30	⎬ from the environment 5–65 per cent
		+ inorganic (sand, etc.)	2–35	⎭
	+ Clean dry wool		20–80	⎫
	+ Sebaceous gland secretions (wax)		15–65	⎬ from the animal 35–95 per cent
	+ Sudoriferous gland secretions (sweat)		3–30	⎭

The chemical composition of wool fibres varies a good deal and over twenty minerals may be present, often in very small amounts. Burns *et al.* (1964) found an average content of 0·42 per cent ash, 15·78 per cent nitrogen, and 3·21 per cent sulphur, with phosphorus, calcium, sodium, silicon, magnesium, and zinc as relatively abundant elements.

The efficiency of wool growth

Since wool is a protein, one relevant way of expressing efficiency is to relate wool growth to the food protein consumed. As Ferguson (1962) has pointed out, efficiency of wool growth is greatly influenced by the level of feeding, and when dietary crude protein (nitrogen multiplied by 6·25) exceeds about 8 per cent (on a dry matter basis), wool growth is chiefly determined by the intake of energy.

Energy can be derived from body reserves also, and as with lactation, production of wool appears misleadingly efficient when the animal is losing weight.

Efficiency of food conversion to wool growth is therefore best expressed in terms of energy consumed and must take body weight change into account.

Ferguson (1958) proposed the following equation for the relationship between wool growth and feed intake:

$$\frac{W}{F} = E - k\frac{C}{F},$$

where W = rate of wool growth,

F = feed intake in units of net energy,

C = rate of body weight change per unit time (not including change in fleece weight), and

E and k are constants.

Since feed intake under hand-feeding conditions is related to body weight, an estimate of gross efficiency can be derived from wool growth per unit of body weight, and Ferguson (1958) also proposed the following equation:

$$\frac{C}{B} = b\frac{F}{B} - a,$$

where B = mean body weight less weight of fleece,

C = body weight change per unit time (not including change in fleece weight),

F = feed intake, and

a and b are constants.

N

The efficiency of conversion of net energy into wool appears to be relatively low (Ferguson 1962), at about 2·25 lb dry wool/100 lb starch weight (about 1 kg dry wool/45 kg starch). The equivalent figure given for milk equals 10·9 (5 kg) and for beef, 5·2 (2·4 kg).

Several consequences flow from the above equations that are of great importance for the natural grazing environment. First, the average efficiency of sheep on a seasonally fluctuating intake would be no less than that of sheep on the same average intake fed at a constant rate throughout the year. Secondly, sheep maintained in different states of body condition, which require different intakes, would show similar efficiencies.

However, it is known that some sheep produce more wool and exhibit greater efficiency of food conversion to wool than other sheep of the same body weight and at the same level of feed intake (Wodzicka-Tomaszewska 1966).

With any population of sheep kept for wool production, efficiency is associated with individuals that grow more wool, with maintenance of adequate body weight and, in a sustained population, a reproductive rate adequate for replacement of breeding stock. An unnecessary number of male lambs will be produced, even when breeding is restricted to a minimal number of ewes, and meat is an inevitable by-product. Since, in general, only maintenance of body weight is required, it is possible to maintain high rates of stocking and efficient utilization of the herbage grown. Thus it is commonly found that, as stocking rates of sheep are increased, meat output per head declines markedly but wool output declines to a much smaller extent (see Table 19.2). Wool production is therefore one of the processes most suited to intensive grazing, and it may be doubted whether it would be possible to improve economically on this method of wool production on relatively cheap land.

Recently (Ferguson 1968), dramatic increases in wool growth have been obtained following direct infusion into the abomasum of small amounts of casein, or sulphur-containing cystine, or methionine (Reis and Schinckel 1961, 1963, 1964), and the development of methods of protecting dietary protein from microbial degradation in the rumen (Ferguson, Hemsley, and Reis 1967). Ferguson (1968) sees 'no theoretical obstacle to feed supplements being developed which will economically raise fleece weights up to 20 lb (approx. 9 kg) while the sheep are still on a maintenance intake'.

TABLE 19.2

Carcass and wool production per ewe per year in an experiment comparing two stocking rates ($H = 11 \cdot 25$ ewes/ha, $L = 7 \cdot 5$ ewes/ha) of Scottish half-bred ewes and their Suffolk cross lambs over a 5-year period (Spedding et al. 1967)

Production from the higher stocking rate has been expressed as a percentage of that produced at the lower stocking rate ((H/L)× 100) (From Spedding 1967)

	Production	
	Carcass	Wool
1959	83	93
1960	58	74
1961	64	90
1962	71	97
1963	88	109

World production of wool

A recent estimate (Verrinder 1967) of the world output of wool showed that its contribution to total industrial fibre production had declined from 19 per cent around 1922 to 8 per cent in 1966. The total production of the four main fibres (cotton, wool, silk, and man-made fibre) amounted in 1966 to 38 844 million lb, of which wool amounted to 3275 million lb. The contribution of the synthetic man-made fibres (polyamides, polyesters, and methacrylates) that compete more directly with wool than do others, amounted to 5458 million lb, 60 per cent more than that of wool.

The number of sheep in the world was estimated to be 950 millions in 1961 (as compared with 350 million goats), the majority kept for wool production (see Table 19.3).

TABLE 19.3

Percentage of world sheep population (1961) *kept for meat, wool, and fur production* (From Schinkel 1963)

Fine and medium wool	Meat and wool	Meat and hair	Carpet wool	Dairy/meat/ carpet wool	Fur	Total
28·8	26·3	9·8	28·3	5·1	1·7	100

It will be noted that sheep fur represents only a small proportion of the total; it may be extremely important to a particular locality, however. Karakul or Persian lamb, for example, is an important export from some regions. Bokhara, in Russia, is reported to produce 4–5 million skins a year (Hosseinion and Jordan 1966) and Afghanistan over a million; the United States of America imports over a million annually from these two sources. The ewes have a fat tail which may contain 8–12 kg of fat, and they give considerable quantities of milk. The male lambs are removed at birth (Bertone 1966), since licking by the dam opens the curl in the wool, and most are slaughtered between 24 and 48 hours after birth. The skins are processed and dried in the sun; the main wool colours are black and grey and some brown.

Other animals also produce wool. The alpaca, llama, vicuna, and huanaco (Auchenidae) of the Andes produce fleece weights of 3·3–11, 3·3–7·7, 0·4–0·7, and 2·2–4·4 lb (1·5–5, 1·5–3·5, 0·18–0·32, and 1–2 kg), respectively (French 1966).

Mohair

This is produced by the Angora goat, chiefly in the United States of America, Turkey, and South Africa. In 1959 world production was 24 000 tons, of which Turkey produced 42·6 per cent, from a population of 5–6 million goats. These mostly graze dry pastures of little value for other purposes and consume a variety of plants, including oak leaves (Sönmez 1965). Meat and milk are also produced but mohair is the main product; it is chiefly exported, more than half of it to England, and accounted (1965) for nearly 5 per cent of Turkish exports.

Skins and hides

The domesticated (and wild) animals of the world produce a great variety of skins and hides, and these are processed for use in many different ways. They are important as sources of leather, for footwear and upholstery, and for articles as varied as coats and receptacles for carrying water.

The proportion of the live weight that is represented by the hide is often considerable. For example, cattle reared for slaughter at 18–24 months of age may weigh 500 kg and the weight of the hide may be 27 kg (approximately 5 per cent). Intensively fed cattle reaching a slaughter weight of 400 kg at 10–12 months of age give lighter hides of about 22 kg (again approximately 5 per cent).

The quality of the product may be affected by the way animals are grown, but age is probably the biggest factor. The collagen content of the skin of cattle and sheep increases with age, and at the same time the collagen itself gradually becomes more stable. Rapid growth leads to increase in collagen content for a given age, and this collagen is relatively less mature (Bowes and Raistrick 1966).

The environment may also influence the quality of skins and hides; the skin may be damaged by grubs of the warble fly, for example, and the insecticides used to control pests and parasites may also interfere with the quality of the hide or with the processes applied in tanning or other methods of preservation.

References

BARNARD, A. (editor) (1962) *The simple fleece*. Melbourne University Press and Australian National University.
BERTONE, E. (1966) *Wld Rev. Anim. Prod.* **3**, 77–88.
BOWES, J. H. and RAISTRICK, A. S. (1966) *J. Soc. Leath. Trades Chem.* **50**, 181–92.
BURNS, R. H., JOHNSTON, A., HAMILTON, J. W., McCOLLOCH, R. J., DUNCAN, W. E. and FISK, H. G. (1964) *J. Anim. Sci.* **23**, 5–11.
CARTER, H. B. (1961) *N.S.B.A. year book*, pp. 48–54.
DONEY, J. M. (1966) *J. agric. Sci., Camb.* **67**, 25–30.
FERGUSON, K. A. (1958) *Proc. N.Z. Soc. Anim. Prod.* **18**, 128.
—— (1962) *The simple fleece* (editor A. Barnard), chapter 11, Melbourne University Press and Australian National University.
—— (1968) *Span* **11**, 43–6.
—— HEMSLEY, J. A. and REIS, P. J. (1967) *Aust. J. Sci.* **30**, 215–17.
FRENCH, M. H. (1966) *Wld Rev. Anim. Prod.* **3**, 89–94.
HOSSEINION, M. and JORDAN, W. J. (1966) *Br. vet. J.* **122**, 308–10.
LIGHTFOOT, R. J. (1967) *J. Agric. West. Aust.* **8**, 2–8.
McFARLANE, J. D. (1964) *Aust. J. exp. Agric. Anim. Husb.* **5**, 252–61.
MULCOCK, A. P. (1965) *N.Z. vet. J.* **13**, 87–93.
REIS, P. J. and SCHINCKEL, P. G. (1961) *Aust. J. agric. Res.* **12**, 335–52.
—— —— (1963) *Aust. J. biol. Sci.* **16**, 218–30.
—— —— (1964) *Aust. J. biol. Sci.* **17**, 532–47.
ROSS, D. A. (1965) *N.Z. Jl agric. Res.* **8**, 585–601.
RYDER, M. L. (1963/4) *Scott. Agric.* **43**, 114–18.
—— and STEPHENSON, S. K. (1968) *Wool growth*. Academic Press, New York.
SCHINCKEL, P. G. (1963) *Proc. 1st Wld Conf. Anim. Prod.*, Rome, **1**, 199–239.
SÖNMEZ, R. (1965) E.A.A.P. Comm. Meet., Noordwijk, June 1965.
SPEDDING, C. R. W. (1967) *Proc. 9th int. Congr. Anim. Prod.*, pp. 174–87. Oliver & Boyd, Edinburgh.
—— BETTS, J. E., LARGE, R. V., WILSON, I. A. N. and PENNING, P. D. (1967) *J. agric. Sci.* **69**, 47–69.
VERRINDER, N. A. (1967) *J. R. agric. Soc.* **128**, 53–62.
WODZICKA-TOMASZEWSKA, MANIKA (1966) *N.Z. Jl agric. Res.* **9**, 909–15.

20

The Contribution to Man

A COMPREHENSIVE treatment of the past, present, and future contributions of grassland to man is quite beyond the scope of this book. Nevertheless, there are many wide implications to the well-being of mankind that arise out of the foregoing discussions and that cannot be completely ignored. It is proposed in this chapter to deal briefly with the more important of these. As a concise summary of the situation, it is worth quoting McDonald (1968): 'The principal contribution of ruminants to man's economy is the conversion of nitrogenous substances in plants to animal proteins—meat, wool, hides, and milk proteins; the use of ruminants as energy converters, with the provision of mechanical work or animal fats, is tending to take an increasingly minor role in the world's agriculture.'

Work

An early service of grassland animals to man was to provide power and this is still important in many parts of the world. This power was harnessed (literally) for a great variety of purposes, not all agricultural by any means, including tilling the soil, cultivating and cutting the crop, transporting the products and the consumers, driving machinery (as in thrashing, grinding, and water-drawing), and even taking part in war. This has applied to many different animal species, from llamas to buffalo, but the part played by the horse has probably been outstanding. It will doubtless be mystifying to a future generation to discover that powerful engines are rated by 'horse-power', and it is interesting that so specialized an animal should have proved so widely useful.

It is to be expected that the animal will steadily be displaced as a direct source of power.

Clothing

The use of skins, hair, wool, and fur for clothing must have made an enormous contribution to the well-being of man, and enabled him to withstand colder climates than he could otherwise have tolerated. Whilst animals are kept in large numbers for meat, skins and their coverings will be available as by-products. It is difficult to estimate the likely contribution from this source to the total clothing required by man (clothing here includes carpets and other domestic uses of animal fibres), or the extent to which it would come from grassland animals.

Quite a lot of the present contribution, however, comes from animals kept primarily for this purpose (such as wool under Australian conditions). It is in this context that competition from synthetic fibres must be considered. It may be assumed that, ultimately, synthetic fibres will probably be able to provide the same qualities, and that the result will be determined largely on economic grounds.

One of the most noticeable features of this kind of animal production is its relative cheapness, in the sense that it can be carried out in harsh environments under conditions that are not easily tolerated for other agricultural purposes. These biological factors are not the only ones that determine the cost of production, however, and in the long term the contribution of the grassland animal to clothing may decline to very small proportions.

Food

It is not easy to estimate the contribution of grassland to the world's food; Table 20.1 illustrates one way in which this can be assessed, as the proportion of one man's diet that can be attributed to animals fed primarily on grassland (in this case, a man in the United Kingdom). In the United States of America, the mean daily consumption of dietary energy is about 3 Mcal per head, of which about one-third comes from animal products (Duckham 1968).

The possibility that this may change was mentioned in Chapter 18. Millions of human beings derive little of their diet from meat or milk now, and it is perhaps unlikely that the proportion doing so will increase.

As standards of living rise, more meat may be eaten (Tanner 1968), although it will not necessarily be produced from grassland; the question is—and it is a sobering one—for what proportion of the human race will standards of living rise?

The argument that food production must increase at least at the same rate as does the population does not apply necessarily to all foods. If the population expands *faster* than the increase in food production, it is likely that meat will play a smaller part.

TABLE 20.1

Distribution of energy (E) and protein (P) in standard United Kingdom diet (Table prepared by J. L. Monteith 1969, from the following sources: (*a*) Ministry of Agriculture. *Monthly digest of statistics*; (*b*) Ministry of Agriculture. *Domestic food consumption and expenditure*; (*d*) Davies 1960)

	Meat	Milk	Butter	Cheese	Total E	P
(*a*) Percentage of diet that is home produced†	66	100	8	43		
(*b*) Percentage in diet of different sources of						
E	15	10	7	2	34	
P	26	18	–	4		48
(*c*) Percentage home produced in the diet = (*a*) × (*b*)						
E	10	10	0·6	0·9	21·5	
P	17	18	–	2		37
(*d*) Percentage contribution of U.K. grass to animal feeds					46‡	67§
(*e*) Percentage of diet from U.K. grassland (*c*) × (*d*)					*10·7*	*24·3*

† Assuming home-produced and imported meat have same energy and protein content per unit weight.
‡ Calculated from starch equivalents.
§ Calculated from dry weight assuming protein equivalent is fixed fraction of weight for major foodstuffs.

In trying to take a global view, there is always a risk that the individual may appear unimportant, especially if he belongs to a group which is not very numerous; by world standards, even small nations may not seem very large units. The importance of a particular component in the diet cannot altogether be measured by the number of people who consume it, even though one measure of its importance must be the contribution that it makes to the nutrition of mankind as a whole.

Nor is it necessarily reasonable to assume that population growth will outstrip food production, or that the population cannot be controlled at a level that can be fed in any fashion that man chooses. Indeed, the case for stabilizing human populations at levels, often lower than current ones, for which *all* resources are adequate, is extremely reasonable (see Hutchinson 1967).

The future for meat and milk may therefore be determined by quite other considerations. Amongst these may be strictly commercial reasons, changing values of the consumer, and changing preferences for a way of life on the part of the producer.

The possibility certainly has to be faced, in the long term, that attractive food may be based on completely synthetic products and that these may be cheaper or associated with ways of life that are more attractive, for many reasons, to the producer. It is quite possible already to visualize protein produced from petrol, by micro-organisms, or from methane gas, by bacteria (Blount 1968). The position has been put as follows (Cooper 1968): 'There is, in fact, a new food technology around the corner that does not require cows and hens in an elongated chain of food production and dis-regards the crops we prize today.' The possibility also has to be considered that people may not wish to consume the products of animals, or that they may not wish to support the methods of animal production that are most economic—or indeed to support any methods at all that are based on the deliberate keeping of animals just for food. It is not necessary to assume that fundamental issues of right and wrong are involved, merely that some ideas are less attractive than others. There is, for example, little doubt that many fewer people would eat meat if they had to be closely concerned with all aspects of its production. In parenthesis, it is probably as true to say that very few people would wish to be personally involved with surgery.

Efficiency and intensification

It is extremely difficult to predict the extent to which any of the fore-going will really be of significance in the future, and it is even more difficult to predict the rate at which any change will occur. Whilst an important part of man's food is derived from grassland, the general concepts of efficiency that have recurred throughout this book appear likely to remain of great consequence. The importance of other factors has been repeatedly stressed, however, in applying biological concepts within an economic context. What is now being suggested is that yet other factors, which may be termed 'social' or even 'moral', must also be included, not merely because they may affect the demand for grassland products but because the use of land must ultimately concern all men.

What are the possible functions of grassland apart from the production of food and clothing? Agriculturally, grass crops are often grown as part of a rotation and may benefit subsequent crops by reducing the build-up of pests and diseases, by increasing the organic-matter content of the soil, or by improving its structure. They would not be so used, of course, if they could not be converted profitably to animal products. Clearly, there are other ways of controlling pests and diseases and of increasing soil fertility. The question here is whether these methods, and future developments of them, are the best or even the cheapest in the long term. It may be that a balanced approach to agriculture, as opposed to monoculture, for example, will prove to be the most satisfactory. It does not automatically follow that grassland would play a significant part in this. If it did so, it is probable that it would be utilized in an extremely intensive manner. After all, if the success of intensification is measured over a long period, and does not merely represent short-term exploitation, it is synonymous with efficiency. What has to be recognized is that other values have to be taken into account; the community also has to make its calculation of efficiency in terms of what it derives from the resources used. If some of the consequences are wholly undesirable, no amount of efficiency in terms of components will necessarily outweigh the effect of these consequences. In other words, a complete calculation must consider the means as well as the ends and the beginnings. Methods of animal production must satisfy the community as a whole, and there is no reason to suppose that this will necessarily involve any inefficiency at all. Indeed, it will be more efficient to develop methods that do satisfy all reasonable criteria. If the world's nutritional problems were simply too many people and too little food, and no methods were ruled out, then a great many absurd or totally unacceptable solutions, including cannibalism, might be considered.

The fact is that everybody really accepts the principle involved and the discussion is always one of practice.

Furthermore, everyone really accepts that feeding people is not the whole purpose of life, however important a base-line it represents. There are other important aspects of man's life and the land forms the natural backcloth against which they must be viewed. It matters greatly, then, even to the well-fed man, what is done with the land.

Land use

When thinking about food production, the problems of land use are much the same as those involved in the use of sunlight, and a good deal of this book has been concerned with what happens to the incident sunlight and how efficiently it is used. Leaving these matters aside, it is obvious that land use involves other similar activities (such as mining and forest production) concerned with man's wealth and welfare; it is also clear that sheer space is an important attribute. People wish to move about, even if they prefer to do so in crowds, and it is likely that open spaces will be directly preserved and created for human recreation. If land is not required for agriculture, many more acres may be devoted to leisure, and it is possible that grassland would be a form of land use entirely consistent with this.

There is thus a prospect of large areas of grassland, which would support a large population of grazing animals, which might have to do so if it was to remain grassland (and not become woodland, for example), and which could be managed to support even more.

Indeed, there are several social questions here, as to whether man would prefer his open spaces to be populated by an abundance of animals or not, whether the animals should control their numbers by starvation, predation, and parasitism, or whether they should be managed in such a way that meat production and population control were synonymous. It is worth mentioning, at this point, that even in the short term there are good prospects of such combined land usage. This is most readily visualized in terms of open grassland sustaining large flocks and herds of breeding animals, with removal of most of the progeny at an early age to more conventional agricultural situations.

Looking to the future, then, the land will support animals unless the environment is rendered unsuitable for them. They will increase where they can and they will die from many causes; their proper management could contribute food and a degree of control of nature that should improve it. Our own respect for animal life, thrusting cynicism aside, already exceeds that of nature; should it ever do so for plant life our philosophical problems will certainly become insoluble.

Finally, this ecological willingness to range widely in space and time should not obscure the enormous and quite certain short term contribution of grassland to man's food. The need to feed hungry people in the next decades or centuries is not in any way diminished by the longer-term probabilities.

References

BLOUNT, W. P. (editor) (1968) *Intensive livestock farming.* Heinemann, London.
COOPER, M. M. (1968) *Economic change and agriculture* (editors J. Ashton and S. J. Rogers), chapter 18. Oliver & Boyd, Edinburgh.
DAVIES, W. (1960) *Proc. VIIIth int.Grassld Congr.*, Reading, pp. 1–7.
DUCKHAM, A. N. (1968) *Chemy Ind.* 903–6.
HUTCHINSON, Sir J. (1967) Symp. Br. Ass., 1967, Leeds.
MCDONALD, I. W. (1968) *Aust. vet. J.* 44, 145–50.
MINISTRY OF AGRICULTURE (1968) *Monthly digest of statistics*, Central Statistical Office Agric. Stats.
—— (1967) *Domestic food consumption and expenditure.*
TANNER, C. C. (1968) *Outl. Agric.* 5, 235–40.

Appendix

Models in Grassland Ecology

A MODEL is simply a representation of reality, designed for a particular purpose. There are innumerable purposes for which models are made, varying from extremely detailed replicas to greatly oversimplified representations; they may be solid, to scale, miniature, working, transparent, mathematical, or mental. The kind of model is chosen to suit the purpose, although this is not always consciously recognized. Mental models, for example, are employed by all of us in conversation. If we discuss aeroplanes or ants, we hold in our minds a sufficiently good, general picture of these objects to make conversation possible. Our mental models will be simplified but correct in essential details. If A informs B that he saw an aeroplane with four engines, both assume, until more detail is specified, that it also had the usual complement of wings, controls, wheels, etc.

When it becomes necessary to be more specific about objects, and to attach precise values to parts and relationships between them, mental models will no longer serve. Descriptions in words become lengthy and difficult to comprehend as a whole; this is why illustrations are often provided in association with detailed descriptions. Descriptions can be abbreviated by use of suitable technical terminology, and the ultimate in this is the use of mathematical symbols. These have the great advantage that they can be readily manipulated, not only by all those with some facility in this direction but also by all the technical aids developed in recent years, including, most importantly, the modern range of computers.

Models may be grouped in many different ways: the two most useful categories for our purposes may be termed (1) real, and (2) abstract.

Kinds of model

For other purposes, quite different categories would be more useful. One obvious distinction is between models that are static and those that are dynamic. Both occur in both (1) and (2). In (1) the dynamic models are represented by 'working' models; in (2) they include those involving 'simulation'.

Another obvious distinction is between qualitative and quantitative models, but the difference is in fact largely one of precision; a model in which the dimensions are grossly inaccurate is not a useful model. It is important to realize that the amount of detail and the precision with which it is given are determined solely by the purposes for which the model is built and the nature of the information available.

Real models

The purpose of these is to present a picture, almost at a glance, of the structure or function of a real object or process.

The most common forms are solid, whether working or not, but pictorial forms also fall within this category, including drawings in two or three dimensions, diagrams, plans, histograms, and graphs. All of these can be quantitative but are not necessarily suitable for quantitative manipulation. A good example of an exception to this is the structural model, such as that currently used by molecular biologists; in these models precision is important and they can be quantitatively manipulated.

Abstract models

The main object of these is to represent reality with precision, in a form susceptible to manipulation. The most primitive version is the mental model. This can be manipulated easily enough, but the degree of precision depends upon the individual mind. Clearly, some people can appreciate mathematical formulae directly (just as others appreciate pictures) or indirectly (formulae giving rise to, say, a graphical picture in the mind). Mental models arrived at in this way may possess great precision, but in general will not. A distinction must be made between precision and accuracy. The mathematical model, which is the most useful of the abstract forms, may be no more accurate than a solid model, but it is obliged to be precise about each quantity it includes. It must also be precise about what is or is not included, whereas solid models are not always meant to be taken too literally as to the precise dimensions at any one point, and they often have 'grey' areas.

The latter may be sketched in where the situation is unclear, where information is lacking, or the area relatively unimportant.

The use of models

The many different reasons for making models have already been indicated; having made a model, it is also helpful to consider what use can be made of it.

1. If it truly represents reality, it follows that the information was already available (or was partially derived from the model-building activity); when completed, therefore, the model can be used for instruction or demonstration, to convey to others what the model-builder knows.

Any completed model allows the value attached to components to be varied and a study made of many different combinations. One common reason for this sort of exercise is to 'read out' from the model the 'best' combination for some purpose. This can be done to obtain the most productive version of some system, or to obtain the combination that will prove most profitable. This is usually the object of the technique known as 'linear programming' (see Roberts 1968).

2. If the model does not correspond with reality, an experimental test may reveal this; it may not reveal in exactly what way it is wrong but this is a matter of skill in experimentation. A model may be wrong and still give the same over-all answer as a test in the real situation, due to errors cancelling out or to the particular error being unimportant in that particular situation.

3. Any model represents what its builder knows, and clearly confronts him with this reflection. It is therefore an aid to clarity in thinking, and will expose some gaps in his information of which he may not have been aware before. On the other hand, the model cannot by itself indicate gaps in the whole conception. Only suitable experimental tests can do this, but in any case, a list of the main components is the first stage in building any model, and this list can only be derived from experience in the real situation.

Model construction

There are a great many different ways of constructing models, varying with the kind of model to be made. Typical static models, and the way they can be built up, were dealt with in Chapter 14. Little has been said, however, of dynamic models involving simulation, and these are of great importance and value in grassland ecology.

The first step is to list the main components of the model. The second is to construct a flow diagram showing how these components are related. The third is to associate actual values with the components and their relationships.

There are several different ways of proceeding in detail, although the principles are basically similar; the choice of method depends chiefly upon how the model is to be used. Generally speaking, complex models will be dealt with by computers, and the model has to be expressed in a language appropriate to the particular type of computer available.

The example illustrated below, taken from the work of N. R. Brockington at the Grassland Research Institute, is a model of pasture contamination, described in the computer language *Dynamo* (suitable for such computers as IBM 70/94).

The following detailed explanation of the steps used in the construction of such a model has been specially written by Brockington. This simple version of the model has been superseded by others, but it has been used here as a convenient example; furthermore, it is concerned with a very important component process in grassland ecology.

Pasture contamination: an example of mathematical simulation of a biological system

The model described here was built as a first simple approximation in considering the problem of pasture contamination by the excreta of grazing cattle. Later and more sophisticated versions of the model illustrated in this exploratory study are thought to be closer to real life, but this example has been chosen to illustrate some of the principles and techniques used in such work in as simple a way as possible.

The simulation language used was *Dynamo*, which achieves an effectively continuous simulation of growth and decay processes by advancing time in small discrete steps, and in which differential equations are replaced by the first-order approximation of 'difference' equations. This language was originally developed at the Massachusetts Institute of Technology to simulate business activities (Forrester 1961, Pugh 1963) and has since been found to be suitable for modelling biological systems (Radford 1967, de Wit and Brouwer 1968).

Flow diagram

The first step in constructing such a model in *Dynamo* is to set out in a flow diagram the various components of the system and their interrelationships. The symbols in Fig. A.1 are the standard ones described by Forrester (1961) in his book on models of business systems.

The square or rectangular boxes are used for *levels*, representing physical quantities that could, at least theoretically, be measured at any given time if the system were brought to rest. The levels are joined by solid lines to indicate physical flows of material and the *rates* of flow are represented by valve-like symbols across the solid lines. If the system were brought to a standstill the rates would be zero by definition. Where a level is on the boundary of the system being studied and its value is not specified then it is shown as a symbol with an irregular outline denoting simply a *source* or *sink* as appropriate. The dotted lines represent flows of information as distinct from physical flows, and the circular symbols, known as *auxiliaries*, are used to indicate interactions and 'feed-back' loops, and to simplify the algebraic expressions for rates where necessary so as to fit in with the standard equation forms used in the actual computer programme.

Thus in Fig. A.1 the rate of contamination feeds from an unspecified source to produce the level or area of contamination on the pasture. It is postulated that the rate of contamination is related to stocking rate, which controls the proportion of the area contaminated per day. However, the auxiliary called 'potential contamination' is not only related to stocking rate but is also influenced by multiple deposition which in turn depends on the deposition pattern in space and on the area already contaminated. Since the model was designed to depict the process on one, representative, paddock of a rotational grazing system, the auxiliary 'potential contamination' only becomes translated into actual contamination when triggered by the 'grazing index' mechanism at appropriate times as specified by the rotational grazing scheme.

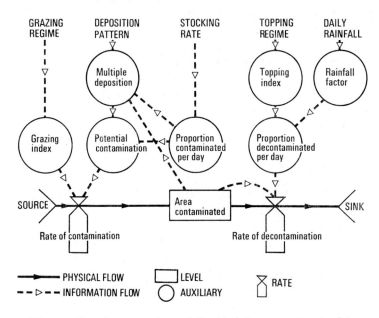

Fig. A.1. Flow diagram to show relationship between components of the system.

Similarly in the process of 'decontamination', which is here defined as equivalent to herbage becoming palatable to the grazing animal once more, the proportion decontaminated per day is shown as being influenced by rainfall and by whether the pasture is 'topped' to remove surplus herbage after each grazing period. In order to translate the proportion of decontamination into an absolute rate the area contaminated at any given time is taken into account, and this is indicated by the dotted line joining 'area contaminated' with 'rate of decontamination' in the diagram.

Computer program

Having set out the supposed relationships in the flow diagram, the next step is to translate them into the actual equations of the computer program. This is done by writing one equation or set of equations for each symbol in the flow diagram, and a print-out of the program for this example is given in Fig. A.2.

```
PAGE 1    200 NRB

*IC ID = 10012005.DYN. BROCKINGTON. G.R.I., 2,   3000                    1000
                       SWARD CONTAMINATION                               2000
                                                                        2001
                                                                        2002
1L      ARCN.K = ARCN.J+(DT) (RCN.JK−RDCN.JK)   AREA CONTAMINATED       2100 (A)
6R      RCN.KL=RCNX.K                      RATE OF CONTAMINATION PER DAY 2101
18A     RCNX.K = (GI.K) (PRCD.K−PRDD.K)                                 2102
58A     PRCD.K =TABHL (TPRCD, STRT.K,0,4,1)  PROPORTION CONTAMD PER DAY 2103
C       TPRCD*=0/.017/.03/.04/.05                                       9103
12A     PRDD.K=(ARCN.K) (PRCD.K)     PROPORTION DOUBLE CONTAMINATION    2104
        DISTRIBUTION CONTAMINATION ASSUMED TO BE RANDOM                 2105
51A     GI.K=CLIP (0,1,G,C*2.K,26)           GRAZING INDICATOR          2106
35B     GC=BOXCYC (2.GC*2.K)                 GRAZING COUNTER            2107
C       GC*=4/26                                                       9107
6R      RDCN.KL=RDCNX.K                 RATE OF DECONTAMN PER DAY       2108
13A     RDCNX.K=(ARCN.K) (PRDC.K) (RNF.K)                               2109
49A     PRDC.K=SWITCH (PRDCX,PRDCY,TI)                                 2110
C       PRDCX=.02                      DECONTAMN WITHOUT TOPPING        9110 (A)
C       PRDCY=.04                      DECONTAMN WITH TOPPING           9110 (B)
C       TI=1                           TOPPING INDEX                    9110 (C)
58A     RNF.K=TABHL (TRNF.RN.K,0,0.25,0.25)  EFFECT RAINFALL ON DECONTAMN  2111
C       TRNF*=0.5/2.0                                                  9111
59A     RN.K=TABLE (TRN, TIME,0,181,1)   DAILY RAINFALL FROM APRIL 15  2112
C       TRN*=.42/0/.14/.26/28/.22/.61/.25/0/0/0/.14/.14/.03/0/.17/.16/.03  9112
X1      /.01/0/.09/0/0/0/.04/0/0/0/0/0/0/.11/0/.28/.34/.05/.16/0/0/0/0  9112
X2      /.01/0/.50/.76/.02/0/.26/0/.19/.28 /0/0/0/0/.86/.23/0/0/0/.34/.46/. 9112
X3      13/.01/.02/.0/0/0/0/0/0/0/0/0/0/0/0/0/.18/0/.08/.18/.10/1.84/0/  9112
X4      .05/0/0/.02/.12 /0/0/.01/0/0/0/0/.01/0/0/0/0/0/0/0/0/0/0/0/0/.03/  9112
X5      .10/0/0/0/0/.01/0/.06/.10/.13/.26/0/0/0/0/.02/0/0/0/0/0/0/        9112
X6      0/0/0/0/07/0/0/0/0/0/0/.05/.32/.07/.15/0/0/0/0/0/0/.18/0/0/       9112
X7      0/0/0/0/0/0/.14/.20/.11/0/.06/0/0/                              9112
6A      STRT.K=STRTX                                                   2113
C       STRTX=1                                                        9113
6N      ARCN=0                                                        2100 (B)
SPEC    DT=1/LENGTH=181/PRTPER=2/PLTPER=1                              2900
PRINT   1) GI/2) RCN, RDCN/3) PRDD/4)RNF/5) ARCN                       2901
PLOT    RCN=A, RDCN=B/PRDD=C/ARCN= D                                   2902
```

Fig. A.2. Print-out of computer program.

Each line of the program proper, apart from the control cards at the beginning and end of the 'deck', is punched on a single card, and the equation form used corresponds to one of the permitted types listed in the *User's Manual for Dynamo* and identified by a letter or number and letter at the beginning of the line; for example, 1*L* indicates that the equation following is one of the six permitted types of equation to describe a level. Those subscripted *R* are from those forms which may be used to define rates, the letter *A* indicates an auxiliary equation, *C* a constant type of equation giving numerical values for inputs, and *N* is used to indicate that the equation specifies the initial value for a level at the beginning of a run. The subscript *B* is used to show that the following equation will specify a device called a 'boxcar train' in which information generated in the course of running the program or specified at time zero can be stored in a sequential fashion in cells or boxes. The contents of one box are shifted at specified intervals to the adjacent box, and finally they may be extracted and used later in the program as desired. Where there is insufficient space on one line or card for an equation or set of numerical values, as at line 9112, continuation cards may be used and are designated X_1, X_2, etc. The use of a rigid framework, with each equation type identifiable to the computer by its letter and number, allows an excellent error detection system to be built which detects punching and 'syntax' errors before the program is run, and greatly helps in the initial 'debugging' stage.

TABLE A.1

List of abbreviations in the order in which they appear in the computer program

ARCN	Area contaminated
†DT	Delta time, or 'calculation time'
RCN	Rate of contamination
RDCN	Rate of decontamination
PRCD	Proportion contaminated per day
PRDD	Proportion of 'double' or multiple deposition
†TABHL	High/low table
TPRCD	Table of proportion contaminated per day
STRT	Stocking rate
†CLIP	Clip function
GC	Grazing counter
†BOXCYC	Cyclic boxcar train
RNF	Rainfall factor
PRDC	Proportion decontaminated per day
†SWITCH	Switch function
TI	Topping index
TRNF	Table of rainfall factor
RN	Rainfall per day
TRN	Table of rainfall per day
†PRTPER	Printing interval relative to calculation interval
†PLTPER	Plotting interval relative to calculation interval

Time subscripts:

.J	time one calculation interval ago
.JK	the last calculation interval
.K	present time
.KL	the next calculation interval

† Standard *Dynamo* abbreviations.

Up to five symbols can be used in the equations to describe a given quantity in an equation, so that words and phrases shown in the flow diagram are abbreviated to suitable mnemonics to fit into this framework: for example, 'area contaminated' is shortened to *ARCN* in the program, 'rate of contamination' is represented by *RCN*, and 'rate of decontamination' as *RDCN*. A list of these abbreviations is given in Table A.1. There is also a shorthand notation, in the form of subscripts to the quantity abbreviations, which is used to indicate time relative to the small discrete time steps by which time is advanced in the calculation sequence. The subscript *.K* is used for the 'present' time, *.J* for time one *DT* (one calculation interval) ago, and *.L* for one *DT* in the future; for example, *ARCN.J* is the value of the area contaminated one *DT* previously, *RCN.JK* is the rate of contamination over the previous *DT*, and *RDCN.KL* is the rate at which decontamination will occur over the next *DT*.

The numbers at the end of each line of the program are for reference only and are ignored by the computer, as are the comments which may be inserted following the equations on the same cards or on separate 'note' cards as an *aide-mémoire* for the programmer.

Explanation of individual equations in the program

Line 2100 (A). This level equation illustrates the use of different equations for approximate integration. It states that the area contaminated now (at time *K*) is equal to what it was one *DT* ago (at time *J*), plus the time interval (*DT*) multiplied by the rate of decontamination over that interval.

Lines 2101 *and* 2102. The rate equation of line 2101 sets the rate of contamination over *KL* equal to the value of *RCNX* as it is at time *K*. Then, in line 2102, *RCNX* is derived by deducting the value for 'double' of 'multiple' contamination from the potential daily contamination, and multiplying the result by the grazing index. The grazing index is arranged, in lines 2106 to 9107, to take the value 1 when animals are grazing the pasture and 0 when they are elsewhere in the rotational grazing scheme.

Lines 2103 *and* 9103. These equations are an example of how tabular data may be fed into the model. In line 2103 the proportion of the pasture contaminated per day is set equal to a table called *TPRCD*, which depends on stocking rate between the limits of 0 and 4 immature animals per acre, in equal steps of 1. Line 9103 sets out the values for this table corresponding to stocking rates of 0, 1, 2, 3, and 4. *Dynamo* can provide values for *PRCD* for intermediate levels of stocking by linear interpolation between the specified points.

Line 2104. Assuming random distribution of contamination in this version of the model, multiple deposition is calculated from the product of the proportion of the total area already contaminated, and the proportion contaminated per day.

Lines 2105 *to* 9107. As already noted, these equations set the grazing index to 1 or 0 at appropriate times during the model run. The details of this arithmetical device are not shown in the flow diagram, but as set up in this example the grazing index remains at 1 for the 4 days of each grazing period, followed by 0 for 26 days, and then 1 for a further 4 days, etc.

Lines 2108 *to* 9110. These equations specify the rate of decontamination in a similar way to those controlling the contamination process. This rate is controlled partly by rainfall (line 2109) and also by topping. The switch function of line 2110 sets the proportion decontaminated per day to 0·02 if the topping index is zero, and changes to the value of 0·04 if the topping index is 1, to signify that surplus herbage is mown after each grazing. The topping index (line 9110 (C)) can be changed in successive runs of the model, as can other 'constant' values to achieve any desired combination of inputs and thus investigate their effects singly or collectively.

Lines 2111 *and* 9111. The rainfall factor used as part of the calculation of decontamination rate is here set to vary between 0·5 and 2·0 according to daily rainfall in the range between 0 and 0·25 in. Again, *Dynamo* will insert intermediate values between these extremes by linear interpolation. This particular table function, known as a high/low table, will also take the extreme values for the rainfall factor if actual rainfall is outside the range quoted. This introduces a smoothing effect, with the rainfall factor not exceeding 2·0, even if the rainfall is greater than 0·25 in on a particular day.

Lines 2112 *and* 9112. The daily rainfall figures are fed into the model in these equations, and in the example illustrated, actual data for the summer of 1964 at Hurley were used.

Lines 2113 *and* 9113. The stocking rate is specified as two beasts per acre for the run illustrated.

Line 2100. Here the initial value for area contaminated is given as zero. While initial values are required for levels, *Dynamo* will generate initial values for other quantity types such as rates and auxiliaries.

Line 2900. This 'specification' card instructs the computer to take a calculation interval (or *DT*) of one, which is read as one day in this context. It also indicates that the length of the run is to be 181 days, and that the results are to be printed out for every two-day interval and plotted for every day. It may be noted that the *DT* of one day is larger than would commonly be thought desirable in such a model, and was used in this case to accommodate the daily rainfall records.

Line 2901. The 'print' card specifies the quantities to be printed. Those separated by commas are printed in the same column while those with a solidus (/) between them appear in separate columns.

Line 2902. Likewise the 'plot' card indicates which quantities are to be shown in the graphical output and assigns symbols to them. If no scales are specified by the user, as in this example, *Dynamo* will select suitable ones and represent those quantities separated by commas on a common scale, while those with a solidus between will be scaled independently if appropriate.

PAGE 2   200NRB

TIME (DAYS)	GI	RCN RDCN	PRDD	RNF	ARCN	QUANTITY ABBREVIATIONS
E+00	E+00	E-03 E-03	E-03	E+00	E+00	} SCALING FACTORS
.00	.0000	.000 .0000	.0000	2.0000	.00000	
2.00	1.0000	16.711 .9112	.2890	1.3400	.01700	
4.00	1.0000	16.207 3.7295	.7925	2.0000	.04662	
6.00	.0000	.000 4.3835	.9315	2.0000	.05479	
8.00	.0000	.000 .9276	.7884	.5000	.04638	
10.00	.0000	.000 .8908	.7572	.5000	.04454	
12.00	.0000	.000 2.2143	.7023	1.3400	.04131	
14.00	.0000	.000 .7807	.6466	.5000	.03803	
16.00	.0000	.000 2.0444	.5951	1.4600	.03501	
18.00	.0000	.000 .7183	.5451	.5600	.03207	
20.00	.0000	.000 1.2780	.5222	1.0400	.03072	
22.00	.0000	.000 .5771	.4905	.5000	.02885	
24.00	.0000	.000 .8202	.4711	.7400	.02771	
26.00	.0000	.000 .5271	.4480	.5000	.02635	
28.00	.0000	.000 .5062	.4303	.5000	.02531	
30.00	.0000	.000 .4861	.4132	.5000	.02431	
32.00	1.0000	16.321 .7988	.6790	.5000	.03994	

FIG. A.3. Part of the printed output from a run of the model. The scaling factors show the power of 10 to which the printed figures should be raised to reconstruct the numbers with the decimal point in the correct position, e.g. E—03 means multiply by 10^{-3}.

Output

Part of the printed output from the example is shown in Fig. A.3, and a portion of the graphical output in Fig. A.4.

In the printed output, very large or very small numbers are divided by some power of ten so that they can be printed with only five significant figures. These scaling factors are set out at the beginning of the printed

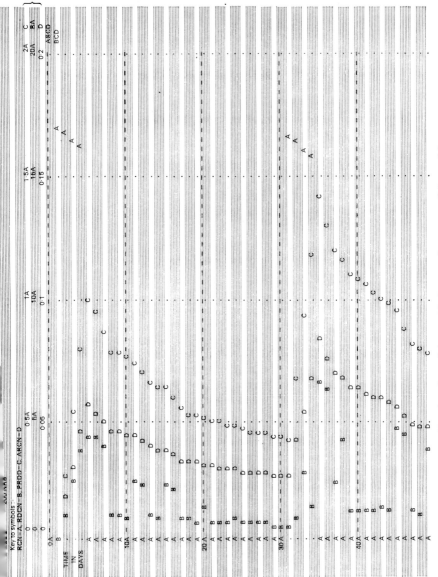

FIG. A.4. Part of the graphical output from a run of the model.

output so that the user may reconstruct the original numbers as required with the decimal point correctly positioned.

In the plotted output the mnemonics for the quantities to be shown in the graph are reduced to single letters or numbers and a key is printed at the beginning of this part of the output to remind the user which symbols he has chosen. In the example, 'rate of contamination' (*RCN*) is plotted as the letter *A*, 'rate of decontamination' (*RDCN*) as the letter *B*, 'proportion of double deposition' (*PRDD*) as the letter *C*, and 'area contaminated' (*ARCN*) as the letter *D*. The time scale runs from top to bottom on the left-hand side of the graph, and the quantity scales from left to right across the top of the figure. In these quantity scales a letter following each number means that the numbers must be multiplied by an appropriate scaling factor, as listed in the *User's Manual for Dynamo*, to restore the decimal point to the correct position. Thus the numbers in the scales for *RCN*, *RDCN*, and *PRDD* all have the scaling factor *A* and must be multiplied by 10^{-3}, whereas in the scale for *ARCN* no scaling factor is shown and the decimal point is in the correct position. Where two or more symbols are coincident on the graph, *Dynamo* plots the first one only and shows those which are coincident with it at the extreme right-hand side of the graph; for example, at time o the symbols *B*, *C*, and *D* are coincident with *A*, and only *A* is printed in the graph.

Use of the model

Simulation studies with the model as described above, and with more sophisticated versions of it, have served to identify some apparently significant gaps in our knowledge of the system, particularly in the 'decontamination' process by which herbage becomes palatable to the grazing animal once more. For example, as presently formulated there is no direct influence of stocking rate on the *proportion* of decontamination per day, although there is an indirect link via the absolute area of contamination. More experimental work is desirable to determine whether such a direct relationship exists, and to check and refine the model formulation in a number of other ways, before it can be accepted as a reliable means of screening large numbers of possible treatment or input combinations to select suitable ones for verification in field studies. Further development is envisaged as an iterative procedure between model or 'hypothesis' and field-work, on the lines of classical scientific investigation but with the essential difference that the precision of a formal mathematical model should make it more useful than a less well-defined verbal model. It may also be noted that there is considerable scope for enlarging the field covered by the model, linking in similar exploratory studies on herbage growth and animal production, towards the ultimate goal of a precise description of ecosystems in an agricultural context.

References

FORRESTER, J. W. (1961) *Industrial dynamics.* M.I.T. Press, Massachusetts.
PUGH, A. L. (1963) *Dynamo user's manual.* M.I.T. Press, Massachusetts.
RADFORD, P. J. (1967) *Annual Rep. Grassld Res. Ins.,* Hurley, pp. 77–85.
WIT, C. T. DE and BROUWER, R. (1968) *Angew. Bot.* xlii. 1–12.

Further Reading

ARCUS, P. L. (1963) *Proc. N.Z. Soc. Anim. Prod.* **23,** 159–68.
BEAMENT, J. W. L. (editor) (1960) *Models and analogues in biology.* Cambridge University Press.
DILLON, J. L. (1968) *The analysis of response in crop and livestock production.* Pergamon Press, Oxford.
DUCKHAM, A. N. (1968a) *Chemy Ind.* 903–6.
——(1968b) *Biological significance of climatic changes in Britain* (editors C. G. Johnson and L. P. Smith), pp. 193–201. Academic Press, New York.
DUNCAN, W. G. (1966) *Proc. Xth int. Grassld Congr.,* Helsinki, pp. 120–5.
FERRARI, TH. J. (1965) *Neth. J. agric.* **13,** 366–77.
GARFINKEL, D. (1967) *J. theoret. Biol.* **14,** 46–58.
GOLLEY, F. B. (1960) *Ecol. Monogr.* **30,** 187–206.
HERBERT, J. R. (1967) *The teaching of ecology* (editor J. M. Lambert), pp. 241–53. Blackwell, Oxford.
HOLLING, C. S. (1966) *Systems analysis in ecology* (editor K. E. F. Watt), chapter 8. Academic Press, New York.
MACFADYEN, A. (1964) *Grazing in terrestrial and marine environments* (editor D. J. Crisp), pp. 3–20. Blackwell, Oxford.
MANN, K. H. (1967) *The teaching of ecology* (editor J. M. Lambert), pp. 103–11. Blackwell, Oxford.
MILSUM, J. H. (1966) *Biological control systems analysis.* McGraw-Hill, New York.
MILTHORPE, F. L. (1965) *The biological significance of climatic changes in Britain* (editors C. G. Johnson and L. P. Smith), pp. 119–28. Academic Press, New York.
MORLEY, F. H. W. (1968) *Aust. J. Sci.* **30,** 405–9.
NELDER, J. A. (1967) *Agric. Prog.* **42,** 7–23.
ROBERTS, P. (1968) Chapter 28 in *Intensive livestock farming* (editor W. P. Blount). Heinemann, London.
SCOTT, D. (1966) *Proc. N.Z. ecol. Soc.* **13,** 1–4.
WATT, K. E. F. (editor) (1966) *Systems analysis in ecology,* chapter 1. Academic Press, New York.
WIT, C. T. DE (1965) *Versl. landbouwk,* Onderz, Ned. 663.
ZIMAN, J. M. (1965) *Nature, Lond.* **206,** 1187–92.

Author Index

208   *Author Index*

Cossens, G. G., 100, 108
Costin, A. B., 52
Cowan, I. R., 16, 26
Cowie, A. T., 160, 167
Cowling, D. W., 32, 33, 35, 42, 43, 46,
  47, 54, 55, 59, 64, 104, 105, 106,
  107
Cragg, J. B., 51, 52
Crawford, M. A., 154–5, 156, 157,
  165, 167
Crisp, D. J., 41, 46, 73, 77, 78, 95, 98,
  109, 117, 118, 119, 137, 205
Currie, J. A., 43, 46
Curry, L., 5, 6
Cushing, D. H., 109, 118
Cutress, T. W., 112, 118, 119

Darwin, C., 53, 59, 70, 77
Davidson, J. L., 40, 47
Davidson, R. L., 104, 107
Davies, A., 40, 47
Davies, H., 99, 107
Davies, W., 1, 2, 6, 48, 52, 58, 59, 68,
  69, 188, 192
Davis, W. E., 11, 14
Denamur, R., 165, 167
Denmead, O. T., 28, 36
Denne, M. P., 41, 47
Deriaz, R. E., 84, 89
Dermanis, P., 43, 47
Diem, K., 160, 167
Dillon, J. L., 205
Dilz, K., 50, 52
Doak, B. W., 102, 107
Dobrenz, A. K., 40, 47
Donald, C. M., 17, 26, 30, 36, 38, 39,
  40, 47, 55, 59
Doney, J. M., 149, 157, 180, 185
Donker, J. D., 111, 119
Douglas, J. Sholto, 59
Dowling, D. F., 155, 157
Duckham, A. N., 187, 192, 205
Dudzinski, M. L., 110, 118
Duncan, W. E., 181, 185
Duncan, W. G., 17, 26, 205

Edmond, D. B., 114, 118
Edwards, C. A., 72, 77, 95, 98
Edwards, R. A., 80, 88, 90, 93, 98
El-Shazly, K., 174, 178
Elton, C. S., 76, 77, 94, 98
England, F., 55, 59
England, G. J., 110, 118
Ennik, G. C., 54, 59

Evans, J. L., 137
Evans, L. T., 100, 108
Evans, S. A., 60, 68
Evenari, M., 29, 36
Eyles, D. E., 91, 92, 93, 98

Fauconneau, G., 168, 178
Fennessy, B. V., 72, 77
Ferguson, K. A., 181, 182, 185
Ferguson, W. S., 80, 88
Ferrari, Th. J., 205
Findlay, J. D., 151, 157
Fisk, H. G., 181, 185
Flatt, W. P., 163
Flook, D. R., 109, 118
Ford, J., 94, 98
Forrester, J. W., 196, 205
Frame, J., 127
Freeman, G. H., 155, 157
Freer, M., 80, 89
French, M. H., 184, 185
Fryer, J. D., 60, 68

Gaastra, P., 34, 36
Garfinkel, D., 205
Garner, R. J., 82, 88
Garwood, E. A., 9, 13, 14, 17, 26, 43,
  45, 46, 47, 105, 107
Gates, C. T., 45, 47
Gause, G. F., 76, 77
Gibson, A. H., 11, 14
Gillard, P., 100, 107
Glenday, A. C., 40, 46
Golley, F. B., 72, 77, 94, 98, 205
Goodall, E. D., 84, 88
Green, J. O., 21, 22, 23, 24, 25, 39, 47,
  64, 104, 106, 107
Green, S. M., 106, 107
Greenhalgh, J. F. D., 80, 88, 90, 93,
  98
Greer, F. A., 12, 14, 15, 26, 30, 35, 36
Gregory, P. W., 147, 157
Gunary, D., 102, 107

Hafez, E. S. E., 103, 107, 110, 118,
  119, 150, 157
Haggar, R. J., 110, 119
Hamilton, J. W., 181, 185
Hammond, J., 103, 107, 147, 157, 160,
  167, 169, 178
Hardison, W. A., 84, 88
Harper, J. L., 39, 47, 53, 54, 58, 59
Harris, C. E., 28, 36
Harris, G. A., 74, 77

Subject Index

PRINTED IN GREAT BRITAIN
AT THE UNIVERSITY PRESS, OXFORD
BY VIVIAN RIDLER
PRINTER TO THE UNIVERSITY